# MYTHS OF THE NATION

# Myths of the Nation

## NATIONAL IDENTITY AND LITERARY REPRESENTATION

RUMINA SETHI

CLARENDON PRESS · OXFORD

# OXFORD
UNIVERSITY PRESS

Great Clarendon Street, Oxford OX2 6DP

Oxford University Press is a department of the University of Oxford.
It furthers the University's objective of excellence in research, scholarship,
and education by publishing worldwide in

Oxford New York

Athens Auckland Bangkok Bogotá Buenos Aires Calcutta
Cape Town Chennai Dar es Salaam Delhi Florence Hong Kong Istanbul
Karachi Kuala Lumpur Madrid Melbourne Mexico City Mumbai
Nairobi Paris São Paulo Singapore Taipei Tokyo Toronto Warsaw

with associated companies in Berlin Ibadan

Oxford is a registered trade mark of Oxford University Press
in the UK and in certain other countries

Published in the United States
by Oxford University Press Inc., New York

© Rumina Sethi 1999

The moral rights of the author have been asserted

Database right Oxford University Press (maker)

First published 1999

British Library Cataloguing in Publication Data

Data available

Library of Congress Cataloging in Publication Data
Sethi, Rumina.
Myths of the nation: national identity and
literary representation/Rumina Sethi.
Includes bibliographical references and index.
1. Indic literature (English)–History and criticism.  2. Nationalism and
literature–India–History–20th century.  3. Politics and literature–India–
History–20th century.  4. Literature and history–India–History–20th century.
5. Gandhi, Mahatma, 1869– 1948–Influence.  6. Group identity in literature.
7. Nationalism in literature.  8. Raja Rao.  Kanthapura.
9. Narration (Rhetoric)  10. Myth in literature.  I. Title.
PR9485.5.N27S48   1999   891'. 1–dc21   98–51996
ISBN 0–19–818339–9

1 3 5 7 9 10 8 6 4 2

Typeset in Sabon
by J&L Composition Ltd, Filey, North Yorkshire
Printed in Great Britain
on acid-free paper by
Bookcraft Ltd, Midsomer Norton, Somerset

FOR MY FATHER

# Acknowledgements

MY RESEARCH on this book began while I was at Trinity College, Cambridge. Much of it was written while on a research fellowship at Wolfson College, Oxford. I am grateful to the British Academy, without whose support the book could not have been completed. I must thank as well the Wolfson College fellows and staff for the ambience of intellectual stimulation and warmth which made my work enjoyable.

I am deeply indebted to Tim Cribb from Churchill College, Cambridge, for his enduring support and constructive advice. Sincere thanks are due to Chris Bayly, Gillian Beer, Romila Thapar, and Robert Young for their guidance and valuable suggestions at various stages of my research. They not only read the drafts of my book but also filled in gaps in my analysis. I would like to express my particular gratitude to Sophie Goldsworthy and Matthew Hollis, my editors, for thier extreme patience, kindness, and encouragement. Jon Stallworthy, Rajeswari Sunder Rajan, and Sarah Barton, meticulously read the manuscript, and gave many useful suggestions which helped me shape my argument. Sir Raymond and Lady Hoffenberg deserve a special mention for their warmth and friendship which made my years at Wolfson very pleasant and memorable. I am grateful to the succeeding president of the college, Sir David Smith, for his generous support. C. D. Narasimhaiah, Uma Chakravarti, Lynn Innes, Kumkum Sangari, Sudipta Kaviraj, and David Richards were always forthcoming with their careful criticism. Adrian Hale, librarian, Wolfson College, was extremely helpful in arranging inter-library loans and procuring many articles for me at short notice.

The English Faculty libraries at Cambridge and Oxford, the Nehru Memorial Museum and Library, and Dhvanyaloka were most supportive during the project's completion. Fellowships and grants from Smuts, Beit, and Le Bas Foundations allowed me the time and resources to finish my research and revisions.

The introduction to the book and chapter four first appeared in *Modern Asian Studies*, 31.4 (1997), and the special issue on postcolonial studies in the *Journal of Gender Studies*, 5.3 (1996). I thank the editors and publishers for permission to reuse and rework this material.

Finally, I owe special thanks to Shelley who read the manuscript with exacting care, and my parents who have given me so much in so many ways. My work is a tribute to my family and the values they have handed to me.

This book is substantially based on my research in Karnataka, Delhi, London, Cambridge, and Oxford. I have benefited extensively from my fieldwork in the Hassan district of Karnataka, India, where I 'found' the fictional village in the novel. It is a hamlet, Harihalli, in Kenchamma Hoskere *taluq*.

# Contents

# Contents

# Introduction
## Narratives of Nationalism

> The Congress then is a National organization that knows no difference between British India and Indian India, between one province and another, between the classes and the masses, between the towns and villages, between the rich and the poor, between agricultural and industrial interests, between castes and communities, or religions.
>
> Pattabhi Sitaramayya, *The History of the Indian National Congress* (Bombay: Padma Publications, 1946), 30.

This book is about the construction of models of nationalist ideology in the cultural sphere. The study seeks to underscore what lies behind the writing of 'true' and 'authentic' histories of the nation by treating historical fiction as the literary dimension of nationalist ideology. I have traced nationalism from its abstract underpinnings to its concrete manifestation in historical fiction which underwrites the Indian freedom struggle. The construction of identity through mythicized conceptions of India is examined in detail through Raja Rao's first novel, *Kanthapura* which, I should indicate, is not singled out for being some kind of 'national allegory'.[1]

The key concept governing this study is that of representation which allows me to consider how history slides into fiction. I am interested in historical fiction primarily because it combines in itself both fiction and history, and seems a good enough genre for examining the construction of nationalism which, while being a subject of history may, at the same time, be taken 'outside' into the framework of fiction. The 'fictional reality' of the nation is, anyway, a much debated issue. Secondly, the analysis of nationalist ideology within the genre of historical fiction will allow more room for imaginative speculation when it comes to examining the motives governing the

---

[1] Frederic Jameson, 'Third-World Literature in the Era of Multinational Capitalism', *Social Text*, 15 (1986), 65–88.

writer's ideology, without having first to deal with the anxieties of well-intentioned historians. Lastly, historical fiction is useful when claiming the validity of many of the nation's myths without having to battle with the charge of essentialism which fiction manages to circumvent more easily than does history, simply because it is fiction. In subservience to my thematic study, I have not thought it necessary to provide a chronological literary history of writing that precedes the publication of *Kanthapura*.

*Kanthapura* is a text of the Civil Disobedience Movement of the 1930s that takes for its central concern the participation of a small village in the national struggle at Gandhi's call. Imbued with nationalism, the villagers sacrifice all their material possessions in a triumph of the spirit. In the end, there remains 'neither man nor mosquito in Kanthapura'.[2] Rao's novel is significant in that it is both a cultural tract which rewrites 'true' history as against the 'inauthentic' historical accounts compiled by Europeans,[3] and also wrests the 'nation' from the aggressor by effecting a cultural revival through the use of indigenous themes and motifs. A faithful history and a national awakening is indeed an effective strategy for bringing together people of diverse religions, languages, and lifestyles to demand home rule.

The 'recovery' of an 'authentic' Indian tradition is briefly examined against orientalism which has provided an impetus to much Indian writing. I take orientalism as a convenient point of departure because it fixes a variety of cultures in a single position as the Other. When I deal with colonialism and nationalism, the economic and political imperatives are so obviously the main motives that orientalism cannot but be relegated to a relatively minor level. It comes back into the foreground when I turn to literature. History is chosen as a sort of middle ground. In this introductory chapter, I attempt to show how nationalist fiction-writing undermines some of the essentialist representations of the orient, but in turn, creates India-centred histories that thrive on culture-specific ideals engineered through myths about

---

[2] Raja Rao, *Kanthapura* (Delhi: Orient Paperbacks, 1938), 258. Subsequent quotations from this edition are indicated in the text parenthetically by page number.

[3] James Mill, *The History of British India* (London: Baldwin, Cradock, and Joy, 1817); Mountstuart Elphinstone, *The History of India*, 5th edn. (1841; London: John Murray, 1866); and Vincent A. Smith, *The Early History of India* (Oxford: Clarendon, 1904) were popular histories of India in the 19th and early 20th cents. See R. C. Majumdar, 'Nationalist Historians', in C. H. Philips (ed.), *Historians of India, Pakistan and Ceylon* (London: Oxford University Press, 1961), 416–19.

language, religion, race, caste, and gender. The background of the construction of an idyllic village community that serves as a foundation for Rao's *Kanthapura*, based on interpretations of villages by a virtual tradition of orientalists and nationalists, will also be seen in the above context of ideological formation and form the backdrop for the subsequent chapters.

Chapter 1 examines how the problematic pan-Indian identity is posited by indigenizing the English language, and raises questions about the part played by a small minority of the intelligentsia in educating the westernized Indians in what is believed to be a timeless and pure 'Indian' tradition. *Kanthapura* is an appropriate text for the ensuing study not simply because it shows the peasantry's awakening to national consciousness but also because it is written in English which can be seen as both a potential and a problem. While the use of English certainly constitutes a problem in any study of nationalist representations, its use as a link language or as the language of administration is acknowledged by proponents of nationalism on the rationale that it is unificatory in the multilingual Indian context. Being perhaps the only language that is wholly Indian, it paradoxically makes *Kanthapura* an Indian novel. On the other hand, literature existing in the regional languages can hardly ever become 'national' because its dissemination again depends on English translations so that English is bound to become 'the language in which the knowledge of "Indian" literature is produced'.[4] A study of *Kanthapura* is also relevant from the point of view of the class of people who constructed it, a *national* intelligentsia grounded in the study of English language and literature, and co-opted, to a large extent, by western thoughts and ideas. My choice of *Kanthapura* is influenced mainly by these considerations.

The apotheosis of Gandhi into an avatar in Rao's novel turns contemporary politics into a religious saga in an attempt to build a homogeneous national-popular movement in a society acutely divided by language, caste, and class. Chapter 2 critically examines how Rao builds up associations with Gandhian philosophy, stretching it to its extreme in an overarching Hinduism, rather than with Gandhi's political strategies. Bringing fictional representation to a collision with subaltern history of peasants and women involved in the

---

[4] Aijaz Ahmad, *In Theory: Classes, Nations, Literatures* (Delhi: Oxford University Press, 1993), 250.

national movement, Chapters 3 and 4 comment on the author's inclusion of what did not occur, or at least not entirely, to create an agreeable and uniform history that demands an acceptance of the motives and principles which fashion its ideology. I use the dramatic qualities of the novel and juxtapose them with its governing ideology to show cracks in the homogeneous discourse of nationalism. Although it may be alleged that Rao writes history into the novel form which thus precludes it from being assessed by the parameters of history, it is precisely because the 'actual' and the 'fictional' coalesce in *Kanthapura* that I am able to examine the reconstruction of a usable past by both historians and fiction-writers comprising the intelligentsia, a reconstruction which, in retrospect, appears to be a misrepresentation of 'actual' events for political purposes. Since the existence of self-representations on an imaginary plane in the novel is an ideal that successfully manipulates large numbers and diverse kinds of people, it allows us to contemplate the nature of history-writing and its proximity to the creation of fictions in nationalist representations.

Of course, the intelligentsia becomes a very productive category for any study about representations. Here I should clarify that the nationalist intelligentsia were political figures, statesmen, and intellectuals engaged in social and political activities or reform movements to start with, without necessarily having nationalism as their primary concern. With the consolidation of the Indian National Congress in the late nineteenth century, many activists and intellectuals came into mainstream national activity. Save for their affiliation with the Congress which made them 'nationalists', they were not identified by a homogeneity of interests or grounded in any common theory of nationalism. On the other hand, the Congress witnessed a nationalism of every kind—of Hindu revivalists, who excluded the minorities while promoting their own regional groups, and who desired a hasty coalition based on religious exclusion; of social reformers who saw the national movement as a panacea for their ills; and of anti-imperialist agitators who believed national unity to be the precursor of national liberation signifying the end of imperial rule. The absence of a common ground became one of the primary reasons for importing western nationalism into India, assisted by English education which, on its own plane, served to unite them. It was the Congress which managed to combine in itself many of these descriptions. Under the auspices of Gandhi's policies especially, the national struggle sought to unify the various strands of nationalism and

introduce some degree of homogeneity. I demonstrate that nationalism was a mixture of all these aspects, in which different characteristics were thrown up in different circumstances even though the
national *movement* tended to be more specific, faced as it was by
the practical considerations of gaining independence.

I focus mainly on cultural nationalism which is a selective and
partial category, and where imagination and manoeuvre play a vital
role in fashioning identity.[5] Cultural nationalism derives its strength
from the past—mainly folk traditions, religion, rural dialects, which
I discuss in detail—in order to demonstrate cultural uniqueness and
thereby stimulate national consciousness. However, when culturally
reified structures collide with the processes of modernization and
social reform in the attainment of political ends, cultural nationalism
shows its regressive aspect. The requirements of a modern state and
the aspirations of the masses are hardly compatible with a nostalgic
retreat into culture. This is very relevant in anti-colonial struggles
where a culturally imagined unification must work side by side with
mass mobilization, the primary motive being the establishment of an
independent nation-state. The emerging nation-state, consequently,
witnesses rapid appropriation of workers, peasants, minorities, and
the lower orders, and enlists their participation. But often we discover, as in India, that although we have a political nation-state, the
nation itself is yet to be born. From this viewpoint, we can say that
the intelligentsia remains separate from the subaltern, and the field of
writing or rhetoric from the field of political action, although nationalist ideology tends to cover up its differences. While nationalism, as
espoused by the intelligentsia, was not a homogeneous category, it
includes all the connotations of a popular bourgeois ideology, and has
both affinities with and differences from European varieties of nationalism in my references to it.

[5] For an understanding of cultural nationalism, see Anthony D. Smith, *National
Identity* (Harmondsworth: Penguin, 1991), 71–98; John Plamenatz, 'Two Types of
Nationalism', in Eugene Kamenka (ed.), *Nationalism: The Nature and Evolution of an
Idea* (London: Edward Arnold, 1976), 24–7; Isaiah Berlin, *Vico and Herder: Two
Studies in the History of Ideas* (London: Hogarth, 1976); Hans Kohn, *The Idea of
Nationalism: A Study in Its Origins and Background* (New York: Macmillan, 1944),
351–2; 381; John Hutchinson and Anthony D. Smith (eds.), *Nationalism* (Oxford:
Oxford University Press, 1994), 122–31; Thomas Hylland Eriksen, *Ethnicity and
Nationalism: Anthropological Perspectives* (London: Pluto, 1993), 99–104; and in
particular Elie Kedourie (ed.), *Nationalism in Asia and Africa* (London: Weidenfeld
and Nicolson, 1970).

The fifth chapter which takes stock of the body of Rao's later fiction is added mainly as a comparative study. Although it does not merit as much detail and data as *Kanthapura*, a consideration of these later novels becomes especially important because they were written after independence when the political motives of national integration were lost with the attainment of the nation-state, and in view of the comparisons one can draw with the recent 'Hindutva' wave in India.[6] The sixth and concluding chapter brings all these aspects together and conceptualizes the domains of history and fiction: how real is history? What are 'actual' events? Studies of literary representations of nationalist ideology tend to privilege historical inquiry since history is the accepted empirical repository of truth. I have, instead, tried to show how 'third-world' identities can be ideologically represented as variously in history as they have been in the writing of fiction. What both fiction-writing and history-writing have in common is their basic concern with understanding past cultures and common problems in relation to evidence, interpretation, and analysis.

In the last decade or so, historians, especially those centred around Subaltern Studies, have attempted to demythologize the histories of the national movement and highlighted the role of the subaltern in terms of agency, which is diminished in the interests of a homogeneous nationalism. It is equally important to have a reassessment of key literary figures who have created popular histories based on culture-specific ideals. Interestingly, some of this literature has a considerable role to play in the production of a nationalist ideology and thereby can be an important source for historians in showing how that mythical conception is constructed. In the light of my concerns with representation and ideology, it seems important to me to focus on textual practice, both nationalist and subaltern, and posit them against each other. When I refer to the struggles of insurgents in the subaltern context to highlight the aporias of narratives of nationalism, I allude to the textual reproduction of those instances of rebellion without making any claims for the validity of subaltern history as it must have happened. I hope, however, that my inquiry into the shaping of nationalist narratives will be seen, in itself, as its critique, not requiring comparisons with subaltern or other histories for its exposé.

Nothing of a definitive nature has been written within Indian

---

[6] For an elaboration of the ideology of 'Hindutva', see Ch. 5.

writing in English about the construction of cultural identities in periods of nation-building. My task has been made especially difficult as the historical works and literary criticism on nationalist literature as yet contain hardly any commonly accepted views as to the specific nature of the 'reality' of nationalist phenomena in India. Further, while the many rewritings of colonial discourse theory, including my own, have debunked nationalism variously as elitist, totalizing, essentialist, and coercive, few have spoken of the composition of its deductive, persuasive, and even progressive form, and its consequent reach towards 'reality'. It has to be admitted, in spite of my dismantling of nationalist structures, that nationalist discourse does succeed in creating its own reality. The many examples of co-operation, bloodshed, and sacrifice are instances of the 'imagined community' intersecting real time. Again, the glorification of the peasantry is an appropriation by the nationalist intelligentsia of that site of subalternity which is untouched by the culture of imperialism. By escaping modernity and Enlightenment, the peasantry remain outside discourse-making, thereby, quite justly, getting alloyed with unadulterated and pristine reality. Curiously, both Subaltern historians and deconstructive poststructuralists themselves appropriate that very field of the uncorrupted but voiceless native in their critiques of humanism. In fact, orientalists, nationalists, Marxists, subalternists, and poststructuralists, have all, in their own celebratory or benevolent ways, used the disenfranchised subproletariat in their works. What I find useful in poststructuralist practices, however, is that subaltern identities are imbued with heterogeneity, thus splitting open an authoritarian and definitive nationalism, and a continuing neo-colonialism.

In the present generation, when colonialism as direct political control has largely lost its hold, and postcolonial cultures are seeking new ways of expression, such a study gains immense relevance, particularly since it aims not simply at interrogating nationalist history but in showing *how* it gets written. This is done by conducting independent assessments of the employment of early epics, the use of local dialects, the emphasis on ancient rituals and practices, oral tradition, and other theoretical relations revealed through literature, rather than the common practice of accepting an analytical framework in which to structure the specific material. This view of the text permits the recovery of a cultural matrix for the text, and at the same time, opens up a space for an interrogation of the assumptions upon which it is grounded.

I

As a background to the study, it is important to address western configurations about the orient as well as highlight some instances of indigenous writing as a response to these representations in order to throw light on the motives of political expediency that govern and shape ideological constructions. This exercise would raise questions concerning the role of the nationalist intelligentsia in shaping a nationalist consciousness by establishing a strong link between a lost past and the current political malaise. While the national freedom struggle comprised many forms of resistance, the creation of nationalist sentiment was an important, sometimes dominant, feature of its politics.

We are by now reasonably well aware that the creation of orientalist stereotypes was part of the intellectual exercise that strategically made colonialism possible and legitimized it.[7] In the interest of colonialism, the orient was a creation which played a vital role in constituting the variety of religious, political, and aesthetic positions of European imperialists.[8] For those legitimizing colonialism as a channel of advancement, imperialism was the prerequisite to progress and an antidote to feudalism.[9] As Nandy maintains:

Not only the arch-conservatives and the apologists of colonialism were convinced that one day their cultural mission would be complete and the barbarians would become civilised; even the radical critics of Western society were convinced that colonialism was a necessary stage of maturation for some societies.[10]

From within this perspective, academic orientalism can be interpreted in the light of Said's hypothesis which links scholarship and power,

[7] Edward W. Said, *Orientalism* (London: Routledge, 1978).
[8] Marx has noted that the ideas of the ruling class are in every epoch the ruling ideas. These ideas comprise the 'ideal expression' of the ruling material relationships of that class. Marx's views on the interests of the dominant groups in society forms, generally, the basis of Antonio Gramsci's theory of *hegemony* which gives the most thoroughgoing understanding of how a ruling group exercises and sustains domination through consent and persuasion. In other words, the ideas of the ruling class are not directly imposed through coercion over subordinate groups but permeated in society through a consensus of subordinate will in order to appear legitimate and normal.
[9] See, for instance, Karl Marx, 'The British Rule in India' (1853), in *Collected Works of Marx and Engels* (London: Lawrence and Wishart, and Moscow: Progress Publishers, 1979), xii. 125–33.
[10] Ashis Nandy, *The Intimate Enemy: Loss and Recovery of Self under Colonialism* (Delhi: Oxford University Press, 1983), 14.

since orientalism, in Said's terms, was not limited to its role as a romantic discipline for disinterested seekers. Thus viewed, Sir William Jones's conscious and magnanimous intention of trying to lay the foundations for the inherent translatability of cultures would also have enormous significance in terms that establish advantage over the natives. To take an example, Jones's continual emphasis on learning Sanskrit was bound to have its uses in inhibiting the authority of the pandits who argued their legal battles in Sanskrit which was a linguistic proficiency unavailable to the British.[11] In fact, Jones's *A Grammar of the Persian Language* (1771) was designed for East India Company employees in India, where Persian was the diplomatic language used in administration and the legal system until 1837. Along with effecting the awareness of common principles underlying different cultures, oriental learning was to help make accessible the profits of British academic and mercantile trade in India.[12]

The lines along which British rule in India had fashioned itself were severely attacked by James Mill in *The History of British India*. Mill argued not only that Jones's orient was 'the product of an undisciplined imagination, but that the Orient, as Jones and others had conceived it, underpinned notions of the imagination which were dangerous on epistemological and political grounds'.[13] According to Mill, oriental learning had been a failure since it encouraged self-indulgence and despotism.[14] A staunch proponent of the science of utilitarianism, Mill argued that any ideas opposed to the utilitarian system of learning would hinder British aims of administration and governance since all ahistorical studies of the orient could only breed immorality and licentiousness among both the ruler and the ruled.

It is difficult to situate Said's theory of the all-pervasive nature of power within Mill's critique of the romantic orient. The nature of British rule in India, which apparently did not operate within a single idiom, runs counter to Said's ahistorical conception of orientalism.[15]

---

[11] Javed Majeed, *Ungoverned Imaginings: James Mill's 'The History of British India' and Orientalism* (Oxford: Clarendon, 1992), 6. See also Nicholas Thomas, *Colonialism's Culture: Anthropology, Travel and Government* (Cambridge: Polity, 1994), 39.

[12] Gauri Viswanathan, *Masks of Conquest: Literary Study and British Rule in India* (New York: Columbia University Press, 1989), 28–9.

[13] Majeed, *Ungoverned Imaginings*, 6.

[14] Viswanathan, *Masks of Conquest*, 38–9; 122.

[15] The status of the East India Company as a trader, regent, or revenue collector, for instance, was not as unambiguous as Said would have us believe. On the contrary, in the

Despite his strong critique of the colonial structure, he is guilty of constructing universalizing notions and essentializing types, what Bhabha describes as the contradiction between 'content' and 'form', the former identified as 'the unconscious repository of fantasy, imaginative writings and essential ideas' and the latter as 'the historically and discursively determined diachronic aspect'.[16] In other words, where on the one hand Said states that orientalism in the academy spurred and encouraged political conquest, he also says that the representation of the orient bears scarcely any resemblance to the 'real' orient.[17] This would be an instance of the real intersecting the representation, or time intersecting timelessness, the latter 'unreal' category actually effecting historical change. In Bhabha's view, it is important to understand 'the *productive* ambivalence of the object of colonial discourse' by scrutinizing forms of both identification and difference: 'despite the "play" in the colonial system which is crucial to its exercise of power, colonial discourse produces the colonized as a social reality which is at once an "other" and yet entirely knowable and visible,' what he calls 'phobia and fetish'.[18] It is thus that colonial discourse can never be unambiguously one-sided. Rather, it is open-ended, comprising of both fear and attraction, sameness and difference, and, within Said's context, both manifest and latent orientalisms. As against Said's advocacy of the binariness of these categories, Bhabha emphasizes their fusion and inseparability. Said has also addressed orientalism from an exteriority, limiting the role of the 'oppressed', and thus ignored, in Bhabha's words 'those terrifying stereotypes of savagery, cannibalism, lust and anarchy which are the

late 18th cent., British rule rather sought to justify its presence by abiding, as far as possible, with the customs and manners of the people, exemplified in Hastings's new cultural policy in which the British Civil Service elite were expected to 'learn to think and act like . . . Asian[s]' in order to avoid breaking the rapport between the ruler and the subject and the consequent collapse of the empire. As Kopf writes, 'Whatever their intent upon arriving in India, whatever their motivation in mastering Indian languages and then translating them for profit, the first generation of Orientalists left India with a tradition of public service and cultural empathy which for the most part was lacking in the generation they replaced.' See David Kopf, *British Orientalism and the Bengal Renaissance: The Dynamics of Indian Modernization 1773–1835* (Calcutta: Firma K. L. Mukhopadhyay, 1969), 17–18; 31; and Nandy, *Intimate Enemy*, 5.

[16] Homi K. Bhabha, 'The Other Question: Stereotype, Discrimination and the Discourse of Colonialism', in *The Location of Culture* (London and New York: Routledge, 1994), 71–2.

[17] Robert Young, *White Mythologies: Writing History and the West* (London: Routledge, 1992), 129–30.     [18] Bhabha, 'The Other Question', 67; 70–1; 72.

signal points of identification and alienation, scenes of fear and desire, in colonial texts'.[19] While orientalism will remain a discursive construction, the part played by the subject in his or her own enunciation cannot be separated from the discourse of the colonizer.

Said's invariable view of the imperial power as a compelling force offers few compromises. Even within the understanding that orientalism is a set of representations which need have no correspondence to the actual, one cannot lose sight of the way in which a culturally fragmented and politically heterogeneous country like India combined and reassembled its multifarious societies under the onslaught of colonialism.[20] The intricacy of the relationships that existed between the Indian populace and British rule in India speaks for the inhabitants who were active agents, and not passive victims in the creation of colonial India.[21]   Many of the policies that British rule administered were derived, for instance, from the indigenous literati. Furthermore, Said's analysis of the collaborative design of the imperialists to combine knowledge with power is questionable since orientalism as a romantic study was already on the decline by the 1830s when imperialism in India was in its ascendancy.

Despite the shortcomings, Said has advanced one of the earliest challenges to Enlightenment history within colonial discourse analysis. In general terms, he has done much work to expose the creation of the subject as the 'other'. The conglomeration of various cultures into a single position, however homogeneous, facilitates an understanding of counter-strategies of representation. Even though he has not outlined any programme for circumventing the assumptions of orientalism, his model is useful in analysing what Sadik Jalal al-'Azm has called 'orientalism in reverse'.[22] In other words, the circularity of Said's argument can be used to explain how indigenous idioms, fashioned to wrestle with orientalist assumptions, in fact correspond closely with the orientalist problematic. This brings me to examine how indigenous identities often turn out to be relational rather than

[19] Ibid. 72.
[20] See Lisa Lowe, *Critical Terrains: French and British Orientalisms* (Ithaca and London: Cornell University Press, 1991). Lowe rejects any totalizing framework that gives orientalism its specific authority, arguing, on the other hand, for the heterogeneity and the contradictions of the orientalist object.
[21] Christopher A. Bayly, *Indian Society and the Making of the British Empire* (Cambridge: Cambridge University Press, 1988), 5.
[22] Sadik Jalal al-'Azm, 'Orientalism and Orientalism in Reverse', *Khamsin: Journal of Revolutionary Socialists in the Middle East*, 8 (1981), 6.

oppositional categories of orientalism. In this regard, the importance of the nationalist intelligentsia in constructing a national conscious-ness cannot be underestimated.

The nationalist exercise of reviving the past paradoxically re-establishes the unchanging Sanskrit Indic civilization of the oriental-ists. If the early orientalists perceived their origins in Sanskritic India, the nationalists used that very India to fix the origins of the modern nation-state.[23] To rationalize the paradox, the scholarship of 'sym-pathetic' orientalists like Max Müller and Sir William Jones became honest and impartial treatises on India's glorious past. India, in any case, was known to have a 'golden age', the Gupta rule from AD 320–540, which had seen remarkable progress under the aegis of Hindu-ism.[24] It was the Muslim invasions of the eleventh and the twelfth centuries that were believed to have robbed India of its plenitude and wealth.[25] Not only is the notion that India had been glorious in ancient times not strictly true, there had also not been a geographi-cally and politically united India during the Gupta period. India did not exist as a single polity for the people of the land mass until the nation-state was born later out of its history as a single colony.

While Indian nationalism in general was perhaps engendered by the very imposition of a rule that for the first time planted the notion of an integrated identity, the ensuing nation-state was shaped and struc-tured by its intelligentsia, by a 'selective appropriation of the notions of the Orientalists'.[26] The nationalists believed it to be their duty to sever their new-found selfhood from its roots in colonialism, to question orientalist constructions and authority, to judge its adequa-cies, or rather inadequacies, for representing reality, and interpret

[23] Gyan Prakash, 'Writing Post-Orientalist Histories of the Third World: Indian Historiography Is Good to Think', in Nicholas B. Dirks (ed.), Colonialism and Culture (Ann Arbor: University of Michigan Press, 1992), 358–9.

[24] Kopf, British Orientalism, 22–42.

[25] It was the later decline of Hindu India from the 8th to the 18th cents. that was perhaps responsible for Muslim invasions, and thus the commonly held notion believed by many 19th-cent. historians that Muslim rule in India was one of despotism and tyranny.

[26] See Somnath Zutshi, 'Women, Nation and the Outsider in Contemporary Hindi Cinema', in Tejaswini Niranjana, et al. (eds.), Interrogating Modernity: Culture and Colonialism in India (Calcutta: Seagull, 1993), 91. One of the themes the nationalists maintained from Max Müller was the Aryan past of the present Indians. While Müller, of course, lamented the ruin of the Indian civilization that had lost its European connection, the nationalist project maintained that the blue-blooded Aryans had not perished through miscegenation and intermarriage but remained strong in upper-caste Hindu elites.

history from a nationalist position.[27] The underlying strain of an essentialist and undivided entity and a commitment to the idea of Indian nationalism, necessary for revisionist history, were provided by the intelligentsia comprised largely of western-educated Indians.[28] Nationalist history resembled an amalgam consisting of western practices of rationality and liberal thinking, and representations of what were regarded as authentic Indian traditions. While the inclusion of western modes symbolized progress, the Indian were retained as marks of identity. The confluence of both resulted from a feeling of being culturally at a disadvantage for being colonized, yet believing that they possessed the cultural equipment to overcome that disadvantage.[29] Constantly having to make compromises, the elite conceptualized a nation where 'advancing modernity' (change) and timelessness (resistance to change) were engaged in 'the most ferocious of historical conflicts'.[30] These two assumptions characterize the writings of the early decades of the nineteenth century: the rationality of European thought combined with an inability to relinquish the influence of traditional classical Sanskrit drama and epic poetry, folk comedy and parody, and, most of all, oral traditions and Hindu mythology.

Guha cites the examples of Ramram Basu, Rajiblochan Mukhopadhyay, and Mrityunjoy Bidyalankar who wrote the first books on history in Bengali during the first decade of the nineteenth century, marking the beginning of an independent and self-supporting Indian historiography.[31] The inevitable drawbacks are fairly evident in Bidyalankar's *Rajabali* (1808) in its depiction of princely lives. His

[27] For instance, the 1857 revolt in north India had always been regarded as a 'mutiny' since it was an insurrection of soldiers; it was not until 1909 that V. D. Savarkar wrote *The Indian War of Independence of 1857* and thereby 'corrected' history. In a similar manner, the Hindu historian substitutes 'wars' for 'riots', enabling the creation of heroes which would not be possible in situations of rioting. See Gyanendra Pandey, 'Modes of History Writing: New Hindu History of Ayodhya', *Economic and Political Weekly*, 29.25 (1994), 1525.

[28] Prakash, 'Writing Post-Orientalist Histories', 360.

[29] Plamenatz, 'Two Types of Nationalism', 24–7. Also see Isaiah Berlin, *The Crooked Timber of Humanity: Chapters in the History of Ideas*, ed. Henry Hardy (London: Fontana, 1991), 246–7. Berlin attributes the representation of a rich cultural past to 'inferiority-ridden peoples' who dream of a glorious future, as in the German romantics, the Russian Slavophils, the people of Poland, Central Europe, the Balkans, Asia, and Africa.

[30] Zygmunt Bauman, *Modernity and the Holocaust* (Cambridge: Polity, 1989), 45.

[31] Ranajit Guha, *An Indian Historiography of India: A Nineteenth-Century Agenda and Its Implications* (Calcutta: K. P. Bagchi, 1988), 28–32.

history begins with the installation of the first Indian king by god in the *Satyuga*[32] and ends with the regime of another king, again delegated by god some fifty years before the time of writing.[33] The interaction between the secular and the supernatural, and between fact and fiction departs from any semblance of 'reality', and it is easy to note that the writer takes a lot from traditional mythological modes of storytelling.[34] Nevertheless, the effort to demythologize the past is equally strong. Despite the myths and mythological elements, *Rajabali* is a history that takes off from the present. This is particularly so because it was intended to be a document for the officials of the East India Company divulging knowledge about the disposition and mental outlook of the eighteenth-century Bengali literati. The writer was perhaps conscious of the practical use to which the manual was to be put and refrained, to some extent, from giving his history a mythical orientation, so that the final impression left with the reader is that of a work in which historicity supersedes its mythical antecedents.

In the late nineteenth century, Surendranath Banerjee argued persuasively for the writing of 'truthful' narratives, uncorrupted by English influences, by making the following statement in favour of indigenous historiography:

I cannot refrain from alluding . . . to the manner in which sometimes Indian histories are written by English authors. . . . I do not mean to cast any reflection upon those great and good Englishmen, who have done so much toward elucidating the history of our country. . . . Nobody could be more sensible than myself to the difficulties of their task, difficulties which in their case were enhanced by the circumstance that they were foreigners, writing the history of a country of which they could know but little. But although our obligations to English writers may be very great, we owe still higher obligations to truth; and in the interests of truth, it becomes our duty to point out what we conceive to be their errors and their shortcomings.[35]

Further, he makes an appeal to the Hindu cultural past in his rhetoric:

---

[32] Age of Goodness which is believed to precede the modern age.

[33] Guha, *An Indian Historiography*, 31–2.

[34] Commonly known as the *puranic* form of telling stories. The *puranas* consist of Sanskrit writing dating from the 6th to 16th cents. AD, giving a legendary account of ancient times.

[35] Surendranath Banerjea [sic], 'The Study of Indian History', in Kedourie (ed.), *Nationalism in Asia and Africa*, 230–1.

I ask, what Hindu is there who does not feel himself a nobler being altogether, as he recalls to mind the proud list of his illustrious country-men, graced by the thrice-immortal names of a Vâlmiki and a Vyâsa, a Pânini and a Patanjali, a Gautama and a Sankaracharya? I ask, what Hindu is there whose patriotism is not stimulated, whose self-respect is not increased, as he contemplates the past history of his country? For ours was a most glorious past. We were great in literature, in science, in war, but above all, great in morals.[36]

Banerjee, who had been dismissed from the Indian Civil Service at the very outset of his career, was convinced that lack of pride and self-respect among his people was the cause of this treatment at the hands of the British. Hence, his failure to secure advancement within the colonial regime resulted in his radicalization. Banerjee's rejection simultaneously raised questions of cultural identity which had to be rediscovered to compensate for the humiliation of being spurned by his European fellow men with whom he had, up to then, identified. His predicament was shared to a large extent by the Indian intelligentsia who suffered, in many ways, from a sense of inferiority in the face of European views on free initiative, personal responsibility, and moral autonomy. Consequently, they entered the western education system to camouflage the social, economic, and political inadequacies the western colonial regimes had highlighted. Nationalism was among the ideas imbibed from this education. Being products of western education, they were caught between the traditions of two different cultures—alienated from the western through discrimina-tion, and from their own by the pulls of modernization. Whether their 'recovery' resulted from being rebuffed by the west or from the plain fact of being colonized, the nationalists' appeal was made primarily to the 'glorious past'. Returning to indigenous gods and rituals, to a communal past, and to ethnic histories as a means of both restoring injured identity and evoking a patriotic response from within themselves and their countrymen was a preoccupation of the late nineteenth-century intelligentsia. Prominent among them was Bankimchandra Chatterjee who drew from the past to compensate for the 'dark night' of Bengali history. For him, the writing of history became the site for an ideological encounter between the colonizer and the colonized. Believing that it was the absence of history that robbed Indians of national pride, he wrote:

[36] Ibid. 235.

National pride comes mainly from creating and developing people's history. Both social science and social idealism rely on history as a source. A nation without history is foredoomed. There are some poor unfortunates who are not aware of their ancestors, and some races who are ignorant of their glorious forebears.[37]

Bankim uses the words 'creating' and 'developing', hinting at invention rather than objective recapitulation. He links national pride first to the construction of such an history, and then significantly, to the loss of knowledge of one's forefathers and parents, thus relating the absence of history with the ignorance of one's past. His search for a potential history, in fact, has to do with the disappointing nature of Bengali history where he was unable to find any tales of heroic defiance against an oppressor.[38] 'There exists no history of Bengal,' Bankim writes with frustration in another essay, 'what we have does not amount to history; it is partly fiction, and partly the biographical account of the non-believing, foreign exploiters. Bengal must have its history, otherwise there cannot be any hope for Bengal.'[39] His endeavour to link the present moment with the past was shaped in *Anandamath*, an early novel in which nationalism acquires political legitimacy within the religious overtones of an insurrection by *sanyasis*.[40] *Anandamath* was later translated into Marathi, Telugu, and English, and the battle-cry 'Vande Mataram' (Hail to thee, Mother) became tremendously evocative in the struggle to free the enslaved 'mother', a symbol rich with meaning but created by freezing women in space and time. It is significant that the Sanyasi Rebellion of the late eighteenth century was not ideologically motivated by the perils of the 'motherland', and that, as Bankim himself confessed, the

[37] Bankimchandra Chatterjee, 'Bangalar Itihasa' (The History of Bengal), in *Vividha Prabandha*, ed. Brajendranath Bandhopadhyay and Sri Sajanikanta Das (Calcutta: Bangiya Sahitya Parishad, 1959), 288–9. My trans.

[38] Sudipta Kaviraj, *The Unhappy Consciousness: Bankimchandra Chattopadhyay [Chatterjee] and the Formation of Nationalist Discourse in India* (Delhi: Oxford University Press, 1995), 112–13. Kaviraj points out that Bankim's disappointment led to the desire to write a 'possible history' where he found 'several choices . . . open to him', one of which might have been the frequent switching between Bengali identity and the larger Indian one when he could not come up with instances of Bengali valour, but could account for several among the Sikhs and the Marathas.

[39] Bankimchandra Chatterjee, 'Bangalar Itihasa Sambandhe Kayekti Katha' (Some Thoughts About Bengali History), in *Vividha Prabandha*, 301. My trans.

[40] Religious Hindu mendicants.

consciousness of nationalism and self-esteem were, in fact, imbibed from the west.[41]

In brief, the writing of indigenous history has appeared to take two self-contradictory courses: configuration within the orientalist constellation by an emphasis on the ancient past, and an urge to break away from that very past. In terms of modernity and development, the nation-state could follow hardly any direction other than what had been modelled by the British. The ambivalence is seen in the abandonment of ancestral culture for a more advanced standard and the demand that the ancient be retained as a mark of identity. Both the reliance on antiquity and the affirmation of modernity persistently held the emerging nation-state within the orbit of orientalism, representing what Partha Chatterjee calls the 'liberal-rationalist dilemma' of nationalist thought.[42]

In recounting the ideological formation of the nineteenth-century nationalist intelligentsia, it must be stressed that the large part of their rhetoric which came from the European variety of nationalism was well assimilated and grounded in Europe's self-conscious and long-established communities, but hardly appropriate to India's plural and inchoate societies. One of the reasons that the 'borrowing' took place had to do with fashioning a language which the colonial rulers could understand.[43] In so doing, the intelligentsia could not disregard the Indian masses for whose consumption the expression would have to be reformulated if it was to have some meaning. Accordingly, nationalism in India was also grounded in difference from the west: India possessed indigenous cultural resources by which it could maintain its independent spiritual identity.[44] The language of nationalism in India in the nineteenth century thus turned out to be composed of a motley collection of local legends grafted on the characteristics of French and German nationalisms, and later on in the early twentieth century on a regularly appropriated understanding of Gandhian principles.

[41] Bankimchandra Chatterjee, 'Bharat Kalanka' (The Shame of India), in *Vividha Prabandha*, 137.

[42] Partha Chatterjee, *Nationalist Thought and the Colonial World—A Derivative Discourse?* (London: Zed Books, 1986), 3–5.

[43] See Bhikhu Parekh, *Gandhi's Political Philosophy: A Critical Examination* (London: Macmillan, 1989), 191–2.

[44] Partha Chatterjee, *The Nation and Its Fragments: Colonial and Postcolonial Histories* (Delhi: Oxford University Press, 1994), 4–6.

II

The writing of indigenous history leads us to examine the character-istics constituting its nationalistic dimension, which find a prominent place in *Kanthapura*. The invocation of the past, as argued, becomes an important resource for initiating nationalist upsurge since the 'ideal images and exemplars' of a lost past serve as 'prototypes and models for social and cultural innovation'.[45] Nationalists also build on the productive link between the past and religion. As seen above, Banerjee, in his desire to exalt the Indian past, found it necessary to establish not only the illustrious and admirable qualities of this past, but also the nationalist sentiments of the ancient Hindus, evoking in them a parochial consciousness as in Herder, who believed that men should be, above all, members of their national folk communities in order to be really creative. Although a passive and internalized feel-ing, religion has the potential to move people beyond dormancy to display active political energy to the extent of sacrificing their lives.[46] Intending to forge a Hindu identity that was readily recognizable, Bal Gangadhar Tilak mobilized nationalist energy through a revival of the Shivaji festival which popularized an anachronistic Mahratta sense of greatness among Chitpavan Maharashtra. The Bhagavad Gita was also employed as a text recommending the virtues of action as a religious injunction against British rule. The Gita, Tilak ana-lysed, was full of the merits of austerity as well as action in attaining salvation: 'Perform thy allotted work', Krishna advises Arjuna, 'for action is superior to inaction.'[47] A tactical interpretation of the Gita thus swayed its believers to submit to the religious legitimacy of terrorism. In the same way, Bipin Chandra Pal valorized religion by recounting his countrymen's hunger for the reappearance of Krishna, the Hindu god, in the present:

[45] Anthony D. Smith, *Theories of Nationalism* (London: Duckworth, 1983), p. x.
[46] A recent instance is the blood-bath over the Ayodhya Ram Janmabhoomi and Babri Masjid issue in the state of Uttar Pradesh. The Hindus insist that a 17th-cent. mosque desecrates the birthplace of their god, Rama, having been built upon the exact spot. The subsequent demolition of the mosque has led to widespread bloodshed as Hindu devotees clash with the Muslim minority to claim their sacred land. In order to legitimize their violence, the peace-loving god, Rama, has been depicted by Hindu fundamentalists as a militant god even though the warrior-aspect forms a very small part of the classical iconography of the *maryadapurushottam*, Rama.
[47] *The Bhagavad Gita*, trans. Eliot Deutsch (New York: Holt, Rinehart and Win-ston, 1968), 48. See also Kedourie, 'Introduction', in id. (ed.), *Nationalism in Asia and Africa*, 72.

[They sought] a practical application of that faith, not as a mere religious or spiritual force, but as a social, and, perhaps, even as a political, inspiration. Krishna stood too far away from the present. As God, he is no doubt present in spirit always and everywhere. What they craved for was his manifestation in the flesh . . . . A fresh cry now went up from the heart of his chosen people for a fresh advent of the Saviour.[48]

It is worthy of speculation whether the 'fresh cry' went up from the masses or was a fabrication of the minority of the western-educated intelligentsia of India who rapidly grasped the hegemonic principles of European political thought.[49] Bipin Chandra Pal goes on to reveal the role of traditional religion and its commonly known relics in urging the masses into political activism. He uses the example of *swaraj*[50] to explain the original religious connotation of a political phenomenon. The word, according to Pal, originally symbolized self-rule or restraint, embodying austere, inactive living that held out the promise of deliverance from the evil cycle of successive reincarnations. Later borrowings between politics and religion modified the concept, indicating, in Pal's view, the individual's attainment of oneness with the Universal, which in turn would establish a feeling of fellowship with every being he came into contact. Interpreted thus, the term came to embody not merely national freedom but universal federation also, which alone could establish 'perfect harmony' between nations.[51] By the time we approach Gandhi, the concept of *swaraj* evolves into a symbol having a very definite political edge signifying self-government, yet alloyed somewhat with an other-worldly sanctity to consolidate public appeal.[52]

It is significant that tradition, generally taken as a fixed referent, is repeatedly shaped and restructured to suit the prevailing political temper. While tradition is an identifiable repository of past culture, its alleged qualities of uniformity and homogeneity are variously interpreted by the very exponents—both imperialist and nationalist—of tradition in changing political contexts.[53] The consciousness of

[48] Bipin Chandra Pal, 'Hinduism and Indian Nationalism', in Kedourie (ed.), *Nationalism in Asia and Africa*, 341–2.            [49] Kedourie, 'Introduction', 74.
[50] Home-rule. By implication, the term represented the nationalists' demand for their own government. In Gandhi's vocabulary, *swaraj* also meant ways of self-disciplining that would build an inner resistance to defy the British non-violently.
[51] Pal, 'Hinduism and Indian Nationalism', 351–2.
[52] Kedourie, 'Introduction', 75.
[53] Geeta Kapur has made use of the term 'tradition-in-use' to refer to the use that the intelligentsia in India have made of the repository of past traditions. She calls

nationalist sentiment thus rests very strongly on the capacity of the intelligentsia to provoke the people into belief as in *Kanthapura* where religion becomes a potent self-definer, providing the very foundation for the existence of the village community, as well as in Rao's later novels where an overarching Hindu metaphysical system edges on cultural imperialism. It is another matter, however, whether there is any truth in the nationalistic environment created by the proponents of nationalism. In fact, what is strikingly apparent in the above instances is the type of history that is evoked, a history which draws on floating myths, local legends, and folklore, and could easily be faulted.[54] In similar ways, *Kanthapura*, as a narrative of nationalism, is also presented at the interface of history and fiction: the past and the present intermingle to shape a staunch national identity. The villagers become the soldiers of the Mahatma, and despite the destruction of the village, look forward to a better future.

It is in the establishment of the link between the past and the future that nationalism finds its sustenance.[55] This is implied in the idea of destiny, in a belief that 'history will not let us down', and that no disaster is irrecoverable. A common destiny unites the national rulers and the ruled, so that their motives, occupations, and interests appear to be alike. The awakening of a national sentiment engenders the illusion of an identity of interests between the intelligentsia and the masses, engineered by appealing to a common ancestry in order to build the impression of a motherland. The past, then, becomes a convenient tool for a like future, and its attendant gods bind the members of the nation into a mass of devotees.

A nationalistic representation may become very nearly a 'world view' in its less abstract meaning, or crudely put, a false conscious-

tradition a mobile signifier, something that is constantly improvised to suit political expediency. What lies beneath tradition-in-use is an ideal and what motivates such usage is convenience. See Geeta Kapur, 'Contemporary Cultural Practice: Some Polemical Categories', *Social Scientist*, 183 (1990), 56. See also Edward Said, *Culture and Imperialism* (London: Chatto and Windus, 1993), pp. xiv–xv.

[54] A good example is the regenerative nature of Bankim's writings on Krishna whom he depicts as a rational god by expelling all references to eroticism from his early dalliances at Vrindavana which have customarily been associated with the mythical figure. See Bankimchandra Chatterjee, *Krishna Charitra*, in *Bankim Rachanavali*, ed. Jogesh Chandra Bagal, 3 vols. (Calcutta: Sahitya Samsad, 1953–69), ii.

[55] Gandhi's concept of *ramrajya* is an example. Linked with the past rule of Rama, symbolizing the qualities of good leadership and perfect justice, the concept anticipates the reversal of imperial rule and looks forward to a future where justice and self-rule would overrule anarchy.

ness. As Althusser remarks, ideology has very little to do with 'consciousness', being 'profoundly *unconscious*' and a 'system of representations' only.[56] Further, it is in their ability to represent 'structures' of images or concepts that these ideological representations are able to impose themselves on the masses, and not through their consciousness. Althusser, in fact, treats the populace as passive and unthinking, one that mindlessly perceives, accepts, and suffers the process of imposition of ideas. The nationalist construction of false consciousness tends to indicate that the ordinary peasant or the subaltern does not have any active role in terms of agency. Although it can be said that the generalizing, transcendent nature of the symbols used by the elite is a construct, it is obviously built on pre-existing notions of religion, sacrifice, or worship that already exist among the folk.[57] The folk, on their part, might find national symbols furthering their ends. There is, thus, a possibility that the participants have their own projects, and are not completely subservient to nationalist ideology, a proposition I take up fully in Chapters 3 and 4 to show that the peasants and the women—the subalterns—cannot be completely subverted within the domain of nationalist politics.

Significantly, women have been used as a prominent trope in the negotiation between the past and the future. In nationalist accounts, representations of women need to be integral to the discourse of modernity which characterizes the new nation, yet cannot be cut off from the traditional past. National movements are thereby accompanied by social reform even as nationalist ideology celebrates the virtues of the Aryan woman who is resurrected repeatedly in homogeneous configurations of goddesses and mothers. I discuss later in this book the premise that women have never been conceptualized as being primary to the national movement. In the domain of gender, nationalism has not proved to be a progressive ideology which revolutionizes sexuality. On the contrary, women who participate in the national movement are seldom empowered by the liberation struggle to emerge from their traditional invisibility.

---

[56] Louis Althusser, *For Marx*, trans. Ben Brewster (London: Verso, 1986), 233.

[57] See Gyan Pandey, 'Rallying Round the Cow: Sectarian Strife in the Bhojpuri Region, c. 1888–1917', in Ranajit Guha (ed.), *Subaltern Studies: Writings on South Asian History and Society*, 9 vols. (Delhi: Oxford University Press, 1982–97), ii. 60–129.

Unitary nationalist sentiment also emphasizes the notion of a common language which not only characterizes a nation-state but also separates it from another: it is 'the eternal and visible badge of those differences which distinguish one nation from another'.[58] Hence the endeavour to keep language pure and unadulterated. In this regard, to speak a foreign language introduces artifice in speech and results in contamination of the very idea of nationalism. Fichte cites the instance of the French who were originally Teutons, but abandoned German for a neo-Latin idiom, and so lost a living language. Original, primitive languages, in his view, are superior to composite, derived languages which suffer from impoverishment, being indebted to a culture that is foreign and unstimulating. It follows that German is an unalloyed and pure language in contrast to the derived French and English tongues. Fichte advocates that any nation speaking an original language must be cautious of the inadvertent intrusion of foreign borrowings that would tend to make language impure and thus unnatural:

All the more, therefore, is it incumbent on a nation worthy of the name, to revive, develop, and extend what is taken to be its original speech, even though it might be found only in remote villages, or had not been used for centuries, even though its resources are inadequate and its literature poor — for only such an original language will allow a nation to realize itself and attain freedom.[59]

From this perspective, Raja Rao's experiment with language, in particular, is a remarkable creation of nationalist identity, following the oral rhythms and narrative techniques of traditional models of writing. It is paradoxical, however, that he plays up the 'Indian' way of life against the new egalitarian ideas of the west in the very language of the west. In spite of the foreign and, to use Fichte's logic, unnatural medium, Rao's intuitive reworking of English into an Indian medium is significant, and a success from the standpoint of communication to a westernized intelligentsia, or that small body of educated Indians for whom English is an intellectual language. What is even more interesting is the way he is enabled through the clever handling of language to extend the boundaries of his little village to embrace that of the country, making it, thereby, a composite nation-state.

[58] Elie Kedourie, *Nationalism* (London: Hutchinson, 1966), 64.
[59] Ibid. 67.

III

With these broad features in mind, it is possible to embark upon the construction of the characteristic colonial stereotype of the unchanging Indian village republic, and its role in generating national solidarity which is significant in the context of the ensuing analysis where Kanthapura, a fictitious Indian village, becomes our object of study. Again, the orientalist and the nationalist views have together effected the idea of India as a land of villages in their efforts to approach its 'reality'. While Europe had already made the transition from the country to the city, the village in India still existed as a living entity. Villages in India were sources of revenue collection and provided a major income to revenue officials. They were not simply artefacts that historians studied, but living, productive, and fertile areas of existence, contributing substantially to the survival of the people.

From the point of view of the civilizing mission of the British, a land chiefly constituted of villages was the antithesis of a modern and progressive Britain. In their logic, the modern (signifying developed society) would dominate the ancient. They argued that the essence of the 'ancient' lay in its inwardly-turned communal societies in opposition to the outward, expanding, competitive, and individualistic 'modern'. Combined with their own nostalgic fantasies, the accounts of Indian village communities by academic orientalists like Sir Henry Maine and Baden-Powell may well have underscored the motives of political and administrative control.[60] However, there was another class of people—the nationalist intelligentsia—who were interested in perpetuating a similar picture of timeless village societies. The reason, of course, was different: their constructions had to do with the founding of an 'alternative society', the world that had been lost.[61] Within the double discourse of nationalism that was both hegemonizing and modernizing, the village was India's answer to western domination. It symbolized indigenous cultural standards as well as the power of antiquity that could stand up to the modern.

Thus village communities were attractive centres of preserved culture for many romantic conservatives. Ordered and stabilized, the

[60] See Henry Sumner Maine, *Village Communities in the East and West* (1871; London: John Murray, 1907); and B. H. Baden-Powell, *The Indian Village Community* (London, New York, and Bombay: Longmans, Green, 1896).
[61] Clive Dewey, 'Images of the Village Community: A Study in Anglo-Indian Ideology', *Modern Asian Studies*, 6 (1972), 292.

village represented permanence in an otherwise disintegrated and chaotic world. The enduring quality of the Indian village was believed to be largely the result of an amazing degree of internal tenacity that resisted any external crisis. Despite stratification into castes, the villagers were mutually bound in various economic and social functions. The clannish nature of the inhabitants, co-operative farming, and joint property in the economic sphere, and the ritualistic character of belief and kinship in the moral sphere enthused romantic conservatives, who visualized the village as the only social unit that could offer a still point in the turning world. There were others who consigned villages to inertia and stagnation, believing them to stifle individuality and thereby economic growth. The different views, nevertheless, did share a belief in the characteristic unchanging nature of the village. The debate, it must be understood, centred more on the question of the desirability of the village character than on the essential features of that community over which there was no disagreement. There was, in other words, scarcely any discrepancy between the two views on the nature of the village itself as an ideal type, even though the triumph of any one view over the other could have resulted in a very different revenue system. This explains why the village has remained 'permanent' and in a state of cultural stasis in its very definition in spite of severe controversies in the late nineteenth and early twentieth centuries.[62]

---

[62] Sir Charles Metcalfe's idealized description of a village community substantiates the commonly held view. According to Metcalfe, '[Indian village communities are] little republics, having nearly everything that they can want within themselves. . . . They seem to last where nothing else lasts. Dynasty after dynasty tumbles down; revolution succeeds revolution; Hindoo, Patan, Mogul, Mahratta, Sikh, English, are all masters in turn; but the village community remains the same. . . . If plunder and devastation be directed against themselves and force employed be irresistible, they flee to friendly villages at a distance; but, when the storm has passed over, they return and resume their occupations. . . . A generation may pass away, but the succeeding generation will return. The sons will take the places of their fathers; the same site for the village, the same positions for the house. . . . This union of the village communities . . . has, I conceive, contributed more than any other cause to the preservation of the people of India.' Generalizing what was basically a comment on the unified Sikh kingdom under the rulership of Ranjit Singh, Metcalfe exaggerates the communal aspect of village existence at the cost of their social organization and economic roots. He emphasizes the permanence of the village even in the middle of invasion and rebellion. At a brief glance, such were the attitudes taken up by the admirers and adversaries of village communities in the second quarter of the 19th cent. The dominant English commentators, however, shared a consensus for the romantic idyll rather than for the utilitarian critique. See Sir C. T. Metcalfe, 'Minute on the Settlement in the Western Provinces', 7 Nov. 1830, in *Minutes of Evidence taken before the Select Committee on the Affairs of the East India Company*, cited in Dewey, 'Images of the Village Community', 296–7.

In fact, the numerous descriptions of villages appear to be part of the same text or of a common family of thinkers.[63] Around 1870, Sir Henry Maine's philological enthusiasm brought forth more exaggerated notions of permanence in his theory of racial diffusion that saw Europe and India as different phases in the same passage of development, with India as the earliest form of European civilization. In this schema, the village symbolized the fossilized remains of the then contemporary Europe, that had remarkably survived and remained intact owing to India's geographical isolation. It became possible, therefore, to substantiate any historical research by the living example of the Indian village that was, in other words, 'the early European village community *extant*'.[64]

The insistence that each village was a pre-historic inner world, economically self-sufficient, and an organic community of peasants persistently dogged both orientalists and nationalist intellectuals as the embodiment of a village community. What we notice is an acute lack of independent inquiry in the reproduction of this single formula definition. The consequence is the conception of an Indian village as a static entity in which we are not permitted to see the play of choices by the inhabitants of that village, either at a simple or a complex level. When Raja Rao constructs his village, the constantly refigured image of Maine and others already existed as a 'tradition' among nationalists who worked, in many ways, on the 'Black is Beautiful' principle. What was ugly and obsolete by western standards became India's strength and identity. Passivity transformed itself into Gandhi's non-violent resistance, while the view that Indians were incapable of governing themselves led to a rejection of state apparatus. The Indian village, nevertheless, continued to be regarded as the idealized antithesis of western civilization in terms of its spirituality and religious norms which were eternal. Beginning in the early nineteenth century from Rammohan Roy's recognition of India as a Land of the Spirit to Swami Vivekananda's advocacy of the Indian instruction in matters of the spirit later on in the century, the assumption of the spiritual potential of India embodied in its villages became a fundamental feature in representations of Indian identity. Other thinkers and writers like Rabindranath Tagore, Madanmohan Malaviya, and

[63] Marx also sees Indian villages as cellular and 'idyllic', largely unchanged before the advent of the British who would prove to be 'the unconscious tool of history in bringing about . . . revolution'. See Marx, 'British Rule in India', 132.
[64] Dewey, 'Images of the Village Community', 307.

Bankimchandra Chatterjee stressed the values imbibed from the family, the village, and its castes. Gandhi, of course, was the later fountainhead of Indian cultural identity which he believed was rooted in its villages.

Literature participated actively in resurrecting the 'pastness' of village societies facilitating the formation of national consciousness, not only through print dissemination but also as a carrier of 'folk character' and 'national language'.[65] The novel, with its epic intentions, served to bring the present in touch with the past, as is reflected in the fiction which was written in the last crucial decades of colonial rule. Many novelists like K. S. Venkataramani, Mulk Raj Anand, and R. K. Narayan conceived full-scale studies of 'real' Indian villages to project 'a microcosmic image of the macrocosmic world'.[66] Narayan's Malgudi, a village on which his novels are based, is a case in point: he presents the river Sarayu in close association with the myths of the Ramayana and the Mahabharata, India's famous epics, and thus celebrates the immemorial in a world of flux. Post-independence writing like K. Nagarajan's *Chronicles of Kedaram* continued to idealize village life by using myths of the past typified by the river Nilaveni and the Temple Kedareswarar.[67] Even Prafulla Mohanty's *My Village, My Life*, written in the early 1970s, privileges permanent village values epitomized in Nanpur, his village in the Cuttack district of Orissa: 'This is the portrait of a village in India. It has been there for a long time. Nobody knows its history. It was never planned. . . . It happened.'[68] To regard Nanpur, Kanthapura, Kedaram, or Malgudi as 'a truer and greater India which is timeless and enduring'[69] amounts to taking the Romantic episteme from orientalism for perceiving the village. Rao's treatment of the subject, in a similar manner, raises questions and provides testimony to the agreement between orientalist and nationalist accounts. He turns the political upheaval of controversial contemporary politics of the freedom struggle into a homogeneous national-popular movement in *Kanthapura*. The quest

[65] Timothy Brennan, *Salman Rushdie and the Third World: Myths of the Nation* (Basingstoke and London: Macmillan, 1989), 7.

[66] K. S. Ramamurti, 'Kanthapura, Kedaram, Malgudi and Trinidad as Indias in Miniature—A Comparative Study', in Avadesh K. Sinha (ed.), *Alien Voice: Perspectives on Commonwealth Literature* (Lucknow: Print House, 1981), 63.

[67] K. Nagarajan, *Chronicles of Kedaram* (Bombay: Asia, 1961).

[68] Prafulla Mohanty, *My Village, My Life* (London: Davis-Poynter, 1973), 9.

[69] Ramamurti, 'Kanthapura, Kedaram, Malgudi and Trinidad as Indias in Miniature', 67.

for identity had to be encoded in age-old principles ostensibly present in village societies that were accepted monuments of the 'essence' of India. Such a representation oddly appeared to be the only means of countering the legacy of colonialism without actually engaging in any real ideological battle with the colonialists.

It is within this context that I explore Raja Rao's *Kanthapura*, believed to be a historical fiction of the very soil of 'real' India in the tradition of *sthala-puranas* or legendary stories of the land. As the story unfolds, the reader gets a taste of the fixed values, of roots, and a sense of place, the fictional and self-conscious nature of which it is my intention to explore. The common denomination of villages to the normative and representative little communities undermines the view that 'each village has a pattern and mode of life which is to some extent unique' and that villages differ even within the same locality, this being a recognized fact of rural existence.[70] Arvind Das, in his detailed study of three generations of mutation in a village in the Darbhanga district of Bihar, speaks of the gradual but definite change despite the backwardness and continuity of life.[71] There have been even more vehement protests against the construction of an idealized village community. Repudiating Gandhi, B. R. Ambedkar, the champion of the untouchables, spoke of the village as 'a sink of localism, a den of ignorance, narrow-mindedness and communalism'.[72] And several years later, Balwantray Mehta, a leader of the Congress Party known for his village development programmes, repeated Ambedkar: 'I would like to point out that villages have never been as they have been depicted by poets and men of letters in their works. They have been what they are. What we find today has been there all throughout the ages. Factions are there, conservatism is there and superstitions are there.'[73] The existing stereotype of the concept of the village as the basis of the Indian society in the manner of Gandhi is here replaced by the development programme of the *panchayati raj* (the rule of the village representatives) which emphasized democratic decentralization based on development and not utopian visions.

[70] M. N. Srinivas (ed.), *India's Villages* (Bombay: Asia, 1955), 2.

[71] Arvind N. Das, 'Changel: Three Centuries of an Indian Village', *The Journal of Peasant Studies*, 15.1 (1987), 3–59.

[72] Cited in Richard G. Fox, *Gandhian Utopia: Experiments with Culture* (Boston: Beacon, 1989), 183.

[73] Balwantray Mehta, 'Reflections from the Chair', in M. V. Mathur and Iqbal Narain (eds.), *Seminar on Panchayati Raj, Planning and Democracy, Jaipur, 1964* (Bombay: Asia, 1969), 87–8.

Nevertheless, the focus on Rao's representation of an Indian village becomes essential in any study of nationalist identity because the image of a village community as a 'peasant society' is still dominant.[74] That fictions constituting such views of history are successful and have a large readership speaks for the kind of audiences who are inclined to receive such constructions favourably.

IV

Undoubtedly, the production of a nationalist ideology in particular narratives and its role in attempting to absorb as many people as possible through its rhetoric is significant. Within the colonial situation, the figuration of a common identity leads to unitary nationalism for it is only through collective religious or linguistic sentiments that political ends can be reached. These strategies are motivated by the desire to dominate, and this is achieved through the imposition of the idea of ethnic superiority of a social group. The rhetoric of nationalism in India has always built on Hindu iconography since Hindus are in the majority so that the creation of 'imagined communities', more often than not, implicitly ignores class divisions and economic distinctions.

If we were to dismantle the notion of a monolithic Hindu identity to develop an alternative perspective on self-representative accounts, we would find various communities and segmented identities distinguished by language, caste, occupation, and geographical location in contrast to the concept of the unified Hindu identity of the modern Indian nation-state. In explaining the homogenizing tendency of Hinduism, Romila Thapar argues that the urge to construct a homogeneous Hindu heartland was legitimized by the expedient twisting of available historical evidence:

The new Hinduism which is now sought to be projected as the religion of this community is in many ways a departure from the earlier religious sects. It seeks historicity for the incarnations of its deities, encourages the idea of a centrally sacred book, claims monotheism as significant to the worship of deity, acknowledges the authority of the ecclesiastical organisation of certain sects as prevailing over all and has supported large-scale missionary work and

[74] Shanin regards the representation of peasantry as an aspect of the past continuing in the present to be still powerful. See Teodor Shanin, *Peasant and Peasant Societies* (Harmondsworth: Penguin, 1971), 17.

conversion. These changes allow it to transcend caste identities and reach out to larger numbers.[75]

Religions outside Hinduism—Jainism and Buddhism—that interrogate brahminical philosophy and practice, have been carefully absorbed into the mainstream of Hinduism by sweeping aside their distinctiveness. What we now know to be Hinduism was possibly a mixture of a large number of sects and cults which observed common symbols, yet followed diverse customs and rituals. The etymological beginnings of the term 'Hindu' as a geographical nomenclature have to do with the region around the river Indus which was referred to as Hi(n)dush, implying that it had neither religious nor cultural connotations. It was rather an all-embracing term for the people of the Indian sub-continent which spanned the river Indus or Sindhu.[76] Al-Hind, therefore, referred to a geographical area, and Hindus were those who lived in it. In the eyes of the newly arrived Muslims, Hindu, thus, essentially came to mean 'the other'.[77] Imperceptibly, however, the meaning shifted to those who were inhabitants of India but embraced a belief that was other than Christian or Islamic. Within such an understanding, 'Hindu' came to comprise the brahmins as well as the other cults including the lower castes. This contradicted the exclusive premises of the brahmins who found themselves clubbed with a host of pagan elements infringing upon their community. As for the large number of non-brahmin sects, the term 'Hindu' must have been equally perplexing, since they lost their distinctiveness and stood assimilated into Hinduism.[78] Even at the turn of the twentieth century, there was a good deal of uncertainty about who comprised the Hindu community, and the meaning of the term 'Hindu', whether Buddhists, Jains, Sikhs, and members of the different bhakti sects, as well as the 'untouchables' and 'tribals', all of whom lived on the borders of settled Hindu society, were to be

[75] Romila Thapar, 'Imagined Religious Communities? Ancient History and the Modern Search for a Hindu Identity', Kingsley Martin Memorial Lecture, University of Cambridge, 1 June 1988. Published in *School of Social Sciences Working Paper Series* (New Delhi: Jawaharlal Nehru University, 1988), 31–2.

[76] T. M. P. Mahadevan, *Outlines of Hinduism* (Bombay: Chetana, 1956), 12.

[77] Quite in the same way, the resident 'Hindus' did not categorize the new arrivals as 'Muslim'. They were referred to variously as 'Yavana' (Greeks), 'Turuska' (Turks), or 'Mleccha' (Untouchables). See Thapar, 'Imagined Religious Communities?', 23–4.

[78] Ibid. 23. Thapar's argument about the assimilation of brahminic and other cults has been made earlier by Sarasvati Chennakesavan, *A Critical Study of Hinduism* (London: Asia Publishing House, 1974), 3.

included among the Hindus.[79] Cantwell Smith goes so far as to call Hinduism an altogether 'false conceptualization' because it is difficult to conceptualize the geographical entity 'Hindu' as a historically constituted unity holding religious and philosophical beliefs.[80] In short, a variety of religious beliefs and practices have been labelled 'Hindu': there is a 'popular Hinduism', a 'temple Hinduism', a 'bhakti Hinduism', a 'village Hinduism', a 'tribal Hinduism', and so on, all of which facilitate the construction of abstract models.[81]

The construction of a Hindu national identity was the nationalist solution to unite a people by appealing to a common consciousness in terms of religious practices. In the vein of dismantling foundationalist history, recent studies have attempted to interpret Indian nationalism in terms of a formation constituted by 'both popular elements from below and manipulative ones from above'.[82] Such studies attempt to show that ideologies and propaganda exist on one level while individual commitment is situated on another, even though the latter might link up with the former. This is seen in the instances of peasant rebellion in Chapter three where national identity combines with the people's set of non-national identifications for its realization, a connection in which nation-formation is not superior to the goal of personal livelihood, and is witnessed within a shifting terrain of loyalties. There is little room in such a scenario for nationalist consciousness. Breuilly has contributed substantially to the idea of the political formation of nation-states by dismissing as 'misleading' the notions of nationalism as a manifestation of national consciousness, as something embodying a national interest or even its relation to class interests.[83] His view would refute Kohn's early argument that

[79] Gyanendra Pandey, 'Which of Us Are Hindus?', in id. (ed.), *Hindus and Others: The Question of Identity in India Today* (New Delhi: Viking, 1993), 246.

[80] Wilfred Cantwell Smith, *The Meaning and End of Religion* (New York: Mentor, 1964), 61. Smith goes on to say that his 'objection to the term "Hinduism" . . . is not on the grounds that nothing exists. Obviously an enormous quantity of phenomena is to be found that this term covers. [The] point . . . is that the mass of religious phenomena that we shelter under the umbrella of that term, is not a unity and does not aspire to be' (63).

[81] Robert E. Frykenberg, 'The Emergence of Modern "Hinduism" as a Concept and as an Institution: A Reappraisal With Special Reference to South India', in Günther D. Sontheimer and Hermann Kulke (eds.), *Hinduism Reconsidered* (Delhi: Manohar, 1989), 87.

[82] Achin Vanaik, *The Painful Transition: Bourgeois Democracy in India* (London: Verso, 1990), 117.

[83] John Breuilly, *Nationalism and the State*, 2nd edn. (Manchester: Manchester University Press, 1993), 1–2; 12–18.

the political formation of the nation-state is linked to the consciousness of nationality. In other words, Breuilly's 'fundamental' point that nationalism is 'above and beyond all else, about politics' opposes Kohn's idea of a cultural entity that first forms largely in the consciousness and *then* gets transformed into the political nation-state (emphasis added).[84] Such a premiss as Kohn's does not consider those who, in Hobsbawm's view, are 'the objects of [the elite's] action and propaganda'.[85]

Furthering our exercise of denying the homogeneity of nationalist accounts, Christopher Bayly's *Rulers, Townsmen and Bazaars* marks another significant turn. Bayly's detailed study speaks of an eighteenth-century India which was characterized by the emergence of successful and dynamic regional societies consisting of Hindu and Muslim entrepreneurs and merchants in the wake of Mughal decline.[86] In very many ways, it was the dynamism of these societies which contributed to the interactive relationship that developed between the East India Company and the north Indian society. In his view, the Indian nation-state was born, not out of an ancient past, but was created in the process of the establishment of a colonial relationship around 1850.

A homogeneous nation-state is difficult to conceptualize in Marxist terms as well owing to the neglected question of class divisions. At the same time, Marxists provide a different explanation of colonialism as a necessary political instrument for mass production and capital accumulation, assisting the emergence of the nation-state. Marx's stance, it has however been reasoned, 'had little to do with a positive preference for European colonialism', reflecting, on the other hand, 'his concern to encourage the emergence in India of indigenous social movements opposed at once to canonical exploitation *and* to the traditional "despotism" which . . . [he] held responsible for India's weakness in the face of European incursions.'[87] Marx's desire 'to chart a third way' towards other political alternatives was resistant to the revanchist creation of a 'golden age

[84] Kohn, *The Idea of Nationalism*, 15; 19.

[85] E. J. Hobsbawm, *Nations and Nationalism Since 1780: Programme, Myth, Reality*, 2nd edn. (Cambridge: Cambridge University Press, 1991), 11.

[86] Christopher A. Bayly, *Rulers, Townsmen and Bazaars: North Indian Society in the Age of British Expansion, 1770–1870* (Cambridge: Cambridge University Press, 1983).

[87] Erica Benner, *Really Existing Nationalisms: A Post-Communist View from Marx and Engels* (Oxford: Clarendon, 1995), 176.

of Hindostan'.[88] Marxist historians in the present, while locating themselves at a fair distance from Marx's eurocentric position, would subscribe to the Subalternist view of presenting powerful indigenous movements among the traditionally non-ruling classes of India to unfix the orientalist/nationalist stereotypes. In writing histories of class-conflict, hierarchy, and contest, Marxists also seldom find themselves free of the charge of foundationalism since these privileged themes bring language, religion, caste, and gender completely under erasure. It is thus that the Marxist principles underlying the Subaltern Studies group have been criticized by Spivak for eliding the specificities of the individual subaltern.[89] It cannot be denied, however, that the Subaltern School of historians have challenged homogenizing discourse and targeted the primary constituents of nationalism fashioned by the elite by positing the subaltern as a point of opposition. The question they pose is: when it comes to nationalist representations, how far are the subalterns the subjects of the nation-in-the-making? The Subaltern collective has tried to make a case for the actual instances of subaltern insurgency and the absence of a suitable representation of these instances in nationalist accounts.

History-writing, then, is not a single act but a variety of discourses based on different contextual positions, and must necessarily be addressed with scepticism. To argue for the orient as a different region with its indigenous definition of religion, culture, or essence is, as examined, as debatable as any explanation that precludes the native from grasping the inner sense of his or her own orient. The 'real' orient is not simply one that is created by an oriental just as a representation of blacks by blacks or of Muslims by Muslims would not bring forth a truer or an unprejudiced account, though it would be undoubtedly true for the blacks or Muslims. Towards the conclusion of *Orientalism*, Said expresses a concern with finding alternatives to homogenizing tendencies as long as there is ambiguity in the representation and definition of a culture. He is optimistic that it is not entirely impossible to conceive of a scholarship that neither 'corrupts' history nor is indifferent to human reality:

[88]  Marx, 'British Rule in India', 126.
[89]  Gayatri Chakravorty Spivak, 'Subaltern Studies: Deconstructing Historiography', in *In Other Worlds: Essays in Cultural Politics* (New York and London: Routledge, 1988).

If we no longer think of the relationship between cultures and their adherents as perfectly contiguous, totally synchronous, wholly correspondent, and if we think of cultures as permeable and, on the whole, defensive boundaries between polities, a more promising situation appears. Thus to see Others not as ontologically given but as historically constituted would be to erode the exclusivist biases we so often ascribe to cultures, our own not least. Cultures may then be represented as zones of control or of abandonment, of recollection and forgetting, of force or of dependence, of exclusiveness or of sharing, all taking place in the global history that is our element. Exile, immigration, and the crossing of boundaries are experiences that can therefore provide us with new narrative forms or . . . with *other* ways of telling.[90]

Said thus rejects the possibility of an authentic history of the orient. He considers identity from a vantage point not external to the actuality of relationships between cultures or from a privileging epistemology centred in unequal relationships, but '*within* the actuality, and as participants in it'.[91] By implication, India could be constituted in a variety of unstable identities.

From a Marxist historian's point of view, Said has been criticized most recently by Aijaz Ahmad for his 'reactionary anti humanisms', presumably poststructuralism and postcolonialism, which have cast suspicion on the truth value of any representation of reality, owing to the medium of language.[92] One of Ahmad's severe criticisms of Said is his investment in the Nietzschean idea that any representation of reality is not an exact representation. Ahmad draws lines between the two powerful discourses of Nietzsche and Marx. While the former rules out the possibility of making true statements, the latter sanctions it. As Ahmad writes:

[Said] is affiliating himself with a new kind of history-writing, which was emerging more or less at this time, which goes far beyond the empirical historian's usual interrogation of and scepticism about the available evidence and the accepted modes of interpretation; and enters the Nietzschean world of questioning not merely positivist constructions but the very facticity of facts, so that it will eventually force a wide range of historians around the globe . . . to start putting the word 'fact' in quotation marks.[93]

Let us examine Ahmad's first argument about Said's scepticism which puts 'reality' in question. Undoubtedly, there does exist a reality, but

---

[90] Edward Said, 'Representing the Colonized: Anthropology's Interlocutors', *Critical Inquiry*, 15.2 (1989), 225.    [91] Ibid. 217.    [92] Ahmad, *In Theory*, 194.
[93] Ibid.

it is only available to us through the narrativization of events. In a well-argued essay, Menon has shown that 'no fact presents itself to us innocent of narrative structures which give it the meaning it has for us'.[94] Hence it is prudent to question 'the facticity of facts'. Linked to his misgivings about the relationship between discourse and reality is Ahmad's second apprehension about the Nietzschean position Said adopts, which, in his view, is to deny meaning altogether. Ahmad's emphasis on real history seems to deny that all narratives are discursively constituted through language. This does not imply that all representations are misrepresentations or that there is a reality 'out there' which is being misunderstood simply because it has undergone transformation in the act of writing. Nietzschean scepticism must be read only as a pointer towards greater self-consciousness among those who write history. This is not to say that there are no good or bad histories. The ones which approximate most to our conception of the real, and offer substantial reasons for being so, would be better than those which do not. As Derrida has argued, 'When one attempts, in a general way, to pass from an obvious to a latent language, one must first be rigorously sure of the obvious meaning. The analyst, for example, must first speak the same language as the patient.'[95]

Ahmad's chief concern is to rescue 'history' from being co-opted by poststructuralism in any academic exercise of a search for identity. Both third-worldist cultural nationalisms and recent postmodernisms, in his view, subvert reality by false explanations:

[A] theoretical position that dismisses the history of materialities as a . . . 'myth of origins', nations and states . . . as irretrievably coercive, classes as simply discursive constructs, and political parties themselves as fundamentally contaminated with collectivist illusions of a stable subject position—a theoretical position of that kind, from which no poststructuralism worth the name can escape, is, in the most accurate sense of these words, *repressive* and *bourgeois*.[96]

It is quite surprising that soon after making such a claim, Ahmad himself deconstructs Jameson's celebrated essay, 'Third-World Litera-

[94] Nivedita Menon, 'Orientalism and After', *Economic and Political Weekly*, 27.39 (1992), 2135.
[95] Jacques Derrida, 'Cogito and the History of Madness', in *Writing and Difference*, trans. Alan Bass (London: Routledge, 1990), 32–3; cited in Menon, 'Orientalism and After', 2135.          [96] Ahmad, *In Theory*, 35–6.

ture in the Era of Multinational Capitalism'.[97] Ahmad has shut out the possibility of an emancipatory discourse through corrosive criticisms of poststructuralist politics of cultural displacement and Said's anti-essentialist works leaving no room for the multifarious speaking positions which have put history and meaning in a state of flux.

Even though the later Said has distanced himself from some of his earlier views and also expressed reservations about Foucault,[98] his research on orientalism, as I see it, is extremely useful in breaking down the category of the 'nation' which is no longer available to us in the forms we are accustomed.[99] Undoubtedly, as Ahmad argues, the break-up of the nation-state described by Said is 'frequently delivered alongside resounding affirmations of national liberation'.[100] Yet the two should not be seen as oppositional or mutually inconsistent but as complementary movements: the fixing of identity in all latter cases is a means to understanding historical formation at the same time as the former gives us access to rapidly dissolving categories, all of which is happening simultaneously. To take one example, the revolt of the nationalists in Northern Ireland can only serve to remind Southern Ireland of the limits of decolonization as they move into 'post-colonial' structures like the European Union.[101]

---

[97] See Ibid. 95–122. Jameson, in this essay, clubs together the countries which have been subjected to colonialism and imperialism as the 'Third World', allocating the nomenclature 'First' and 'Second' worlds respectively to the capitalist countries and those that earlier constituted the socialist bloc. It is Jameson's contention that 'all third-world texts are necessarily . . . *national allegories*', thus limiting their experience to colonialism and imperialism. In other words, they have nothing else to write about but their slavery and the consequent nationalist ideology. But, as Ahmad alleges, if the common experience of colonialism binds the third world, surely the common experience of imperialism must dictate nationalist allegories among the first world too. Ahmad believes that there are more reasons to homogenize the experiences of France, Germany, or Britain, and to produce a single narrative form for them than for India and Iran, or for Afganisthan and Uruguay. In the case of third-world nation-states, it is hardly likely for there to be any commonalty between the various kinds of nationalisms they experience. Secondly, he argues, why should socialism, or indeed, capitalism be the privilege of the first two worlds alone? The specific purpose of Jameson's argument might have been to homogenize the third world and posit it as the singular Other. See also Jameson, 'Third-World Literature'.

[98] Ahmad, *In Theory*, 199. See also Edward Said, 'Traveling Theory', in *The World, the Text, and the Critic* (London: Faber, 1984), 243–7.

[99] See Menon, 'Orientalism and After', 2133.

[100] Ahmad, *In Theory*, 201.

[101] Liam O' Dowd, 'New Introduction', in Albert Memmi, *The Colonizer and the Colonized* (London: Earthscan, 1990), 34–60. While the Catholic Nationalists

Interestingly, literature as a discipline has shown a lot more re-silience and promise when faced with the explosion of identities. Said himself speaks of the emerging 'praxes of . . . humanist activity' and 'new theoretical models that upset or at the very least radically alter the prevailing paradigmatic norms'.[102] Prominent among these would be the imaginative works of Salman Rushdie whose fiction and criticism is self-consciously written against the cultural stereotypes and representations commanding the field. Literature is a significant source for witnessing the shifting nature of identities just as it is a viable genre to study the ideological construction of narratives. It is, however, seldom considered capable of providing evidence germane to the understanding of history. In the following chapters, I have attempted to show how Raja Rao represents a particularly evocative kind of history through a literary idiom for the kinds of political purposes that have already been explored. What is striking about Rao's project is the effectiveness with which he is able to use myths convincingly. The study is significant in exploring the configuration of a timeless Indian community of the nationalist intelligentsia. At the same time, it throws light on the role of historical fiction and its potential for an understanding of the nature of historical inquiry.

Literary representations will always suggest a fresh range of histor-ical investigation. But like other forms of historical evidence, litera-ture has to be treated with caution, its language fully comprehended and analysed as a social and ideological structure and its biases taken into account, for often 'how it really was' can get translated into 'how it shall be remembered'. With this in mind, the genre of Indian nationalist fiction should be seen by historians as documents for understanding important events in the political, social, and intellec-tual life of pre-independence India. It may also be of interest to those who work in the highly specialized area of historical inquiry because such novels offer particularly interesting case-studies of novelists who employ historical perspectives to explain, and even influence, con-temporary reality.

continue striving for independence, the Irish Republic, having passed through similar phases of conflict now paradoxically seek assimilation in socio-economic relationships of dependence. Said's position of both abetting national liberation struggles and mistrusting national identity may be illustrated in the Irish context.

[102] Edward Said, 'Orientalism Reconsidered', in Francis Barker, *et al.* (eds.), *Europe and Its Others: Proceedings of the Essex Conference on the Sociology of Literature*, 2 vols. (Colchester: University of Essex, 1985), i. 24.

Part I

# Representations and Identities

# 1  The Nativization of English

## I

Since sections of the intelligentsia participated actively in the institutions of the colonial state—its administration, its teaching, its law, and trade—there developed a curious correspondence between English and other Indian languages, significantly referred to as 'regional'. The very institutionalization of English by the nationalist elite extended a 'national' character to the language of state administration, enabling only works in English to assume the status of a national literature while the regional languages occupied a less national character. The recognition of the position of English in India did not lead to the exclusion of regional languages. On the contrary, it allowed regional languages to exist side by side, and, in fact, enabled the intelligentsia to be comfortably bilingual. In our context, it is fair to say that bilingualism was a trait (and still is) of these sections of the intelligentsia who practised these linguistic variations to suit different circumstances. Gandhi and Nehru belonged very much to this 'polyglot' tradition of bilingualism.[1] In effect, the use of English in India could never be seen markedly to jeopardize or displace indigenous languages, even as the influence of English continues to be irresistible.[2] Despite the opposition to colonial rule and its impositions, it was English that enabled the intelligentsia to effectuate the modern nation-state in terms of linguistic homogeneity, apart from its use-value in commanding an elite status in society. Above all these

[1] Aijaz Ahmad, *In Theory: Classes, Nations, Literatures* (New Delhi: Oxford University Press, 1993), 75–6. Nehru, in fact, saw the 'best guarantee of a unified nation in the continuance of English.' See Badri Raina, 'A Note on Language, and the Politics of English in India', in Svati Joshi (ed.), *Rethinking English: Essays in Literature, Language, History* (New Delhi: Trianka, 1991), 287.

[2] For an interesting discussion of the position of English in India, see Rajeswari Sunder Rajan, 'Fixing English: Nation, Language, Subject', in ead. (ed.), *The Lie of the Land: English Literary Studies in India* (Delhi: Oxford University Press, 1992), 7–28. See also Svati Joshi, 'Rethinking English: An Introduction', in ead., *Rethinking English*, 5–6.

practical considerations, it could also not be denied that for the Indian mind, the appreciation of the English literary canon as an ideal cultural artefact was able to override its other hegemonic function associated with the exploitative aspect of colonialism.[3] Thus removed from history, the 'mental output' of English rule was able to exist on a plane separate from the 'material reality' of subjugation,[4] and thereby debilitate the native effort to critique the ruthlessness of colonial politics through the gentle persuasion of English education.

Within the national context, the sovereign character of regional languages could not be abandoned altogether. The regional languages were a connection with the past which the nationalists wanted to maintain.[5] In spite of being led by an English-speaking nationalist elite, some common indigenous language was the only medium appropriate for national integration. At the same time, the use of any one of India's many regional languages, like Bankim's employment of Bengali, could only be a vehicle for cultural chauvinism. An interesting example of the uses to which language can be put for the expression of a unitary identity defining nationalism is found in Raja Rao's *Kanthapura*. In this novel, Rao conducts a unique experiment with both Kannada and English sentence structures to produce a kind of syntax that plays up the 'Indian' way of life against the imported and imposed values of the west. The contradiction, remarkably muted by the 'Indian' flavour infused into English speech, contributes to the tension of the novel and presents a potential subject for analysis in our study of nationalist representations.

It becomes important, therefore, to explore the manner in which the experimental use of the English language is geared towards the

---

[3] Narayan's *The English Teacher*, for instance, brings out the conflict between the hero's anti-colonial sentiments and his sincere appreciation of English literature. While Krishna's resignation letter attacks 'a whole century of false education' which has created a 'nation of morons', he cannot shrug off his admiration for English literature: 'What fool could be insensible to Shakespeare's sonnets or the *Ode to the West Wind* or "A thing of beauty is a joy forever"?' See R. K. Narayan, *The English Teacher* (1946; Mysore: Indian Thought Publications, 1973), 205; 206.

[4] Gauri Viswanathan, *Masks of Conquest: Literary Study and British Rule in India* (New York: Columbia University Press, 1989), 20.

[5] Though Bankimchandra Chatterjee wrote his first novel, *Rajmohan's Wife* in English, all his subsequent novels were written in Bengali. See Bankimchandra Chatterjee, *Rajmohan's Wife* (1864), in *Bankim Rachanavali*, ed. Jogeshchandra Bagal, 3 vols. (Calcutta: Sahitya Samsad, 1953–69), iii.

definition of a cultural identity. Rao emphasizes the nativization of English and its new identities in the foreword of the novel:

The telling has not been easy. One has to convey in a language that is not one's own the spirit that is one's own. One has to convey the various shades and omissions of a certain thought-movement that looks maltreated in an alien language. I use the word 'alien', yet English is not really an alien language to us. It is the language of our intellectual make-up—like Sanskrit or Persian was before—but not of our emotional make-up. We are *all* [emphasis added] instinctively bilingual, many of us writing in our own language and in English (5).

Evidently, Rao is anxious about the use of an 'alien' language but he circumvents the risk by assuming his readership to be intuitively bilingual, speaking both English and an Indian language of which we are not certain. Rao perhaps refers to Kannada, the language spoken in Karnataka, and there could be two reasons for that: the language and speech mannerisms used in the novel are close to those of Kannada, and Rao is, himself, a native speaker of the language. But in not specifying the exact location of the language, the reader is at liberty to infer that the foreword is, perhaps, indicative of his or her own particular language, which is presumed to be shared by the author owing to the subtle construction of community suggested by first person plurals. The concealed information not only removes the difficulty of employing any single language in a multilingual country, it also legitimizes the use of English. This enables Rao to evoke a response from all readers so long as they speak and read English and one Indian language. By establishing English as the lingua franca, he can go on to write an Indian novel in English with convenience.

The acculturation of English and the formation of multicultural identities is steadily developed in the second section of the foreword which deals with the indigenization of the foreign language and the construction of a new native technique of writing that would be a mixture of the English and the Indian:

We cannot write like the English. We should not. We cannot write only as Indians. We have grown to look at the large world as part of us. Our method of expression therefore has to be a dialect which will some day prove to be as distinctive and colourful as the Irish or the American. Time alone will justify it (5).

Rao would like to incorporate the foreign into the indigenous and create a multiculturalism which would nonetheless include within itself a localism. Though he realizes that English 'is the language of our intellectual make-up—like Sanskrit or Persian was before—but not of our emotional make-up' (5), he feels that the foreign language can be indigenized if it is dressed up with Indian mythology, presented as a rich *sthala-purana* or a legendary history of the country in the novel. An experiment using the intellectual character of one language and the emotional of another would hold added appeal for the bilingual people comprising Rao's reading public.

Before I address the question of readership, I would like to point out that the 'instinctively bilingual' among Rao's readers can include only those who are literate and competent in both English and an Indian language. Outside elite politics, this would not only sacrifice the concept of linguistic homogeneity necessary for national integration but also exclude the vast multitudes of illiterate or semi-literate masses of India. The illiterate would not be able to read even in the language of their speech, and certainly not in English. Paradoxically, then, Rao's 'Indian' language for village India cannot be understood by the majority of village Indians since they are not bilingual. For the Indian writer, thus, the issue of literacy must precede that of language.[6] Whatever language is used in his or her writing, it is the question of literacy which first confronts the writer. Since Rao's reading public is limited to the bilingual elite, the majority of whom in the period that we are examining were educated in English, he becomes obliged to create a literary form compatible with the 'cultural and literary expectations' of this section of society.[7] But for a novel of nationalistic dimensions where English must serve to unite the people rather than pose a partition, it becomes equally important to not exclude the masses. This Rao achieves through the employment of oral tradition which enables the illiterate masses, though only on the level of literary technique, to become 'participants in the act of communication'.[8] While the novel addresses the literate few, the style of oral story-telling brings within its reach the peasantry of India, who are excluded in the reading of it.

At this point in the foreword to the novel, Rao has already called for an expectation of a different version of English. He next moves on

---

[6]   Sunder Rajan, 'Fixing English', 17.
[7]   U. R. Anantha Murthy, 'The Search for an Identity: A Kannada Writer's Viewpoint', in Guy Amirthanayagam (ed.), *Asian and Western Writers in Dialogue: New Cultural Identities* (London and Basingstoke: Macmillan, 1982), 78.
[8]   Ibid.

to stylistic transcreation: 'After language the next problem is that of style. The tempo of Indian life must be infused into our English expression, even as the tempo of American or Irish life has gone into the making of theirs' (6). The aspect of the 'tempo of Indian life' introduces the oral quality of the novel: the interminable length of the stories, yet their quick pace. The long tale and the suggestion of rapid movement prepare the ground for the oral narrator whose mnemonic skills are used by Rao to narrate the story of Kanthapura. Gradually, Rao shifts from his hybrid variety of Indo-English speech to a specifically Indian perspective when he considers the cultural conventions of narrative, those culture-specific discourse strategies which are not part of the traditional stylistic repertoire of English:

And our paths are paths interminable. The *Mahabharata* has 214,778 verses and the *Ramayana* 48,000. *Purana*s there are endless and innumerable. We have neither punctuation nor the treacherous 'ats' and 'ons' to bother us— we tell one interminable tale. Episode follows episode, and when our thoughts stop our breath stops, and we move to another thought. This was and still is the ordinary style of our story-telling (6).

Rao here makes a cultural claim to his inheritance by classifying his narration with the epic and the traditional ways of ancient storytelling in India, believing these forms to continue even into the present.

In the light of his new paradigm for creativity, it is important to assess the literary influences that shaped and structured the language of *Kanthapura*. The novel was written after Rao had experimented with both a 'Macaulayian English' and a native Kannada.[9] He recounts:

A South Indian brahmin, nineteen, spoon-fed on English, with just enough Sanskrit to know I knew so little, with an indiscreet education in Kannada, my mother tongue, the French literary scene overpowered me. If I wanted to write, the problem was, what should be the appropriate language of expression, and what my structural models.[10]

For a writer who was attempting to write seriously and 'authentically' about India, his references are surprisingly eclectic although the literary mind at the time of writing could scarcely have avoided the debt of European influences.[11] From Rao's own account, a suitable

---

[9] Raja Rao, 'Entering the Literary World', *World Literature Today*, 62 (1988), 537.
[10] Ibid. 537–8.
[11] See Raja Rao, 'Books Which Have Influenced Me', in M. K. Naik (ed.), *Aspects of Indian Writing in English* (Delhi: Macmillan, 1979), 45–9.

medium had to be devised to recreate a natural mode of literary expression. Rao diffuses the crisis by seeking justification from the Irish who

had done it, not only with Yeats, but again with Frank O'Connor and Sean O'Faolain. Further, Joyce had broken in, as it were, from the side-wings, giving us sound and symbol structures that seemed made for almost the unsayable. So why not Sanskritic (or if you will, Indian) English?[12]

The influence of the Irish experiments ties up with the foreword, where Rao speaks of modelling the style of his novel in the manner of the Americans and the Irish. The foreign contribution to the type and mode of fiction he has constructed must, therefore, be acknowledged in the transcreative experiment he attempts in *Kanthapura*:

In such a world of linguistic ferment, at that time there were also going on experiments with form. Kafka had broken the crust of realism and given fabled meanings to man's fears. The Surrealists having abolished the natural as the concrete gave earth wings upwards, and even more, bore blind fold downwards into subterranean fires. And suddenly Malraux burst in on the scene, upsetting all intellectual stratagems, and giving the world an international dialect of, as it were, pure gesture and metaphysic meaning. For an Indian therefore who wanted to forget Tagore (but not Gandhi) to integrate the Sanscrit tradition with contemporary intellectual heroism seemed a noble experiment to undertake.[13]

Having gone to France at an early age and witnessed its experiments in the arts, his literary style was naturally influenced by European thought. The distance it afforded also generated an increased 'love for India'.[14] This discovery drew him back to India within a short period, and though he did not make India his home, his occasional visits were 'attempts to replenish his inner resources by vitalizing contacts with his motherland and its traditional values'.[15] This endeavour included Rao's visits to Sri Aurobindo at his *ashram* in Pondicherry, Ramana Maharshi at Tiruvannamalai, and Narayana Maharaj at Kedgaon. He also visited the Premayatana *ashram* of Pandit Taranath and Mahatma Gandhi's *ashram* at Sevagram with Maurice Frydman. Significantly, the personages mentioned here are guru-figures who

[12]  Rao, 'Entering the Literary World', 538.
[13]  Raja Rao, *The Policeman and the Rose* (Delhi: Oxford University Press, 1978), pp. xv–xvi.
[14]  Cited in M. K. Naik, *Raja Rao* (New York: Twayne, 1972), 20.
[15]  Ibid.

assume significance in the light of Rao's religious treatment of nationalism, as also in the development of his later metaphysical fiction.

## II

Rao's discovery of India within his multicultural experience reflects his self-conscious use of English as a medium of storytelling. His first collection of stories, *The Cow of the Barricades*, forms the transitional period of the development of his style, when he was switching over from Kannada and French to English.[16] What makes the collection of short stories interesting is the author's confession of the intuitive 'translation' they have undergone, presumably from Kannada thought into English prose.[17] This could account for the non-standardized use of English that predates the stylistic experimentation so characteristic of *Kanthapura*. 'Kanakapala', for instance, has a female narrator, as in *Kanthapura*, who uses colourful figures of speech to impart an Indian flavour to the English language:

He had refused bride after bride, some *beautiful as new-opened guavas*, and others *tender as April mangoes*.[18]

Oh! To have had a father with a *heart pure as the morning lotus.*[19]

Kanakapala knew the true from the false, *as the rat knows the grain from the husk.*[20]

They looked hale and *strong as exhibition bulls.*[21]

The experiment initiated in the short stories is explored more fully in *Kanthapura* where Achakka, the grandmother-narrator, performs the function of mnemonic acculturation for the benefit of an audience who have lost the world of primitive cultures. Correspondingly, the written English of the novel from the outset seeks to initiate primary-speech by means of a sentence structure that attempts to reproduce the Kannada language spoken in the area of Karnataka:

---

[16] Raja Rao, *The Cow of the Barricades and Other Stories* (London: Geoffrey Cumberland: Oxford University Press, 1947). These short stories were published separately during the 1930s, then collected in 1947.

[17] At the literal level, 'The Client' is the only story in the collection first written in Kannada.

[18] Raja Rao, 'The True Story of Kanakapala, Protector of Gold', in *Cow of the Barricades*, 55. The emphases added to these examples are my own.

[19] Ibid. 61.    [20] Ibid. 64.    [21] Ibid. 67.

High on the Ghats is it, high up the steep mountains that face the cool
Arabian seas, up the Malabar coast is it, up Mangalore and Puttur and many
a centre of cardamom and coffee, rice and sugarcane (7).

In several ways, this sentence is a corruption of Kannada: 'the reversal
of word order, so that the verb precedes the subject, and the abandoning of the verb in two of the clauses suggest a sentence structure
which is typical of Kannada.'[22] To take another example:

Kenchamma is our goddess. Great and bounteous is she (8).

This sentence can be translated into Kannada and then back into
English to reveal local rhythms in English writing. Gemmill has
conducted this linguistic experiment with the following result:

Kenchamma our God. Great she, that asked (for) giving one she.

The second clause of the original sentence, indicates Gemmill, gives
us the fundamental pattern of a Kannada sentence: adjective-verb-
subject.[23] The likeness between the word order in *Kanthapura* and
the ordinary Kannada syntax reflects how the author laboriously
recreates the nuances and rhythms of spoken Kannada in English
writing. The process involves the deliberate and literal translation
of Kannada sentences into English to effect a mode that would retain
the flavour of south Indian speech even as it is written in English.

There are, in fact, several instances of literal translation of Kannada into the English language. Taken in categories, the first consists
of Kannada expressions which can be understood with ease and do
not require an explanation or a situational reference.[24] The sentence
can stand on its own to reveal the meaning. In the following
instances, the meaning and the associative connections are relatively
alike in both Kannada and English:

He goes from village to village *to slay the serpent of the foreign rule* (22).[25]
'So you are a *traitor to your salt-givers!*' (25).
'Otherwise brahminism is *as good as kitchen ashes*' (45).
'I am no *butcher's son* to hurt you' (45).

---

[22] Janet P. Gemmill, 'The Transcreation of Spoken Kannada in Raja Rao's *Kanthapura*', *Literature East and West*, 18 (1974), 194.     [23] Ibid.
[24] Chandrashekhar Patil has discussed some of the categories that I examine. See
Chandrashekhar B. Patil, 'The Kannada Element in Raja Rao's Prose: A Linguistic
Study of *Kanthapura*', *Journal of the Karnataka University (Humanities)*, 13 (1969),
149–51.
[25] The emphases added to these and subsequent instances from the text are my own.

Our Rangamma is no *village kid* (46).
Rangamma stood by the door, *helpless as a calf* (59).
'O Maharaja, we are the *lickers of your feet*' (70).
Tell me, does a *boar stand before a lion or a jackal before an elephant*? (84).
'I said to him, the Mahatma is a holy man, and I was not *with the jackals but with the deer*' (100–1).
'We shall *eat mud* and nothing but mud' (101).

Another category comprises cultural expressions which can scarcely be comprehensible to those who do not belong to that culture. Though these phrases are available to the reader in an English translation, it is doubtful whether their meaning would be evident to a western reader. This yardstick, however, does not necessarily eliminate Rao's Indian readership who are expected to recognize the 'emotional' import of English speech:

Purnayya has a grown-up daughter, who will '*come home soon*' (37).
(A girl's attainment of puberty.)

The youngest is always the *holy bull*, they say, don't they? (51).
(Often, after a rich man dies, a bull, bearing his name, is let loose in the village. It moves around freely and without fear, and is fed by everyone.)

I shall offer them a *jolly good blessing-ceremony* in the choicest of words (56).
(The meaning here is ironic and has to do with raking up mischief.)

He walked out to preach the '*Don't-touch-the-Government campaign*' (99).
(A boycott of the government with the allusion to caste defilement, an expression that Gandhi himself would not have approved of.[26])

'This is all *Ramayana* and *Mahabharata*; such things never happen in our times' (172).
(In spite of being sacred to the Hindus, the two epics also imply endless and ideal narration since they are full of fantastic stories.)

'Oh, no more of this *Panchayat*—we ask you again, disperse, and do not force us to fire!' (240).
(A 'panchayat' is the self-governing body of the village. In the context of the

---

[26] This insight occurs in Rao's own explanation to the phrase given in the glossary to the American edition of *Kanthapura* (New York: New Directions, 1963), 217. Knippling has pointed out that the presence of a glossary 'de-nativizes [Rao's] nativizations'. However, it must also be remembered that the glossary appeared in the 1963 edition by which time the nationalist project was over. The absence of a glossary in the early editions helps us clarify the kind of audience—westernized rather than western—Rao must have first written for, from whom an understanding of these expressions was expected. See Alpana Sharma Knippling, 'R. K. Narayan, Raja Rao and Modern English Discourse in Colonial India', *Modern Fiction Studies*, 39.1 (1993), 182.

novel, it indicates a needless and purposeless argument. This is an ironic comment and can be understood only by those familiar with the term.)

Nevertheless, such expressions are used sparingly owing to the possible risk of incomprehension, thus indicating that the readership Rao addresses may not be completely familiar with local idioms.

At other times, Rao uses a Kannada equivalent of an English proverb or an idiom when the English one could have conveyed the meaning as adequately. Of course, the Kannada phrase as it stands is first translated by displacing standard English. Rao restricts himself to recognizable deviations from the English idiom so that he can limit the risk of mystifying the reader by unintelligible speech. In the following instances, he avoids the exact English equivalents but takes care not to cross the boundaries of comprehensibility:

'Nobody who has eyes to see and ears to hear will believe in such a *crow-and-sparrow story*' (27).

Though a 'cock-and-bull story' would have been appropriate, the phrase 'crow-and-sparrow story' evokes a particular legend common among Kannada children.[27]

Every *squirrel has his day* (112).

The phrase is apparently constructed by displacing the proverbial 'dog', and is used by Bhatta to characterize Moorthy as both gentle and small. The presence of squirrels is also common in agricultural communities.

'The Swami is worried over this pariah movement, and he wants *to crush it in its seed*, before its cactus-roots have spread far and wide' (44).

The English substitute 'nipped in the bud' is avoided to make the reader pause and consider the alternative 'crush it in its seed', which appears to be a more original and culturally different expression when it is seen outside regular English speech. Again:

And then there is such a silence that a *moving ant could be heard* (110).

The obvious parallel is to hearing a pin drop. There are other similes picked up from the very soil of the village: 'Venkamma plants herself like a banana-trunk in front of her' (57); 'darkness grows thick as sugar in a cauldron' (76); or 'Every enemy you create is like pulling

---

[27] Patil, 'Kannada Element in Raja Rao's Prose', 151.

out a lantana bush . . . . The more you pull out, the wider you spread the seeds . . . . But every friend you create is like a jasmine hedge. You plant it, and it . . . bears flowers' (102).

Rao's conscious employment of images and vocabulary that impart a rooted quality to the story stretches to a whole repertoire of idioms, beliefs, greetings, oaths, speech mannerisms, name tags, abuses, blessings, and so on, all related to the culture that he intends to represent through his narration. There are words that arise more from habit than from the actual sense they make, but are significant in determining the speech-community of the speaker. Correspondingly, the readers who recognize these expressions also acknowledge themselves as being within the fellowship evoked by common speech. The following sets of expressions, for example, reflect basic harmony among the villagers that is carried successfully to the reader:

Your voice is not a *sparrow voice* in your village (44).
(A powerful person. This expression does not seem to be translated into English from an Indian language, and is probably the author's own creation.)

You cannot put *wooden tongues* to men (49).
(One cannot stop people from gossiping.)

'The *leaf is laid*' (64).
(Food is served.)

But this *stomach that has borne eight children* cannot forget it (164).
(An experienced and worldly-wise person.)

And they get a *coconut and betel-leaf good-bye* (190).
(A traditional leave taking.)

The villagers also have abuses and curses that are part of their culture, yet easily recognizable by a non-Kannada or even a non-Indian reader as being derogatory. Rao, therefore, makes no concessions for his readers in such instances:

'If her parents are poor, let them *set fire to their dhoti and sari* and die' (11).

'See whether those *sons of concubines* are planting well' (24).

'Ah, you will *eat blood and mud* I said, you widow, and here you are!' (119).

'May my *limbs get paralysed and my tongue dumb* and my *progeny for ever destroyed*!' (103–4).

Extremely contextual, the first instance is recognized as an abuse from a vindictive neighbour, and the second as a curse from a master to a servant. The third is addressed to women only, while the fourth, surprisingly, to oneself. The relationship between the addresser and the addressee is clear in all instances, and it is thus possible to classify them culturally in terms of religion, caste, or social status.

The exercise of infusing native spirit into an alien language includes, for Rao, the use of graphic nicknames to evoke a distinctive identity for the characters. This manoeuvre characterizes a person, reveals his or her social status or caste group, and thus represents them as memorable Indian characters. It is not easy, for instance, especially for western and westernized readers, to forget Waterfall Venkamma and Nose-scratching Nanjamma, aided by their half-English names. The device is useful, again, in making the vices of Snuff Shastri and Drunkard Dhirrappa, and the disabilities of Left-handed Madanna, Bent-legged Chandrayya, Gap-toothed Siddayya, and Pock-marked Sidda self-evident. Thus people, fields, and houses can be recognized by identifiable tags: Corner-House Moorthy, Fig-Tree-House people, That-house people, Post-Office-House people, Haunted Tamarind tree field, Bhatta's Devil field, and so on; and occupation or status by names like Cardamom-field Ramachandra, Four-beamed-House Chandrayya, Maddur Coffee-Planter Venkata-narayana, Carpenter Kenchayya, Husking Rangi, Agent Nanjun-daiah, Trumpet Lingayya, Betel-seller Maddayya, and Patel Rangè Gowda. Achakka's use of address—Moorthappa or Bhattarè for Moorthy and Bhatta—suggests the modes of behaviour indigenous to a south Indian society as well as the caste distinctions where Bhatta or Moorthy are a shade higher than she is. In our context, the depiction of such a society amply indicates a village sensibility remote from western currents of decorum and urbanity.[28]

By the 'culturalization' of language, Rao succeeds, to a large extent, in presenting what appears to be the natural idiom of south Indian speech and locution. The 'authenticity' of the south Indian tradition, however, relies on how far the English language can be harnessed to the author's cause without damaging those words and phrases that have meaning only in the native tongue. For when Rao discovers that religious terms which are most culture-specific refuse

[28] As Rao says, 'It is a purely Mysore (Karnataka) tradition; Kannada tradition, I should say. For example, my grand-uncle was living in Hyderabad and you say that house. You don't say grand-uncle's house. You say that house with the platform in front. It is a pure, authentic South Indian tradition.' See Shiva Niranjan, 'An Interview with Raja Rao', in K. N. Sinha (ed.), *Indian Writing in English* (New Delhi: Heritage, 1979), 21.

translation, he resorts to Kannada or Sanskrit. Words such as *Narayan*, *harikatha*, *gayathri* and the use of the names of gods and their festivals—'Kartik Purnima' when gods are to pass by Kanthapura, 'Dasara' or the 'Gauri' festival—as they would occur naturally in speech are used to preserve the cultural unity of the work, apart from their function in familiarizing the reader with certain unfamiliar aspects of Indian village life. The use of natural speech also provides an immediate contrast to the alien language and gets 'elevated into a symbol of identification with the authentic nation.'[29] Undoubtedly the writer feels hampered by standard English; he is rescued, on the other hand, by words which refuse translation into English, thus infusing local colour into the foreign language.

It must also be kept in mind that although the analysis of the vocabulary used in *Kanthapura* is carried out with Kannada in mind, readers other than Kannada may find themselves responding equally to the language and speech-mannerisms in the novel. That the author does not intend to appeal only to a limited, provincial Kannada readership is evident from his promotion of Hindi within the small, Kannada-speaking village in Karnataka:

[Sankar] said Hindi would be the national language of India, and though Kannada is good enough for our province, Hindi must become the national tongue, and whenever he met a man in the street, he did not say 'How are you?' in Kannada, but took to the northern manner and said 'Ram-Ram' (143).

The stress on Hindi clarifies the nature of the bilingual reader, who is now recognized as speaking English and Hindi, both of which are unificatory languages used as mediums for addressing people from platforms, since more people in India are likely to understand these two than any other. Rao's transcreation of Kannada does not hinder the assumption about Hindi since the premisses established in the foreword allow an easy interchangeability between Kannada and any other Indian language. Further, Hindi might be able to unite people 'emotionally' since English, as Rao points out in the foreword, is the language of our 'intellectual' make-up. It does come as a surprise that the advocacy of Hindi should appear in the work of a novelist who hails from the south since the proposal that Hindi should not only be the official but also the national language of India

[29] Bruce King, *The New English Literatures: Cultural Nationalism in a Changing World* (London and Basingstoke: Macmillan, 1980), 44–5.

caused alarm in the non-Hindi belts, particularly in the Dravidian south, where the promotion of Hindi was taken as a sign of domination by the north.[30] English, by this logic, becomes a protection against the imposition of Hindi which is seen as a threat to local cultures.[31]

Significantly, the dilemma of writing an Indian novel in English exists already in Lal Behari Day's novel *Govinda Sámanta*.[32] For Day, the nativization of a foreign language is a stylistic predicament for any non-native writer of English. He feels that his 'authentic' account is obstructed by his Bengali peasants who speak better English than even uneducated English peasants:

> Gentle reader, allow me here to make one remark. You must perceive that Badan and Alanga speak better English than most uneducated English peasants; they speak almost like educated ladies and gentlemen, without any provincialisms. But how could I have avoided this defect in my history? If I had translated their talk into the Somersetshire or the Yorkshire dialect, I should have turned them into English, and not Bengali, peasants. You will, therefore, please overlook this grave though unavoidable fault in this authentic narrative.[33]

Rao avoids Day's 'defects' and nativizes the English language so that his peasants speak neither the Queen's English, nor the provincial English dialects of English peasants. They speak in an Indian English which is appropriate to their character as peasants. To make a comparison with Narayan, it may be said that while Narayan manages to make his people speak as they would speak if English were their language, Raja Rao 'succeeds in making his characters speak as they would speak if English were Kannada itself'.[34] Rao, in fact, owes the success of his characterization precisely to the way in which he has dealt with language.

---

[30] Gandhi also made an appeal in this direction: 'We should hear only Hindi words, not English. . . . I shall struggle all my life to bring this about.' See Mohandas Karamchand Gandhi, 'Speech at Muzaffarpur', 11 Nov. 1917, in *Collected Works of Mahatma Gandhi, 1884–1948*, 90 vols. (Ahmedabad: Navajivan, 1958–84), xiv. 80–1. Much before Gandhi, Bharatendu Harishchandra (though some say it was a Hindi poet, Pratap Narain Mishra) had linked language with religion to coin an evocative slogan: 'Hindu-Hindi-Hindustan' (one culture, one language, one nation). This phrase makes every non-Hindu, as also every non-Hindi-speaker, a non-Indian.

[31] Sunder Rajan, 'Fixing English', 15–16.

[32] Lal Behari Day, *Govinda Sámanta: Or, The History of a Bengal Ráiyat* (London: Macmillan, 1874).    [33] Ibid. 89.

[34] G. S. Amur, 'The Kannada Phase', *Journal of Karnataka University (Humanities)*, 10 (1966), 42.

The creation of an Indian–English vocabulary is not simply a linguistic flight; nor is it an inadequate representation of an acquired language. Rao's Indian collocations can be viewed as 'deviations' from standard English.[35] Such 'deviant' uses of English words and phrases constitute the major part of the effort of 'indianizing' into Indian English. Examples range from 'reduplication' as in *hot, hot coffee* or *different, different things* to 'hybridizations' such as *lathi-charge, Upanishadic, Harikatha-man, pariah-quarter, sudra-street*, or *brahminhood* in order to manifest culture or 'context bound' elements, and in the process achieve a distinctive Indian character.[36] What makes these 'Indianisms' interesting is that not many of them violate any rules of English grammar 'though the rules of usage may have been violated here and there'.[37] A violation of usage usually results from Rao's reliance on the 'aural' rather than the 'visual' quality of the narrative.[38] Kantak cites two instances of Rao's pre-occupation with aspects of sound where words of similar sound and rhythm that ostensibly seem to achieve no more than an alliterative effect are yoked together: the first example is that of the rain which '*poured* and *plundered* all the fields and the woods' (145) on the day Ramakrishnayya died. Again, in an instance depicting the clash between the British soldiers and the *satyagrahis*, Rao refers to the soldiers '*grunting* and *grovelling* at us, bayonets thrust forward' (247) in complete disregard of the visual imagery this evokes. 'Grunting and grovelling' might agree acoustically but not when we think of a soldier ready to strike. Though semantically disconsonant, the two pairs appear to be appropriate simply because Rao offers them together on the basis of their sound pattern. Within his design of deviating from standard English to produce a distinctive and colourful 'thought-movement', his liberties with grammar become meaningful. And so, while it is not difficult to conceive of the 'pouring' of torrential rain, its 'plundering' becomes significant within the cosmos of a tropical India where the wild, beating quality of nature is personified in an act of looting. In the same manner, 'grunting and

[35] Braj B. Kachru, *The Indianization of English: The English Language in India* (Delhi: Oxford University Press, 1983), 2.
[36] Ibid. 79; 82; 112. Reduplication is a linguistic habit with Indians, used either for greater emphasis or to establish continuity. In the same way, hybridizations are also indicative of colloquial speech.
[37] Shreesh Chaudhary, 'Indianness in Indian Writing in English: Towards a Descriptive Approach', *Journal of Indian Writing in English*, 18.2 (1990), 57.
[38] V. Y. Kantak, 'Raja Rao's *Kanthapura*', *Chandrabagha*, 13 (1985), 38.

grovelling' are related terms from the vantage point of retrospective storytelling by the grandmother where the soldiers are, with hindsight, seen to grovel in penitence for their earlier grunting.[39] In other words, standard language shifts to 'recall' oral cultures untouched by writing.[40] A more 'English' construction might sound less deviant, but then it would also be less 'Indian', and consequently, less effective.

For the western reader, the Indian collocations would appear to be extremely unusual or uncommon when addressed through the English language, because these deviations would not function in the absence of the context within which they are used in India. While a comparison of breasts with April mangoes, for instance, is not deviant in terms of the context, or even the structure, the conjunction of 'mango-breast' would undoubtedly be an unusual compound for the native speakers of English. It is the absorptive quality of English, however, that enables the writer to arrange culture-specific items within a foreign medium to make it distinctive. So complete is its assimilation of Indian culture that, at times, the borrowing is almost unconscious or intuitive, and devoid of the realization that the item transferred belongs to an Indian language.

Surprisingly, while English has been demonstrated to be an absorptive language, the reverse is not true since none of the translations of *Kanthapura* into Kannada have been successful.[41] The premisses established in the foreword, of the mixed quality of Indian speech and the presupposition of a bilingual readership, can have scarcely any meaning in a novel written in Kannada or in any Indian language for that matter. The whole paradox of invented authenticity relies on it being presented in a language which is not Kannada. Written in France, this Kannada story has been thought out entirely in English. The infiltration of 'Indianisms', therefore, serves to highlight an Indian cultural context, which in its very location within English, receives a new orientation. The reader begins to acknowledge the hidden dimensions of a language pushed in new directions. It follows that this new 'Indian' method of expression is compatible with a novel about 'authentic' village culture without having to surrender the English language which alone can absorb linguistic difference and

---

[39] V. Y. Kantak, 'Raja Rao's *Kanthapura*', *Chandrabagha*, 13 (1985), 38–9.
[40] Walter J. Ong, *Orality and Literacy: The Technologizing of the Word* (London: Methuen, 1982), 31; 73.
[41] Patil, 'Kannada Element in Raja Rao's Prose', 148.

serve the purpose of consolidating a nation.[42] The privileging of English, ironically, dismisses the commonly held notion that 'the most powerful candidates for nationhood in India have been religious, not linguistic communities', judging from the partition of India which ran along religious lines, where Hinduism, and not Hindi, fashioned the nationalist consciousness.[43] While language played a vital role in the rise of nation-states in the west, the enormous significance of English in fashioning the ideology of the Indian elite and thus constituting a linguistic unity of another kind is often lost. In cases such as *Kanthapura*, the use of English is the panacea in that a completely new idiom is fashioned in which a non-communal linguistic medium forms the basis of a pan-Indian nationalism so that the emergence of the Indian nation-state does not stand divided along linguistic lines as the nationalists feared, but where a common, though artificial, language in fact leads to a sacerdotal unity.

This takes me back to the question of the specific composition of Rao's readership. Despite their bilingual nature, it is still not clear whether the readers are Indian, non-Indian, or just Kannada. The peasantry of Kanthapura can, of course, be ruled out since the physical presence of the narrator surrounded by a group of eager listeners lacks credibility when we see how Rao's use of English changes our conception of the audience. However well the Irish and the American may have performed successful experiments in the art of writing, the poor in India, unlike them, do not speak in English. In fact, in spite of being pan-Indian, English poses the 'most visible divide between the ruling classes and the ruled'.[44] Were it not for Rao's shrewd fusion of the 'intellectual' and the 'emotional' within the same language, his motives would not be realized. Another detail that merits pointing and indicates who the targeted reading public could be comes from the publishing details of the novel. *Kanthapura* was sold for five rupees in the 1930s. Its readers could only have been upper class, English-speaking, and reasonably prosperous. Our

---

[42] Aijaz Ahmad points out that while he can think of several texts in the English language which focus on the experience of colonialism or imperialism, he cannot think of any such texts in the last 200 years or so, of much significance and length, in the Urdu language. See Ahmad, *In Theory*, 118.

[43] Achin Vanaik, *The Painful Transition: Bourgeois Democracy in India* (London: Verso, 1990), 6. See also id., *India in a Changing World: Problems, Limits and Successes of its Foreign Policy* (New Delhi: Orient Longman, 1995), 118.

[44] Sunder Rajan, 'Fixing English', 15.

conception of the readers is also shaped by Achakka in the very opening sentence of *Kanthapura*, and gradually gains strength as we read the novel: 'Our village—I don't think you have heard about it—Kanthapura is its name, and it is in the province of Kara (7).' It is evident that the narrator introduces an oral situation in which the presumed audience are not the usual listeners who should have heard her story already. The listeners have to be other than her regular audience from the village, referred to as 'newcomer[s]' in the fore-word, who are unaware of what befell Kanthapura. What emerges from the opening gambit, then, is an invitation to a guided tour of India possibly for the bilingual, westernized, educated Indian, or perhaps for the Indian elite situated abroad.[45] The endeavour to familiarize the audience with the environment and to tell them at the outset that the story exists for their consumption alone, is quite obviously the intention of the author, for a traditional narrator would start in *medias res* as an inevitable way to proceed rather than go through a formal introduction. Rao's voice is, perhaps, underlying that of the grandmother's, forcing her to start at the beginning, in consideration for an audience of strangers.

Insofar as Rao's readership is made up of elite Indians (who alone can be bilingual), the use of a distorted form of English not only creates the comprehension of an Indian experience but also highlights, to an extent, their unfamiliarity with that very culture, and, by implication, with the rooted qualities of the land, with brotherhood (or sisterhood, since the story is narrated by a woman to women), and with the glorious past embodied in village life. The reader, in acceptance of his or her inexperience, rationalizes from his or her background, and submits, within limits, to Rao's deviations from both English and Kannada.[46] We might infer that what would, at first glance, appear to be distortions turn out to be effective props for the reader, facilitating the comprehension of an indigenous cultural experience from which there is a danger of becoming distanced.

The bilingual nature of readership also points rather strongly to the composition of the colonial state, to a class of people who, in Macaulay's words were 'Indian in blood and colour, but English in

[45] *Kanthapura* was first published simultaneously from Delhi and London.
[46] The readers' acceptance of deviations also arises naturally from the atmosphere of oral storytelling where occasional errors are accepted by the audience as normal aberrations. See Albert Lord, *The Singer of Tales* (New York: Athenum, 1976), 38.

taste, in opinions, in morals, and in intellect.'[47] The intelligentsia alone could have been bilingual in its function of mediating between the English-speaking ruling elite and the masses over whom they ruled. Their bilingualism, in turn, would ensure for them a prominent position in the colonial state. It was, furthermore, the bilingual intelligentsia who could have access to the 'models of nationalism, nation-ness, and nation-state produced elsewhere in the course of the nineteenth century', facilitated through print capitalism.[48] Rao also realizes that it is only in a 'literary culture' that the literary artefact is fixed, permanent, certain, and independent. The writing of oral narration, therefore, gives a certain fixity to the transitoriness of Achakka's storytelling and stabilizes it into a sacral image of the past fundamental in conceptualizing a nation-state. Further, while the indigenization of the language raises the consciousness of those who belong to this area, the print medium increases the awareness of countless readers, in their particular language-field, of this speech-community.[49] Rao thus constructs, through print, a particular, invisible but nationally-imagined community.

The grandmother narrator is useful in bridging the gap between the written and the oral, or, in other words, between the foreword and the rest of the narration in her function as the 'governing consciousness' of the novel.[50] Her concrete presence complements the author's overall governance of the novel and helps him succeed in keeping within the intentions outlined in the foreword. Both the oral-emotional and the literary-intellectual properties are serviced by the coexistence of the author and the narrator. The grandmother's incessant narration in which 'episode follows episode' is clearly in tune with the author's manifesto outlined in the foreword. Their camaraderie is evident in the breathlessness of her voice, rapidly relating a concourse of events which refuse to be contained in writing. For Rao's purposes, the foreword serves a dual function: while it separates the author's comment from the fictional tale and makes his remarks credible, it also gives him the occasion to ghost the narrator's voice

---

[47] Thomas Babington Macaulay, 'Indian Education: Minute of the 2nd of February, 1835', in G. M. Young (ed.), *Macaulay: Prose and Poetry* (Cambridge, Mass.: Harvard University Press, 1967), 729.

[48] Benedict Anderson, *Imagined Communities: Reflections on the Origin and Spread of Nationalism*, 2nd edn. (London: Verso, 1991), 116; 139.    [49] Ibid. 44.

[50] Sholomith Rimmon-Kenan, *Narrative Fiction: Contemporary Poetics* (London: Methuen, 1983), 86.

and realize the premisses established in the foreword. For having read the foreword, one is willing to suspend disbelief as required by conventions of orally narrated stories, especially those in the first-person autobiographical mode. With this in mind, it is not difficult to understand Rao's success in recreating a representation of what the milieu of peasant India could be imagined to be. Ultimately, it is Achakka, the grandmother, who handles Rao's readership. Her relationship with the author is seen at three different levels. When Rao and his narrator work in unison, the principles embodied in the foreword are maintained. For most of the story, they do not interrupt each other in hindering the smooth flow of the text. Not surprisingly, then, Achakka is 'the aunt who tells such nice stories' (255). Otherwise, the tale of the destruction of the village would be horrifying, not 'nice'. At another level, Rao ghosts, as it were, the voice of the grandmother. It is then that Rao's own prejudices and loyalties are revealed and his role in the narration becomes evident. An instance would be Rao's approach to his protagonist, Moorthy, who is given heroic speech to rise above the rest of the village in status. At yet another level, as seen in Chapter 4, the grandmother comes alive in her own right as a dramatic character, splitting the text to reveal village life as a rapidly changing, or a recently invented, or perhaps even as an extremely hostile area of popular culture, against Rao's own reified view of village culture.[51]


III


Within the broad framework of examining the role of literature in the construction and elaboration of an 'authentic' nationalist agenda, Rao's technique of mixing the oral and the written compels us to explore the kind of 'reality' he would like to represent. The novel begins by evoking a strong sense of place. As it unfolds, the topographical features of the landscape are revealed: the Kenchamma Hill, the Skeffington Coffee Estate, the temple of Kanthapurishwari, and the river Himavathy, which become 'at once landscape, life, history, people, ideas, and ideals'.[52] What is striking is the hidden quality of

[51] Rimmon-Kenan suggests 'implied authors' to be superior to the real authors in intelligence and moral standards. See ibid. 87.
[52] K. R. Rao, *The Fiction of Raja Rao* (Aurangabad: Parimal Prakashan, 1980), 50.

nature: its presence is not depicted in detail. Nature exists, rather, as a symbol of the rooted quality of the land, exercising tremendous hold over the villagers. The river Himavathy or the red Kenchamma Hill, soaked with the blood of a demon, are presented as animate features of the landscape. Their presence in the village is so organized by Rao that the story is conveyed through powerful myth and legend:

There is no village in India, howsoever mean, that has not a rich *sthala-purana*, or legendary history, of its own. Some god or godlike hero has passed by the village—Rama might have rested under this pipal-tree, Sita might have dried her clothes, after her bath, on this yellow stone, or the Mahatma himself, on one of his many pilgrimages through the country, might have slept in this hut, the low one, by the village gate. In this way the past mingles with the present, and the gods mingle with the men, to make the repertory of your grandmother always bright. One such story from the contemporary annals of my village I have tried to tell (5).

There grows almost a veneration of the ancient traditions which Rao believes to be archetypically 'Indian', alluding always to ancient epic heroes and heroines. This veneration is transferred to the River, the Goddess, and the Hill, rendered believable because they are a permanent part of the reality of the villagers, and not mere topographical features. The characterization too, veers towards the typical, and links man to nature. Moorthy, the virtuous hero; Bhatta, the corrupt and pontifical Brahmin; Badè Khan, the Muslim policeman; and Rangè Gowda, the authoritative Patel or the head-man are depicted as stereotypes of Indian folk life, and represent character only in so far as they cohere to pre-defined notions of identity.[53] Stylistically, Rao's realism does not go into detail like Dickens's, Balzac's, or Flaubert's. His realism centres on the way he makes reality appear to the characters: they see Moorthy, for instance, as 'a noble cow' and Rangè Gowda as 'a veritable tiger'. The realism of Rao, then, appears to be more cultural than what we usually understand to be 'realistic'. Thus, it can be conceived that Rangè Gowda becomes 'as lean as the areca-nut tree' (258) after the destruction of the village, and Narasamma grows 'thin as a bamboo and shrivelled like banana bark' when Moorthy is excommunicated. In the same way, Nanjamma describes her vision of Gandhi: 'No, sister, I do not imagine the Mahatma as a man or a god, but like the Sahyadri Mountains, blue,

[53] Steven Cohan and Linda M. Shires, *Telling Stories: A Theoretical Analysis of Narrative Fiction* (New York: Routledge, 1988), 73–4.

high, wide, and the rock of the evening that catches the light of the setting sun' (176). Gandhi, too, is visualized through permanent topography, such as the mountains of Kanthapura, that impart to him a specific cultural association with the Kenchamma Hill and the Himavathy river. Indeed, Rao fashions an imagined community through various figurative devices and techniques which mix history with myth, and men with gods to give current events a timeless significance.

Detailed descriptions of nature feature prominently in the text, evoking associations with ancient modes of storytelling in which nature is personified, and its palpable existence in human lives is described. As in the lyrical passages of the *Bhagavatpurana*, *Kanthapura*, too, has vivid descriptions of nature such as the onset of *kartik* or autumn:

Kartik has come to Kanthapura, sisters—Kartik has come with the glow of lights and the unpressed footsteps of the wandering gods; white lights from clay-trays and red lights from copper-stands, and diamond lights that glow from the bowers of entrance-leaves; lights that glow from banana-trunks and mango twigs, yellow light behind white leaves, and green light behind yellow leaves, and white light behind green leaves; and night curls through the shadowed streets, and hissing over bellied boulders and hurrying through dallying drains, night curls through the Brahmin street and the Pariah street (118).

There are other sensitive descriptions of the day breaking over the ghats, or the coming of the monsoons that indicate the 'real' presence of gods in the midst of men. The belief in the real and animated quality of nature underlines the orthodox, ritualistic, and superstitious nature of the villagers. They live by cosmic time whereby the position of the sun decides when Moorthy would return from Karwar. This also serves to indicate the slow movement of time. The first ploughing and the subsequent harvesting, quintessential traditional activities, are ritually enacted only when the sacred eagle, a bird associated with the goddess, appears in the skies. On another occasion, though advised to take quinine pills by the resident English sahib, the inhabitants of the Skeffington Coffee Estate are sceptical about their curative quality and refuse to take them on the argument that the sahib has no knowledge of their country. Their faith in superstitions governs their actions: to ward off malaria, Siddanna's wife tears 'a rag from her sari fringe, and [puts] into it a three-pice bit and a little rice and an areca nut, and [hangs] it securely to the roof' (79) to appease the resident goddess Kenchamma.

It is largely through the villagers' associations of reality and ortho-doxy that the credibility of myth can be established. While the novel takes up urgent controversial contemporary events of the Civil Dis-obedience Movement, it acquires significance beyond the present by a connection with past legends:

They say the Mahatma will go to the Red-men's country and he will get us Swaraj. He will bring us Swaraj, the Mahatma. And we shall be happy. And Rama will come back from exile, and Sita will be with him, for Ravana will be slain and Sita freed, and he will come back with Sita on his right in a chariot of the air (257).

Achakka's description of Gandhi's visit to England for the Round Table Conference of December 1931, and view of India's later freedom, in terms of the epic serves to mythicize Gandhi in the nature of legendary heroes and heroines, simultaneously evoking parallels with the goddess Kenchamma who has killed a demon to protect Kanthapura.

In terms of the novel, it becomes possible to link Rama, Gandhi, and Kenchamma, each of whom has clashed with the forces of Evil for the ultimate Good. As we ascend the hierarchy, Kenchamma's protec-tion of Kanthapura evokes an analogy with Gandhi's struggle to free India, enabling Kanthapura to reach out to embody all of India. The Kenchamma-myth itself embraces some of the broader myths of the country. Sage Bhagiratha's penance in the *Gangapurana* to bring the river Ganges down to earth for the salvation of his cursed ancestors provides a mythic parallel to the penance of Sage Tripura in invoking Kenchamma.[54] Again, the descent of the goddess Durga to slay the demon Mahisasur in the *Devipurana* is the consequence of the penance of several sages and religious men. Within the determinate Kanthapura, Kenchamma's significance is local, but the associations she evokes with other supernatural deities render the story meaningful

---

[54] There is, however, another myth. A traditional story of how the goddess Kenchamma established herself at Kenchamma Hoskere is thus narrated: The *Sapta-matrikas* (seven mothers or goddesses), in the course of their journey from Varanasi (Benares) to the south, were pleased with the scenic splendour of this area and decided to make it their home. Accordingly, of the seven sisters, three settled at Hassan and another three in a *taluq* called Devigere, also in Hassan, and were called Hasanamba. The seventh settled in a forest near Kenchamma Hoskere and was called Kenchamba or Kenchamma. See *Mysore State Gazetteer, Hassan District* (Bangalore: Government of Mysore, 1971), 1. Rao has ignored this dominant myth, and employed the one of Tripura's invocation of Kenchamma to highlight the parallel myth of Valmiki calling down Gandhi, and thus make associations with national politics.

within a wider context. The political movement and the mythical analogy together enter the cosmos of the Hindu god, Rama, believed to be an incarnation of Vishnu. The story, thereby, gets located within the repertoire of Indian mythology, quite in the nature of an ancient Indian form of storytelling, the *purana*.

It is interesting that Rao works inside the historical mode but keeps alive a romantic iconography. The direction of his body of fiction can be conveniently assessed within the modes of fiction outlined by Robert Scholes and Ulrich Wicks.[55] The two authors locate fiction within ideal types, or what can be called 'primitive' narrative forms:

A fictional world can be better than the world of experience, worse than it, or equal to it. These fictional worlds imply attitudes that we have learned to call romantic, satirical, and realistic. Fiction can give us the degraded world of satire, the heroic world of romance, or the mimetic world of history.[56]

The three modes mentioned here are part of a variety of fictional potentialities which include satire, picaresque, comedy, history, sentiment, tragedy, and romance.

I am concerned with that aspect of the approach which grants universal applicability to these models. Since they are 'applicable to fiction anytime, [and] anywhere'[57] they can be stretched back in time to embrace even pre-novelistic Indian traditions, thus making provisions for the *puranic* form largely governing the narrative structure of much Indian writing. One can engage simultaneously in a different exercise of reintegrating this typology with history and relating Indian structures of writing with western equivalents of fictional types. Both, the liberation from and the integration with history, are useful in defining the traditions Rao works into his writing.

The applicability of the modal approach is useful in examining a work of nationalist fiction since it can help us determine, within the ambivalence characterizing nationalism, how far the novel takes its form from the western tradition outlined by Scholes and Wicks, and

---

[55] Robert Scholes, 'Towards a Poetics of Fiction: An Approach through Genre', *Novel*, 2 (1969), 101–11; Ulrich Wicks, 'The Nature of Picaresque Narrative: A Modal Approach', *PMLA*, 89 (1974), 240–9. The modal approach to Indian fiction has been demonstrated to an extent in S. C. Harrex, 'Typology and Modes: Raja Rao's Experiments in Short Story', *World Literature Today*, 62.4 (1988), 591–5. In following the analogy, I have drawn parallels with indigenous models of storytelling, accommodating them, to a limited extent, within the typology of Scholes and Wicks.

[56] Scholes, 'Towards a Poetics of Fiction', 104–5.

[57] Wicks, 'The Nature of Picaresque Narrative', 241.

the degree to which it refuses categorization within those terms. In formal terms, *Kanthapura* may be called a *puranic* text. Originally, a *purana* would seem to have been a book of origins or a sort of Hindu Genesis. Believed sacred, the *purana*s, to this day, are a source of popular conceptions of creation, time, the universe, the earth, geography, and early history. Their historical nature, curiously, derives from the presence of kings and religious sects who sought to foist their own significance upon some popular *purana* in order to find their way into the hearts of the people. The process seems to have begun, as in the epic, with Krishna. Thereafter, secular documents of several types found their way into the *purana*s, and all of them have possibly been co-opted, to some degree, by various interest groups for religious motives of a sectarian kind, or by secular groups for particular historical purposes. It is perhaps true that every existing *purana* owes its present form and its survival to some sect or overlord. In other words, they have largely been treated as ideological tracts, and there is some significance in Rao's employment of the *puranic* technique of storytelling. The *purana*s are known to have suffered much from rewriting and interpolations so that they scarcely have a settled text. Nonetheless, they are regarded as sacred texts, for their antiquity renders them sacrosanct. It is significant that Rao follows the style of storytelling enshrined in the *purana*s because he can, then, traditionally 'rewrite' an existing *purana* by substituting the hero, and, at the same time, be true to its fixity. In effect, the very nature of the *purana*s permits Rao to write a sectarian narrative with an ancient flavour, enabling the text to achieve the dimensions of a 'pure' Indian narrative. The *purana*s are further characterized by openness, so that men of any caste, and women too, are allowed to read them in a predominantly caste-based and patriarchal society.[58] Undoubtedly, then, their dissemination among all castes and sexes democratizes their meaning, allowing Rao to have a broader canvas in terms of readership.

The strategy of the novel of mixing gods and men is, in fact, achieved by the *puranic* nature of the story. At Ramakrishnayya's death, the swelling waters of Himavathy do not touch the pyre until the body is completely reduced to ashes, soon after which 'a huge

---

[58] Benjamin Walker defines the *purana*s as 'the Veda of the common folk'. See Benjamin Walker, *Hindu World: An Encyclopedic Survey of Hinduism*, 2 vols. (London: Allen and Unwin, 1968), ii. 254.

swell churned round the hill and swept the bones and ashes away' (146). In a typically *puranic* vein, Achakka adds:

'And that night, sister, as on no other night, no cow would give its milk . . . and calves pranced about their mothers and groaned . . . . Lord, may such be the path of our outgoing Soul!' (146).

Ramakrishnayya's death is strikingly similar to that of Karna in the Mahabharata:

When Karna fell, the rivers stood still. The Sun set with a pale hue. . . . The firmament seemed to be rent in twain; the Earth uttered loud roars; violent and awful winds began to blow. . . . The mountains with their forests began to tremble, and all creatures, O sire, felt pain.[59]

In other words, nature becomes a co-sharer in the grief of the village folk as in the *purana*s where it is seen to participate in the social and political functions of the people, and actively shape destinies. The myth-making qualities of the novel are, thus, represented remarkably through pre-existing modes of storytelling. On the level of narrative, the antiquity of the *puranas* and the belief they inspire evidently authenticate the story which itself is one long, interminable oral tale encapsulating other tales, usually digressions within the main narrative, consisting of stories that Achakka has heard in her lifetime. Often her stories begin with the formulaic beginning, 'Once upon a time' or 'And this is how it all began', which are conventional tools of an oral narrator that serve to situate events in a hoary past.

In addition, *Kanthapura* is characterized by an abundance of *puranic* conjunctives and repetitions. There is repeated use of 'and', and Maini has counted up to forty-four in one long sentence.[60] Again, the word 'rush' is used very frequently, especially in the chapter describing the march of the *Satyanarayan puja* by the villagers. The police 'rush' at them, the villagers 'rush' down the Aloe lane and then 'rush' again behind Bhatta's sugar-canes. In the midst of rushing, there is a lot of ducking and rising as they are being chased by the policemen:

And we say, 'Let us rush behind Bhatta's sugar-canes there they cannot catch us, for if they come to one row, we will slip into another,' and we stumble and

---

[59] *The Mahabharata of Krishna-Dwaipayana Vyasa: Karna Parva*, trans. Pratap Chandra Ray (Calcutta, 1889), 379.

[60] D. S. Maini, 'Raja Rao's Vision, Values and Aesthetic', in K. K. Sharma (ed.), *Perspectives on Raja Rao* (Ghaziabad: Vimal Prakashan, 1980), 4. Counted on pp. 65–6 of *Kanthapura*.

rise again, and we hold to our children and the night-blind, and we duck and we rise again, and, our eyes fixed on the soldiers, we rush towards Bhatta's sugar-cane field. . . . and we huddle behind the sugar-cane reeds and we lie along the sugar-cane ditches, and we peep across the dark, watery fields, and the children begin to say, 'I am afraid, I am afraid,' and we say, 'Wait a moment, wait, and it will be over soon' (241).

Stylistically, these aspects in the vocabulary of the novel are meant to impart a fast-paced quality to the prose itself—a sense of time rushing by so rapidly as to escape narration. Recall Rao's foreword where he says, 'We, in India, think quickly, we talk quickly, and when we move we move quickly. There must be something in the sun of India that makes us rush and tumble and run on. And our paths are paths interminable' (6). Curiously, the consequence of the fast-paced action is a sense of continuum and uniformity which comes from the repetitive and coordinative syntax. The disjunction is located in the distinction between oral and written texts. So long as one reads silently, the 'linked colloquial rhythm of the katha and the fable' give the impression of slowness and passivity and establish, as it were, 'the sanctity of the past'.[61] This derives from the timeless tendency of the printed word, impassively communicating the agitation of the temporal. But if read aloud, the voice emphasizes, colours, and differentiates a word like 'rush', and the passage acquires a more agitated life. While the visual act of reading is inclined to approve of immobility and order, the oral emphasizes the dynamism of the event.[62] This appears to be a deliberate negotiation of the relation between the oral and the written by the author who is aware of the hidden community of readers. The convergence of the oral with the written also allows Rao to adapt the imported novel form—perhaps, the Irish or the American—to Indian narrative traditions. But since the novel is only accessible in the written medium, it is the written which translates the oral into timeless metaphysics and subsumes all this rushing and tumbling.

The sense of continuity that results from stylistic devices links the past memories of the grandmother with the present moment of narration. The past and the present thus fuse into each other making the contemporary moment a part of the 'eternal continuum of time'.[63] This is achieved by frequently punctuating the

[61] Ibid.     [62] Ong, *Orality and Literacy*, 32.
[63] Maini, 'Raja Rao's Vision, Values and Aesthetic', 4.

quick flow of action with length-giving devices, as is evident in the following:

And it is the same by the Ganges and the Jumna and the Godavari, by Indus and by Kaveri, in Agra and Ankola, Lucknow and Maunpuri, in Madras, Patna and Lahore, in Calcutta, Peshawar and Puri, in Poona and in Benares—everywhere; and millions and millions of our brothers and sisters have gone to prison, and when the father comes back, the son is taken, and when the daughter is arrested, the mother comes out of prison (228).

We're in the Big field. Where is Ratna? Where is Venkateshia's wife Lakshamma? And Nose-scratching Nanjamma? And Seethamma and Vedamma and Chinnamma and all? 'How are you, Madamma?' I ask (246).

And there is such a confusion that men grip men and men crush men and men bite men and men tear men, and moans on moans rise and groans on groans die out, while the ambulance men are still at work and men are bandaged, and shots after shots ring out and man after man falls like an empty sack, and the women take up the lamentation . . . (249).

And crouching, we creep back through the village lane . . . and the Canal-bund beyond which three thousand men are shrieking and slaying, weeping, wounding, groaning, crawling, swooning, vomiting, bellowing, moaning, raving, gasping . . . (250).

The overall picture is one of confusion. In the first instance, the structural and the philosophical principles of the quotation invoke a parallelism between the rivers of India and its people. In what reads like a litany or an incantation, Rao juxtaposes India's various cities, connecting their different events into a single experience. The arbitrariness of their inclusion and juxtaposition shows that the linkage between them is imagined, not real. Rao appears to suggest a common sanctity between the rivers, cities, and people that together dissolve and make 'India', both within a political and a spatial consciousness.[64] In his later novels, India is shaped as an overt metaphor that can encompass people from anywhere in the world so that 'india' [sic] becomes an adjective signifying universalism. The

---

[64] A similar sentiment is expressed by Rabindranath Tagore as he looks beyond geographical unification: 'Just as we want Bombay, Madras, and Punjab to be near us, similarly we want a direct knowledge of the past of India. Fully aware of ourselves we want to understand our identity both in space and time, as a unified and great nation.' Cited in Meenakshi Mukherjee, *Realism and Reality: The Novel and Society in India* (Delhi: Oxford University Press, 1985), 57.

coexistence of rivers and cities, it appears, has functionality within Rao's personal Hindu metaphysics of oneness between 'indians'.[65] Further, we are told in no certain terms about the number of people in prison. The grandmother simply gives us figures in millions so that there appears to be scarcely any Indian out of prison, thus creating the impression of joint resistance to aggression and common suffering. The second instance is the scene in the Big field which is one of chaos in which Ratna, Lakshamma, Nanjamma, Seethamma, and Vedamma become indistinguishable in the mass of people, thereby enhancing the effect of the presence of millions. The third instance of men gripping men, and men tearing men reads like an extremely long-shot view of the fight where the two sides and their hostilities are lost in the jumble of bodies. The distance is achieved by taking the story back in time. By narrating the story fourteen months after the event, Rao protects history, making it as static and eternal as the grandmother's repertoire of myths arranged in her memory.

Sentences running into scores of lines, as in chapters four and five of *Kanthapura*, and the length-giving devices used therein are evidently intended to heighten the interminable quality of Indian storytelling. They are well suited to the vivid depiction of the slow pace of activity or the vastness of space as in the case of the coffee estate. The graphic potential of such sentences conveys the conversational prolixity and the run-on manner of the narrative which not only imparts vigour to the story but also links it to the stylistic nuances and gestures of oral storytelling, ensuring Rao's success in conveying effectively the immutable and lasting quality of an Indian experience. The conjunctive tone of the *puranic* narration, however, serves as much to dehistoricize the historical moment in the background. Rao's use of the word 'and' at the beginning of the sentences admittedly imparts a sense of continuity to narratives and an eternality to language, but it also conveys a feeling of the timelessness of existence. In addition, the introduction of the *puranic* elements of fantasy, poetry, and folklore turn the current political upheaval initiated by Gandhi into a Gandhi*purana*. The very presentation of Gandhi through a *harikatha*, which Rao explains in a

---

[65] Elsewhere Rao says, '[W]heresoever you go, you always return to the Himalayas, and whatever the rivers that flow, the waters are of the Gangotri.' See Rao, 'Books Which Have Influenced Me', 49.

footnote to be 'literally story of God', is in the traditional *puranic* style.[66]

Rao's depiction of *Kanthapura* as a *puranic* text is deliberate. He intends to turn the historical environment of the 1920s and the 1930s into a glorious past in order to appeal to his readers on the evidence of that past. By situating the incidents beyond their micro level of materiality, he stretches the boundaries of Kanthapura to take on a larger, 'Indian' dimension. The *puranic* nature of the narration, the epic intention, the use of length-giving devices, the technique of orality, the mythicization of real events, all of which are the functions of the grandmother, are, in fact, subtle ways of broadening the area of concentration, and attempts at making Kanthapura a 'miniature version of a larger India'.[67] The subsequent appeal to a common identity is, then, implicit in the homogeneous environment of a collective mythical past. The ensuing traditionalist–nationalist model betrays the desire to preserve or enhance a people's national or cultural identity when it is felt to be inadequate or lacking.[68] Hence, Rao's experiment with language is geared to make *Kanthapura* more a novel of nationalistic dimensions, with all its ideological ramifications, than simply a text of political self-consciousness at the local level.

On Scholes's spectrum of literary modes, such a representation would be farthest from the mode of history although the depiction of real events enables a confluence of 'romance' and 'history' engineered through time. Rao's writing exists at the interface of these two traditions. On the one hand, he deals with nationalist politics and the world of 'real' consequence, constituted by the intervention of time, and on the other, defines those very politics in terms of Hindu philosophy and *puranic* narration which are no less real. The contradiction is also present between the novelistic form and the evidence of a circular Indian tradition which, in being 'endless', is opposed to the

[66] The presence of a footnote draws attention away from the inner circle of narrator and audience to the outer circle consisting of the author and the reader. *Harikatha* being a Sanskrit term, the footnote indicates the writer's responsibility to explain what the narrator may not need to clarify to the supposed village listeners. By implication, the footnote subverts the credibility of the tale as well as the plausibility of the narrator.

[67] K. S. Ramamurti, 'Kanthapura, Kedaram, Malgudi and Trinidad as Indias in Miniature—A Comparative Study', in A. K. Sinha (ed.), *Alien Voice: Perspectives on Commonwealth Literature* (Lucknow: Print House, 1981), 62.

[68] John Plamenatz, 'Two Types of Nationalism', in Eugene Kamenka (ed.), *Nationalism: The Nature and Evolution of an Idea* (London: Edward Arnold, 1976), 23–4.

very idea of linear action. The print medium which sustains the historical context and the oral which altogether denies historical linearity or chronology contribute in perpetuating this opposition.[69] So skilfully are the two strands woven into the novel structure that mythology operates uninhibitedly to evoke a live cultural tradition unviolated by verifiable facts. By the time Rao writes *The Serpent and the Rope*, the romance/metaphysical far outweighs the history/nationalistic model.

However, the modal development in Rao cannot be seen within the terms of Scholes and Wicks alone. Forms of fiction can scarcely adhere to fixed typologies, particularly when they tend to be culture-specific, and consequently cannot correspond to western generic forms. It is only through a procedure of gradual elimination that Rao's writing can be placed anywhere near Scholes's classification of history or romance.[70] There is also the problem of the writer's environment and cultural tradition which would attach unfamiliar meanings to these terms when seen outside the west. In the same way, it is difficult to fix non-European writing completely within western typology.[71] *Kanthapura* has to be different from the 'well-made' realist novel of the eighteenth and nineteenth centuries since it is marked by the absence of linear time-consciousness. While the consciousness of the present determines the representation of reality for the western tradition of novel writing, the characters in myths, romance, or epics are permitted to exist outside historical time. Here again, *Kanthapura* cannot be encapsulated within the process of eventful history, since it develops in the spatial sense. It appears to be closer to the narrative conventions of traditional *kavya* or works of poetry where all time exists as part of a regenerative cosmic cycle.[72] In the west, the invention of mechanical clocks in the fourteenth century, and the emergence of the genres of the newspaper and the novel in the seventeenth and the eighteenth centuries, created the concept of a linear and secular historical time.[73] This marked a break

---

[69] Ong, *Orality and Literacy*, 145–6.

[70] For an interesting treatment of western traditions of realism and the corresponding reality in Indian writing, see Mukherjee, *Realism and Reality*, 9–10; 39–40; 127–8.

[71] For instance, the *maukhik* (oral) narration differs from the western tradition which is mainly a written one. The Indian tradition of oral discourse is espoused by its gurus who consider the written word secondary to *vak* (speech).

[72] Mukherjee, *Realism and Reality*, 9.

[73] Joyce Appleby, *et al.*, *Telling the Truth about History* (New York and London: W. W. Norton, 1994), 52–6.

with the past since such a concept of simultaneous living was 'universal rather than particular to any epoch, nation, or faith'.[74] In the Indian context, on the other hand, a break with the past was a notion unimaginable for the builders of a national agenda since it would discipline history, thus voiding invented traditions.

It also has to be kept in mind that the *puranas* have always been a dominant influence on the genre of the historical novel in India. History here is generally enacted outside chronology in mythic time since the *puranas* are based on the assumption that 'the universe changes through enormous cycles of time', thereby conveying a 'radically different historical sense' from Christian, Jewish, and Muslim writings.[75] There arises, then, the possibility of a history outside time, which demands, more often than not, a suspension of disbelief for its credibility. The inclusion of miraculous happenings and magical deeds and the employment of animal typology are an important feature of this classification. Cultural protagonists are projected in cows, tigers, serpents, birds, and other animals possessing divine power.[76] It is not difficult to trace their depiction to the *Panchatantra* or the book of animal stories in which vices and virtues are manifested through animals. The unconscious and even conscious influence of the *puranas*, bardic literature, tribal memory, epic poetry, and oral tradition which spurred many Indian writers, thus cannot be disregarded in the study of Indian literary traditions. Significantly, the pre-novel narrative tradition in India can find resonance with the ideal fictional types in Scholes's spectrum of possible fictional worlds. For in his very definition, the terms of the given fictional spectrum are abstracted from history, and in that sense, can accommodate Rao's use of indigenous narratives which, too, are outside history and its linear conception of time.

Evidently, Rao demands to be judged on his grounds alone. To see him simply from the standpoint of the western novelistic tradition would amount to diminishing the indigenous categories of narrative he uses to construct his fiction. If the nationalist elite had only western 'modular' forms to choose from, what would nation-states

[74] Joyce Appleby, *et al.*, *Telling the Truth about History*, 55.
[75] C. H. Philips, 'Introduction', in id. (ed.), *Historians of India, Pakistan and Ceylon* (London: Oxford University Press, 1961), 4.
[76] See e.g. Rao, 'The True Story of Kanakapala', 53–69. Some of Rao's stories are narrated by a parrot as in the Prakrit folk tale *Suka-sapati* (AD 950) or *The Enchanted Parrot*. See Raja Rao, *On the Ganga Ghat* (New Delhi: Vision, 1989).

be left to 'imagine'? Anticolonial nationalism was, in fact, character-ized by its difference from the existing 'modular' forms of the national society which are believed to have been already provided by the historical experience of nationalism in western Europe.[77] As Partha Chatterjee writes, nationalism would be reduced to a 'carica-ture' of itself if the indigenous elite had not created a divide between the spiritual and the material.[78] In spite of borrowing ceaselessly on the level of materiality, it was on the spiritual plane that the nation was already 'sovereign', even though the state was controlled by colonial power.[79] Although Chatterjee's own familiar categories of spiritual/material may be easily traced to orientalism, and are thor-oughly essentialistic, he does provide a ground where there was enormous scope for invention, and space for the nation to be ima-gined. Within such an argument, Rao's experiment with English can also be seen as an expression of the 'inner domain of cultural identity' from which the rulers are kept out.[80] It is thus important to under-stand Rao's writing in terms of a classification, however essentialist, emerging from the aesthetics of his own culture. This has far more relevance to his later fiction where his work becomes doctrinal and philosophical. Raja Rao's use of the traditional concept of story-telling for the depiction of real events may then call for an evaluation within a social reality substantially different from the western con-ventions of realism. Apart from being an accepted literary practice in the given social milieu, the adaptation of episodes from the epic and the *purana*s allows the novelist to glorify the timeless, pre-British past. In pre-independence India, this was the cultural and literary inheritance largely employed by the intelligentsia to augment the values of the present generation.

[77] Partha Chatterjee, *The Nation and Its Fragments: Colonial and Postcolonial Histories* (Delhi: Oxford University Press, 1994), 4–5.          [78] Ibid. 5.
[79] Ibid. 6.          [80] Ibid. 7.

## 2  The Ideology of Gandhi:
## A Mass Fantasy

While the intuitive borrowing from language takes place at one level in the novel, at another interconnected level, 'real' India is constructed by enshrining the novel in Gandhian ideology. The response to Gandhi's ideas of *ahimsa* (non-violent resistance) and non-cooperation among villages had been strong: villagers prepared for the struggle by breaking the Salt and Forest laws, picketing toddy shops, and fighting against social evils like untouchability in order to unite in a common cause. Rao treats the history of the freedom movement at the level of hostility between village folk and the police under British rule at a time when colonialism had become intensely heavy-handed during the Civil Disobedience Movement. He has focused on two individual leaders and their beliefs: the actual and the mythicized significance of Gandhi, and his transmutation into Moorthy, the saintly hero of the novel. The interest of the novel lies not so much in Gandhi's doctrines and deeds as in their reflection and alteration in the novel, leading to an understanding of the ahistorical nature of Rao's representation of the contemporary politics of the 1930s.

In the following analysis, I examine Gandhi's veneration of village communities, the significance of his fasts and the Salt March, his treatment of the caste system, and his contradictions and inconsistencies as a person and as a thinker within the overall consciousness of Rao's ritualized adoption of him in the novel. The chapter demonstrates Rao's implicit bias towards brahminism which can be seen as a feature of chauvinist Hinduism employed by revivalist nationalists. As we shall see, the tensions between the brahminic and the Gandhian nationalist-*puranic* models may be neutralized or highlighted in varying political situations. I also review the novel's turn towards socialism, and the author's intervention to 'correct' the historical turn of events by retreating into the Gandhian scheme. Posing a series of contradictions between Gandhi's ideals and principles and the way in which they have been written into the novel, the chapter exposes

Rao's concern with presenting the historical moment in terms of a timeless past. The author's intrusion upon the grandmother's narration should be seen in all the instances where the ideological overwrites the dramatic.


I


Since the village joins the freedom struggle with Gandhi's advent, attention must be drawn to his actual visits to Karnataka and the effect of his appeals. Gandhi first visited Karnataka in 1921 with a view to motivating people into joining the Non-Cooperation Movement. His appeal to boycott courts, schools, colleges, and government offices was taken up enthusiastically. So was the adoption of *khadi* (homespun), the abolition of untouchability, and the prohibition of liquor. During another visit in 1927, he said: 'More is expected of those who give much. I have found so much good in this State that I almost fancy that if you and the Maharaja together will it, you can make the state *Ramrajya*.'[1]

It is conceivable that Gandhi's presence in Karnataka motivated the youth of its cities and villages alike, and, therefore, Moorthy's encounter with the Mahatma, though imaginary, has a context:

He [Moorthy] stood up, and he saw there, by the legs of the chair, the sandal and the foot of the Mahatma, and he said to himself, 'That is my place'. And suddenly there was a clapping of hands and shoutings of '*Vande Mataram, Gandhi Mahatma ki jai!*' and he put forth his hands and cried '*Mahatma Gandhi ki jai!*' And as there was fever and confusion about the Mahatma, he jumped on to the platform . . . and fell at the feet of the Mahatma, saying, 'I am your slave'. The Mahatma lifted him up and, before them all, he said, 'What can I do for you, my son?' and Moorthy said, like Hanuman to Rama, 'Any command,' and the Mahatma said, 'I give no commands save to seek Truth,' and Moorthy said, 'I am ignorant, how can I seek Truth?' and the people around him were trying to hush him and to take him away, but the Mahatma said, 'You wear foreign cloth, my son'. — 'It will go, Mahatmaji.' — 'You perhaps go to foreign Universities.' — 'It will go, Mahatmaji.' — 'You can help your country by going and working among the dumb millions of the villages.' — 'So be it, Mahatmaji'. . . . And when

---

[1] M. K. Gandhi, 'Speech at Citizens' Meeting, Bangalore', *The Hindu*, 29 Aug. 1927, in *Collected Works of Mahatma Gandhi, 1884–1948*, 90 vols. (Ahmedabad: Navajivan, 1958–84), xxxiv. 417.

he came back to the college that evening, he threw his foreign clothes and his foreign books into the bonfire, and walked out, a Gandhi's man (53–4).

The political movement from town to country is marshalled with the Mahatma's appeal. Moorthy, like Rama's devotee Hanuman, agrees to carry the Mahatma's message to the villages and educate the 'dumb millions' in nationalism. His conversion simultaneously implies other definite movements from the literate to the illiterate, and from written to oral, as indicated in the long passage from the text. The repetitive nature of the rallying cry supporting Gandhi, the mixture of direct speech and indirect narration, and especially the ritualistic conversation between Moorthy and Gandhi draw attention to the oral qualities of the text and with it, associatively, to the virtues of natural village life. The movement is, however, paradoxical, since the edification of the village Gandhi speaks of has all the ramifications of mobility and change symptomatic of modernity. If the villages are to be more like cities, the author's counter-ideology of subsuming urbanity into placid village life, and of making the village a representation of India will not succeed. Significantly, Moorthy's contact with the Mahatma is imaginary since he has only seen Gandhi in a vision. This enables Rao to turn the historical moment into a visionary experience, and opens a space for the possibility of assumed politics. Rao is thus free to turn the dialogue in any way, without having to be completely faithful to Gandhi.

Curiously, the strength of the village comes from the purity of its traditions, as opposed to the cities which, in the novel, have thrown open their temple gates to the pariahs as recommended by Gandhi. The dichotomy between cities and villages should then be reconsidered in terms of custom which is not violated in the villages. From this viewpoint, the relaxation of caste-boundaries in the cities is, in fact, polluting and sacrilegious. Yet the action of the novel is against conservative resistance to change since it is Moorthy the nationalist, and not Bhatta the reactionary, who assumes significance. Rao maintains the sanctity of the village at an ideological level, but permits mobility and change to heighten the historical significance of the national struggle. Though the balance between the ideological and the novelistic/dramatic is largely maintained, their tendency to widen and separate will be taken up in the course of the analysis.

On ideological grounds, the city and the village are mutually defined opposites: the city is the den of corruption and deceit in contrast with village purity and truth, ideologically construed as 'the level of changeless meaning'.[2] Since Gandhi's idealized India was non-industrial, the narrative accordingly privileges village existence and celebrates Gandhi's philosophy of *gram raj* or the centring in village authority. Coming under the strong influence of Tolstoy's faith in the value of 'bread labour', Gandhi conceptualized the image of free India in terms of his perception of a traditional Indian culture which tolerated no economic oppression or human degradation of any kind. He related his philosophical premises of Ahimsa and Truth to the life of the 'simple' peasantry.[3] Of a meeting with the peasants of Champaran, he wrote: 'It is no exaggeration, but the literal truth, to say that in this meeting with the peasants I was face to face with God, Ahimsa and Truth.'[4] Post-independence social order was to be built on a more utopian than historical perspective, the vision of a revitalizing and vigorous ancient Indian village community being a dominant constituent of his social philosophy of state, society, and nation elucidated at length in 'Hind Swaraj' in 1909.[5] He would remain loyal to this stand in spite of severe criticism. From this position, village societies were to be independent and self-determined units, promoting only cottage industry for the production of essential commodities. Although he permitted the centralization of important manufacturing industry in recognition of its significance for economic growth, such industry, in his scheme, was allowed to develop only in harmony with the growth of the rural community to prevent capitalists from making profits at the cost of mass unemployment.

Gandhi considered cities to be colonial inflictions in their function of eroding the very base of India's organic social order. 'We are

---

[2] Ronald Inden, *Imagining India* (Oxford: Basil Blackwell, 1990), 159.

[3] Gandhi's conception of village societies finds many parallels with Russian populism, a radical movement widespread in mid-19th-cent. Russia. The populist goals concentrated on the 'martyrs' of Russian society, namely the agricultural workers whose uncorrupted virtue alone could hold the promise of a future Russia. The populist leaders blamed capitalism for peasant dehumanization, and instead idealized an organic society of the village commune. The difference between Gandhi's vision and Russian populism, however, lies in the opposition between non-violence and terrorism in the achievement of complete liberty. See Isaiah Berlin, *Russian Thinkers*, ed. Henry Hardy and Aileen Kelly (Harmondsworth: Penguin, 1979), 210–37.

[4] M. K. Gandhi, *An Autobiography: Or, The Story of My Experiments with Truth*, trans. Mahadev Desai (Ahmedabad: Navajivan, 1927), 344.

[5] M. K. Gandhi, 'Hind Swaraj' (Indian Home Rule), in *Collected Works*, x. 6–68. Pearse was advocating similar ideals in Ireland about this time which were later put into practice by the Irish Free State under De Valera.

inheritors of a rural civilization,' he said.[6] For him, this historically 'accurate' presumption was also a directive for the future: 'If the village perishes, India will perish too.'[7] Moreover, for Gandhi, village existence represented truth and dignity which, he believed, had eluded western culture. Correspondingly, within Rao's framework of village India, political structures are permitted to evolve naturally from the grassroots. Taking the village as the reservoir of spiritual values, cultural prosperity, and social order, he collaborates wholeheartedly with Gandhi's programme for moral and social regeneration at the rural level unimpaired by urbanization.[8] Kanthapura is accordingly constructed virtually on the lines of Gandhi's Tolstoy Farm. Nourished by the waters of Himavathy, the environment of Kanthapura and its distance from the commercial activity of cities evokes a sense of inaccessibility, effectively captured in the text:

High on the Ghats is it, high up the steep mountains that face the cool Arabian seas, up the Malabar coast is it. . . . Roads, narrow, dusty, rut-covered roads, wind through the forests of teak and of jack, of sandal and of sal, and hanging over bellowing gorges and leaping over elephant-haunted valleys, they turn now to the left and now to the right (7).

If Kanthapura is isolated and removed from civilization, it is compensated by an evergrowing cycle of ceremonies, rituals, and festivals. Rao depicts the regular involvement of the villagers in *Sankara-jayanthi*, *Kartik Purnima*, *Ganesh-Jayanthi*, *Dasara*, and the *Satya-narayana Puja* with the intention of conveying a sense of the natural unity and cohesion of village society. Old Ramakrishnayya reads out the *Sankara-Vijaya* day after day and the villagers discuss Vedanta with him every afternoon. Religion, imparted through discourses and *pujas*, keeps alive in the natives a sense of the presence of god; avatars and incarnations are constantly evoked to sustain an inner strength

---

[6] Cited in Richard G. Fox, *Gandhian Utopia: Experiments with Culture* (Boston: Beacon, 1989), 56.                                                                        [7] Ibid.

[8] Rao's faith in Gandhi's village communities can be estimated from his later association with Maurice Frydman, a Polish engineer interested in the village reconstruction movement, with whom Rao had visited Gandhi's ashram at Sevagram in 1941. There is no record of any correspondence or discussions between Rao and Gandhi but there are references to conversations Gandhi had with Frydman. See, for instance, M. K. Gandhi, *Collected Works*, lxiii. 241; lxviii. 52; lxxv. 175–7, 288; lxxix. 173. We do know, however, that Rao was influenced by Gandhi's autobiography, which he read 'as the text appeared, week after week, in *Young India*.' See Raja Rao, 'Books Which Have Influenced Me', in M. K. Naik (ed.), *Aspects of Indian Writing in English* (Delhi: Macmillan, 1979), 48.

and stability among the villagers. Indeed, village unity is at its upper-
most in the description of traditional festivals and celebrations:

Ratna blew the conch from the top of the Promontory, and with the
blowing of the conch rose the *Satyanarayan Maharaj ki jai! Satyanarayan
Maharaj ki jai!* . . . and we marched through the Brahmin Street and the
Potters' Street and the Pariah Street and the Weavers' Street, and doors
creaked and children ran down the steps, and trays were in their hands, and
the camphor was lit and the coconuts broken and the fruits offered. . . .
And shoulder after shoulder changed beneath the procession-throne and
cries of '*Satyanarayan Maharaj ki jai! Satyanarayan Maharaj ki jai!*' leapt
into the air (234).

The barriers erected by caste through the rest of the year are tem-
porarily removed in the abandonment of a festival. The solidarity
evoked through community life and common interests seems to defy
the deep-rootedness of even the caste system.

Within the characteristic rural atmosphere of religious festivity,
the foundation myth of Kenchamma killing a demon[9] is a living
manifestation in the mind of every villager. She is believed to have
waged such a battle on the demon that the hill soaked up his
blood and became red. It is surprising that in a novel ardently
aligned with Gandhian non-violence, the sight of a bloody hill,
obviously a result of violence, should command so much reverence.
The legend of the red Kenchamma Hill exercises a tremendous
hold on the villagers: 'She has never failed us, I assure you, our
Kenchamma' (9). Rooted as the goddess is in an ahistorical past,
she also has enormous power in the present. This is so because the
red hill, a feature of the landscape visible at all times, symbolizes
her palpable presence in their lives. The Kenchamma-myth is thus
both timeless and enduring. Accordingly, the villagers offer orna-
ments to please Kenchamma, begging her for protection from
famine and disease.

With the writer's representation of an essentialist Indian society, the
ground for Gandhi's position among prominent Hindu deities is well
prepared. It is significant that the political figure is first mentioned as
a god, sent down from heavens to 'slay the serpent of the foreign rule'
(22), and commands devotion because of his introduction through

---

[9] According to legend, the demon is, presumably, Rakta Bijasura, who was killed by
the joint efforts of Kenchamma and Goddess Durga. See *Mysore State Gazetteer,
Hassan District* (Bangalore: Government of Mysore, 1971), 648–9.

the religious medium of a *harikatha*.[10] Gandhi's genericized introduction through the oral tradition facilitates his acceptance among the villagers, not, however, as a political figure, but as a reincarnation of the Hindu god Shiva, and appears to be credible because his canonization remains a prominent feature of a large part of Indian literature and history. For Rao, the investment in the sacral nature of Gandhi's appeal lends enormous support to the *puranic* model where gods and men must mingle.

In order to allow an easy interchange between the world of men and the world of gods, between contemporaneity and antiquity, Rao equips his story with a saintly protagonist—an understudy to Gandhi—whose role it is to enthuse the villagers into joining the political cause of India's struggle for freedom without reservation. In order to make village participation in the freedom movement possible, it is important to provide the masses with a charismatic leader at the local level who can act as a conduit between the Mahatma and the village people, or, if need be, assume the very mantle of the Mahatma. Significantly, the deification of the central character allows the author to deepen the emphasis on religion even as Moorthy's prototype, Gandhi, is seen, in contrast, to be more 'human'. The differences between the two can be interpreted as a projection of the author's ideological construction.

Having set up Gandhi as a god, Rao endeavours to present Moorthy in a quasi-divine role.[11] Moorthy practises not only *ahimsa*, but also undertakes severe penance, the hallmark of Gandhi's appeal to the public. His role as the 'small Mahatma' is seen to service two ends: it connects the supernatural and the human, and consequently, transports the present story to the lost world of antiquity. Like Gandhi, Moorthy is depicted as an otherworldly creature who imbibes the saintly quality of penitence and suffering for others' sins: '[He fasts until] a great blue radiance seems to fill the whole earth, and dazzled, he rises up and falls prostrate before the god,

[10] Even today, the *harikatha* is used as a means of religious instruction, where a *pandit* well versed in the epics or the *puranas* weaves a story or relates an episode to point a moral to a village audience. *Harikathas* are often used for political propaganda, even though their outward religious appearance is maintained.

[11] The villagers become loyal servants of Gandhi only because they begin to deify Moorthy as 'our Gandhi': 'The state of Mysore (Karnataka) has a Maharaja, but that Maharaja has another Maharaja who is in London, and that one has another one in Heaven, and so everybody has his own Mahatma, and this Moorthy . . . will be our Mahatma' (109).

chanting Sankara's "Sivoham, Sivoham. I am Siva. I am Siva. Siva am I"' (92). Believing fasting and meditation to be a way of rising 'lovingly to God' and diminishing the 'dross of the flesh through vows' (91), Moorthy attains oneness with the Absolute through self-denial. Even though it is the violence at the Skeffington Coffee Estate that motivates him to fast in the first place, the religious dimension of the fast is evident.

It is relevant here to introduce a comparison with Gandhi's fasts in order to understand their potency in similar circumstances. Originally, Gandhi undertook fasting to support his vow of sexual self-restraint or *brahmacharya*. Born into a Hindu Vaishnava family, and accustomed to his mother's frequent fasts, Gandhi had observed their efficacy in maintaining good health and discipline. At Tolstoy Farm in South Africa, he stretched the significance of the fasts to embrace other religions: Christians and Parsis were encouraged to fast with Muslims in the month of *ramzan*, or with the Hindus in observing *pradosha* (vows) with the view to practising self-denial. It was later that the fasts assumed another dimension, that of penitence for others' sins. A 'moral fall' of two of the inmates of the Ashram led Gandhi, for the first time, to undertake the responsibility for the errors of his pupils: 'I felt that the only way the guilty parties could be made to realize my distress and the depth of their own fall would be for me to do some penance.'[12] It should be indicated that Gandhi's fasts were not undertaken specifically for spiritual motives or for the attainment of god, though such reasons cannot be ruled out entirely. Gandhi was conscious that his fasts pained everybody, but nevertheless succeeded in bringing home to the sinner the dimension of his sin. He also realized that conversion in the sinners would not be possible without a sense of community between the teacher and the pupil: 'Where there is no true love between the teacher and the pupil, where the pupil's delinquency has not touched the very being of the teacher and where the pupil has no respect for the teacher, fasting is out of place and may even be harmful.'[13] Fasting, thus, had a precise function for Gandhi and was undertaken only when a favourable outcome was ensured.

Gandhi's major fasts of 8 May and 16 August 1933 were undertaken explicitly to convince his followers of the importance of removing the disabilities of the depressed classes: 'They must either remove

[12] Gandhi, *Autobiography*, 286.   [13] Ibid.

untouchability or remove me from their midst.'[14] It can be inferred that his fasts were, to an extent, forms of emotional arm-twisting and, thereby, irresistible.[15] Gandhi used the hunger-strike as a technique of disapproval and protest, broadly as an appeal to the villagers and the lower classes. He justified these fasts as answers to his 'inner voice', which, he said, could also be described as 'dictates of reason'.[16] While fasting was compatible with a culture that valued this form of penance, Gandhi introduced an innovation into that same culture by applying fasting to the practical world in quest of political and historical efficacy. In so far as Gandhi's fasting revolutionized orthodox belief in the achievement of present goals, it cannot be situated within conservatism. The suffering he undertook may be positioned outside orthodox Hinduism since it includes certain features of the Judaic tradition. Gandhi's realization of the latent potential of a religious feature of Hinduism in effect creates a syncretic amalgam of the Hindu and the Judaic which is worldly rather than other-worldly. Gandhi also did not elevate Hinduism at the cost of other religions in spite of his abiding faith in Hindu principles; he held Christianity in high esteem and was sorry that the west had deviated from their faith. His religion combined the virtues of action enshrined in the Gita with the Sermon on the Mount. At this level, Gandhi operates outside the problematic of strict Hinduism.

Rao, in comparison, localizes penance within Hindu orthodoxy since Moorthy's fast is self-revelatory and culminates in finding the Absolute. Moorthy's austerities are mystical in nature: he imagines himself to be the child-Krishna who cannot drown, or the victimized Prahlada who is saved by protective gods when hurled down steep mountains, or the ascetic Mira who turned poison into nectar when it was forced down her throat. The mythological characters Moorthy 'sees' in his trance are examples of gods and saints who finally get absorbed into the Almighty. His visions include even Gandhi who appears to him in the very manifestation of god. Moorthy's conversion to Gandhism, as mentioned earlier, is not the result of a direct

[14] Cited in Bipan Chandra, *et al.*, *India's Struggle for Independence* (New Delhi: Penguin, 1989), 292.

[15] While the masses believed Gandhi to be fasting, he did, in fact, consume a certain amount of prescribed food to sustain life. In a letter to Mirabehn, he said: 'I am able to take about 8 meals of this poison-tasting but nectar-like meal. Yet I claim to be fasting and credulous people accept it. What a strange world!' See M. K. Gandhi, 'Letter to Mirabehn', 16 Jan. 1948, in *Collected Works*, xc. 430.

[16] Cited in Chandra *et al.*, *India's Struggle for Independence*, 292.

interaction with Gandhi since Gandhi himself never comes to Kanthapura. For the rest of the village, too, the Gandhi-symbolism is disseminated largely by creating a 'double' in Moorthy, so that Rao can translate the utopian Indian past in terms comprehensible to the simple-minded villagers. For the readers, however, the hierarchical descent from Gandhi to Moorthy is plain. It is also clear that Rao highlights the mythical and the godlike character of Gandhi by the association with Krishna, Prahlada, and Mira. Further down the hierarchy, Moorthy, too, acquires the halo of otherworldliness and assumes the mantle of an avatar, reappearing on earth to fight evil. In terms of identity, the mythicization of historical personages as eternal prototypes appears to be a cultural truism in a society that accepts the coexistence of the religious and the secular.[17] This conforms to the *puranas* which are the best instance of a narrative genre that records the legends of saints and martyrs. While *Kanthapura* may be an example of 'history' conforming to 'romance', or time inter-secting timelessness, the very analogies Moorthy's fasting presents with *moksha*, the Hindu form of salvation, enables the novel to testify to the eternal than to the historically 'real' since the depiction of national history transcends linear time and correlates to an ahis-torical conception of existence marked by an absence of death.

Inside the Hindu world, the laws of *karmic* inevitability are the supreme reality that determine existence.[18] In the west, on the other hand, what we call 'real' is signified by the linearization of time that generates the very concept of history and gives it direction so that religion itself is historicized in the Judaic tradition. The Hindu view of the real would be analogous to what the west would regard as a 'romantic' way of perceiving the concept of time, a prejudice usually associated with orientalism. In so far as Rao uses nationalist history, he subscribes to linear action, but the spiritual/metaphysical trans-mutation of real events can be interpreted as romance. As soon as Moorthy is touched by sainthood, Rao's history summons mythic time and abandons linear time. The constant interplay between his-tory and romance appears to have two advantages: it is both a means of escaping present subjection under colonialism and in turn glorify-ing timeless cultural myths, and a device to bring the educated Indian

---

[17] See Janet P. Gemmill, 'Elements of the Folktale in Raja Rao's *Cow of the Barricades*', *World Literature Written in English*, 20.1 (1981), 155.

[18] *Karma* is the doctrine of causality which derives from action, implying that one's existence in the next incarnation depends upon the actions in this lifetime.

reader in closer touch with an ostensibly Indian 'reality'. From this view, Rao's employment of metaphysical principles or 'Indian romance' redeems 'the evil world of history.'[19] The seductive quality of the western novel form remains to give credibility to his cultural model of nationalism although it has germinated in a very different soil, outside the accepted categories of history and fiction.

In accordance with the ideological undertones of the novel, the villagers' initiation into the Congress is ritualized by administering Kenchamma's oath:

'There is a huge Panchayat of all India called the Congress, and that Congress belongs to the Mahatma, and the Mahatma says every village in this country must have a Panchayat like that, and everybody who will become a member of that Panchayat will spin and practice ahimsa and speak the truth' (105–6).

The reluctant villagers are bludgeoned into submission by the authoritative village headman who supports Moorthy mindlessly:

'If you are the sons of your fathers, stand up and do what this learned boy says,' and Rangè Gowda's words were such a terror to them that one here and one there went up before the sanctum, rang the bell and said, 'My Master, I shall spin a hundred yards of yarn per day, and I shall practise ahimsa, and I shall seek Truth,' and they fell prostrate and asked for the blessings of the Mahatma and the gods, and they rose and crawled back to their seats (110).

The sweeping power of religion and the dread of Kenchamma finally induces them to join the Congress. By depicting the reluctance of the villagers in undertaking Kenchamma's solemn oath to never break the Panchayati law, Rao reveals the apolitical nature of the villagers, even though their apathy serves his ideological purpose of enhancing the cultural character of the village community. Consequently, in the novel, the village opposition to British rule—using the spinning wheel, or *charkha*, to spin their own cloth, toddy picketing, and revolting against the treatment meted out to the coolies of the Skeffington Coffee Estate—is in no way political. The ultimate encounter of the protesters and the armed soldiers, similarly, is *dharmic*, a moral or religious duty, almost an attempt to attain *moksha*, so that even in their defeat the villagers can see only the triumph of Good over Evil. Gandhi's *ramrajya*, too, is not assimilated and recognized within his politics: it is visualized completely in terms

---

[19] S. C. Harrex, 'Typology and Modes: Raja Rao's Experiments in Short Story', *World Literature Today*, 62.4 (1988), 593.

of its mythical and literal signification as a return to the rule of the god-king, Rama.

The correspondence between the present and the timeless is responsible for the depiction of Gandhi's famous Salt March in an entirely traditional way. Since Gandhi had refused to ride on a horse-carriage or a motor-car, preferring to walk instead, Moorthy remarks: '"He says he likes our ancient ways, and like the ancients he will make the pilgrimage on foot," and our hearts gladdened, for no one ever goes like that to far Kashi, do they?' (173). While it is true that Gandhi derived his symbols of appeal from religious tradi-tions, and often sought to politicize isolated rural communities by delivering politics through familiar modes of religion, he also under-stood the march in a sophisticated sense of mediated communication through press, photography, radio, and newsreel.[20] If, on the one hand, the march signified a movement towards rural India, on the other, the entire movement was disseminated through modern com-munication network. His walk was, thus, pure gesture, theatrical: it was an efficient means of establishing an interface between the most basic and the most advanced. Gandhi had wanted to popularize the making of salt, less for the boycott of salt taxes, which were minimal, but rather for the appeal it would hold for the millions in strengthen-ing the Civil Disobedience agitation, and thereby defying the govern-ment. Breaking the Salt Act was a reasonably convenient strategy for trespassing on colonial monopoly. The march was slow in order to gain maximum publicity throughout the journey.[21] The success of the march was ensured by a month of intense preparation: the original five-day programme was stretched to a dramatic twenty-four, and the rest halts were announced and widely publicized three days before the commencement of the march. Scouts were dispatched in advance with questionnaires prepared by Gandhi to collect data from villages which Gandhi was to use in his speeches. His employment of tradi-tional symbology, in the light of his manoeuvres, was intended to

[20] Dennis Dalton, 'The Dandi Drama', in Peter Robb and David Taylor (eds.), *Rule, Protest, Identity: Aspects of Modern South Asia* (London: Curzon, 1978), 135. See also Chris Harman, 'The Return of the National Question', in Alex Callinicos, John Rees, Chris Harman, and Mike Haynes, *Marxism and the New Imperialism* (London, Chicago, and Melbourne: Bookmarks, 1994), 230.

[21] Gandhi originally started off from his ashram in Sabarmati with seventy-nine *satyagrahis*. People from the villages on route and around spontaneously joined the march. By the time the procession neared Dandi, there were thousands of people walking with Gandhi.

heighten expectations and give the movement unprecedented proportions. He declared that the march was 'his Hardwar',[22] and that it was
'the hand of God' that urged them on. But he also announced: 'Everyone
is on the tiptoe of expectation, and before anything has happened the
thing has attracted world-wide attention.'[23] Despite the theatrical
aspect of the march, and the use of traditional symbols, Gandhi declared
plainly that the Salt March would mark the beginning of the Civil
Disobedience campaign. The nationalist press, however, rhapsodized
over their hero, conferred the status of god upon him, and declared
him to be 'Lord Ram on his way to conquer Sri Lanka', comparing
his march to 'Buddha's great march of renunciation'.[24]

Like the nationalist accounts, *Kanthapura* also represents the
legendary aspects of the march, using the metaphor of pilgrimage to
enhance the serene village model. One might concede at the fictive
level that the villagers are unaware of the significance of Gandhi's
march and the repeal of the salt laws, but to depict the intelligent
Rangamma as part of the inert village crowd amounts to situating
political and economic concerns wholly within a sentiment issuing
from religion.[25] Rangamma is educated, rational, and sensible, and is
not expected to mythologize the Salt March to the extent of saying:
'Oh no, the Mahatma need not go as far as the sea. Like Harishchandra before he finished his vow, the gods will come down and dissolve
his vow, and the Britishers will leave India, and we shall be free, and
we shall pay less taxes, and there will be no policemen' (172).[26]

[22] A pilgrim shrine for the Hindus.
[23] M. K. Gandhi, 'Speech at a Prayer Meeting, Sabarmati Ashram', 10 Mar. 1930,
in *Collected Works*, xliii. 37.          [24] Cited in Dalton, 'The Dandi Drama', 137.
[25] Rangamma, we hear, is 'no village kid'. She receives newspapers from the city:
'Tai-nadu' (Motherland), 'Vishwakarnataka' (World of Karnataka), 'Deshabhandu'
(Brothers of a nation) and 'Jayabharatha' (Victory to India) which, presumably, are
nationalistic publications. She knows of the telescope: 'you put your eyes to a great tube
and see another world with sun and moon and stars'; the galaxy: 'each star has a sun
and each sun has a moon, and each moon has an earth, and some there are that have
two moons, and some three'; aeroplanes: 'how in the far-off countries there were air
vehicles that move'; and the radio: 'she spoke to us, too, of the speech that goes across
the air; and she told us . . . you could sit here and listen to what they are saying in every
house in London and Bombay and Burma' (46–7).
[26] According to Hindu legend, Harishchandra, an honourable king, vowed that if a
son was born to him, he would sacrifice him to the gods. After his wish was granted,
however, he kept deferring the promise he had made, and consequently suffered years of
torture and hardship. After an intensely difficult period, the concerned deities appeared
before him. He was subsequently pardoned, and he and his wife secured a place in
heaven.

Gradually, just as Kanthapura is Rao's India in miniature and possesses uniform indigenous characteristics, Gandhi too is indigenized
into a pure symbol: 'high and yet seeable, firm and yet blue with dusk'
(176). The villagers begin to call him 'the Mountain'. Correspondingly, his arrest is seen as an affront to god, and they react by fasting.

For the villagers, the politics of the country are inseparable from
Gandhi, and Gandhi from divinity: 'Rama, Krishna, Sankara and the
Mahatma' are always mentioned in the same refrain. This speaks of
Gandhi's birth as a divine visitation on earth to destroy sin and
sinners alike in order to re-establish the hold of religion. The political
struggle is, thereby, largely ritualized, and nationalism filters down
into the village ranks through religion. Gandhi's mythicization
reveals Rao's intention to depict the cultural character of Indians,
who are perceived to be lacking a chronological conception of time,
and are accordingly conceived by the author. The novel, too, moves on
a plane much higher than its material level of plot and character
would suggest, aiming, on the other hand, at 'transforming the
national self of the countrymen and, in the process, virtually redis-
cover[ing] the Indian soul through Gandhi.'[27] The emphasis on
religion as a conduit to social and political activity largely provides
the underpinning to what is believed to be a dominantly Indian
characteristic, as Sri Aurobindo has remarked that all activity, political and social, begins only as a religious and spiritual movement in
this country.[28] Similarly, Narasimhaiah reiterates that 'religion
becomes the nucleus of social regeneration in Kanthapura in the
true tradition of India where social reformers have been profoundly
religious men'.[29]

Within the historical context of the Indian freedom struggle,
Gandhi himself ritualized politics to an amazing extent, dismissing
even history to protect the power of the 'soul force', or satyagraha, in
his critique of civil society. He believed that the strength of his
satyagraha alone would result in freeing India and establish a system
of pre-capitalist, agrarian village republics. His 'romanticism' was
unlike the dilemma of post-Enlightenment intellectuals, torn between

[27] Shiva Niranjan, Raja Rao: Novelist as Sadhaka (Ghaziabad: Vimal Prakashan,
1985), 43.
[28] Aurobindo Ghosh, The Renaissance in India (1920), repr. as The Foundations of
Indian Culture and The Renaissance in India (Pondicherry: Sri Aurobindo Ashram,
1972), 418.
[29] C. D. Narasimhaiah, Raja Rao (New Delhi: Arnold-Heinemann, 1968), 49.

Reason and Morality, between the rationality of industrial society and the anguish caused by the misuse of scientific temper. Nor was it merely a means of appropriating the subaltern for whom populism would hold immense attraction.[30] While Gandhi's plea for a peasant society was, in many ways, analogous to the elite-nationalist ideology in the representation of uncorrupted peasant consciousness and had a major role to perform in the practicalities of a nationalist-bourgeois movement, he had few ideological affinities with the European brand of nationalists like Banerjee and Bipin Chandra Pal. Gandhi did not unproblematically adopt the idea of a homogeneous nation-state, preferring instead 'the vaguer but politically more relevant and . . . morally more acceptable concept of civilisation' which he articulated in a 'non-nationalist and non-national language.'[31] In seeking to combine the ideological aspect of Tolstoy's thought with the political movement of India's struggle for independence, Gandhism, however, was not free of contradictions and ambiguities. Gandhi's singular achievement lay in the sheer flexibility with which he exercised his experiments with Truth, and combined his apparently irreconcilable objectives. He was thus able to secure political investment in mishaps and calamities which he otherwise emphasized to have been the consequence of divine retribution for wrongdoing.[32]

The nationalist intelligentsia, on their part, used Gandhi's 'spirituality' and its mass appeal extensively to appropriate the masses.[33] An exponent of cultural nationalism, Rao also represents Gandhi purely in terms of his religious appeal so that politics acquires religious overtones to adapt to a kind of society where the preservation of essential 'truths' is of ultimate importance. It is not surprising, therefore, that he departs from the political movement to what can be called the 'iconic' use of Gandhi very much in the nature of the

[30] Partha Chatterjee, 'Gandhi and the Critique of Civil Society', in Ranajit Guha (ed.), *Subaltern Studies*, 9 vols. (Delhi: Oxford University Press, 1982–97), iii. 175–9.

[31] Bhikhu Parekh, *Gandhi's Political Philosophy: A Critical Examination* (London: Macmillan, 1989), 193–4.

[32] The injury to a *satyagrahi*, which was otherwise to be suffered unflinchingly and non-violently, was, in fact, viewed as a political gain. When Jairamdas, a Congressman, was wounded during the Civil Disobedience Movement, Gandhi wired the Congress office saying: 'Consider Jairamdas Most Fortunate. Bullet Wound Thigh Better Than Prison. Wound Heart Better Still.' See M. K. Gandhi, 'Telegram to N. R. Malkani', 18 Apr. 1930, in *Collected Works*, xliii. 282.

[33] Whether the response of the masses was a result of Gandhi's appeal or the effect of a correspondence between Gandhi's principles and their own ambitions and aspirations will be discussed in the following chapter.

depiction of bhakti saints in Indian films whose lives are not seen in terms of realism, nor as the mass appeal of miracles, but as 'socially symbolic narratives' since film representation is made to undergo a process of 'iconographic augmentation'.[34] Not very different from the orientalist fantasy, Rao's representation of India as timeless and passive reproduces Gandhi's nationalist politics in an entirely utopian and unidimensional way.

The religious dimension of national politics, it must be pointed out, was not espoused in a similar manner by other writers of that time. Mulk Raj Anand, for example, effected a forward-looking ideology in comparison particularly to Rao's interest in the past. If Rao is a traditionalist, Anand is a socialist. Anand's treatment of Gandhi, in many ways like Rao's, is significant in drawing attention both to the emotional involvement of the people, which did not always spring from a sound understanding of Gandhi's principles, and their limited interest in those aspects of his appeal which did not affect their routine existence. Nowhere does he give an account of happy and settled villagers who get mixed up with politics and look forward to their doom. Both Bakha in *Untouchable* and Lalu in *The Sword and the Sickle*, impatient for reform, are critical of Gandhi's equation of religious taboos and social evils.[35] Lalu is agitated when Gandhi advocates the virtues of non-violence, spinning, soul force, repression of sexual urges, and the therapeutic values of suffering, none of which are related to his routine problems: he had 'not quite expected the Mahatma to define his religion so narrowly as to call himself a *Sanatani* Hindu, a sect which was notorious for its conservative fanaticism. And he wondered how this man, who had been to Europe and who imbibed so much learning could talk like that'.[36] The perspective we get on Gandhi from Anand is very different from the reverential idolatry of Raja Rao. Anand's Gandhi is an 'inveterate, non-stop talker', deriving evident pleasure in hearing his own voice.[37] His characters conceive of Gandhi as 'a little lop-eared, toothless man with a shaven head, which shone clean like a raw purple turnip

---

[34] See Geeta Kapur, 'Revelation and Doubt: Sant Tukaram and Devi', in Tejaswini Niranjana et al., *Interrogating Modernity: Culture and Colonialism in India* (Calcutta: Seagull, 1993), 22.

[35] Bakha is amazed how Gandhi can talk simultaneously of the emancipation of the untouchables and the protection of cows. See Mulk Raj Anand, *Untouchable* (London: Wishart, 1935), 220.

[36] Mulk Raj Anand, *The Sword and the Sickle* (London: Jonathan Cape, 1942), 192.     [37] Ibid. 195.

. . . dictating something to a black god who sat on his right-hand side'.[38] What makes these comments particularly interesting is Anand's own position. Unlike his characters, he does not consider Gandhi a sham hero. Not for nothing has he edited *The Historic Trial of Mahatma Gandhi*, dedicating the book to 'the immortal memory of our teacher, guide and liberator'.[39] He undoubtedly respects Gandhi's sincerity and honesty but, like his characters, he seems to have little patience with the Gandhian scheme of reform which involves prayers and hopes rather than enforcement.[40] To his critics who accused him of departing from a 'nationalistic' pattern, Anand replies:

Spontaneously, I feel, that the revivalists want to take us back to the filth of Hinduism, to the worship of Sabala the cow, and Hanuman the monkey, to the God-King Rama, who was a casteist and allowed his wife to be consigned to the fire, because the dhobis [men who wash clothes] said she had been abducted by Ravana and had stayed in his ashram. They want to bring back the philosophy which smothered the rationalism of the Buddha and divided India into hierarchies, weakening it, so that it fell before every conqueror who could bring 500 horsemen through the Khyber Pass and descend upon the fertile plains.[41]

While Rao secures national integration through an appeal to the past, generated through sentiment, Anand clearly believes that organized revolution alone can bring change. However, despite Anand's reversal of the traditional pattern of representing identity, his condemnation of the revivalists clearly suggests his own feelings of nationalism, for the passage reveals a passionate desire to protect a frequently invaded country from the ingress of conquerors. It is worth noting that a common nationalist feeling or motive issues from two such evidently dissimilar ideological programmes as offered by Anand and Rao.

It is also equally evident that Anand's representation of national identity does not work within the nationalists' programmes which are believed to administer spiritual weapons to perpetuate a false

[38] Mulk Raj Anand, *The Sword and the Sickle*, 191.
[39] Mulk Raj Anand (ed.), *The Historic Trial of Mahatma Gandhi* (New Delhi: National Council of Educational Research and Training, 1987).
[40] Mulk Raj Anand, personal interview, 19 Jan. 1991.
[41] Mulk Raj Anand, letter to Saros Cowasjee, 5 Aug. 1968, in Saros Cowasjee (ed.), *Author to Critic: The Letters of Mulk Raj Anand to Saros Cowasjee* (Calcutta: Writers Workshop, 1973), 32–3.

consciousness.[42] Unlike Rao, who endeavours to maintain the 'historically conditioned illusions' even after independence by rejecting social change and substituting spirituality for a diffused national sentiment, Anand firmly believes nationalism to be a reactionary bourgeois ideology.[43] However, his condemnation of nationalism as bourgeois is accompanied with a pride in his own cultural tradition which cannot be sustained within a historically determined class consciousness, even though it coexists with the desire to remove exploitation both by the foreign power and the indigenous elite.

Anand's message lies less in an appeal through spiritual or religious reform than in a cutting indictment of the prevailing differences that exist in society leading to the miserable condition of the downtrodden. What emerges is a picture of low Indian life. Correspondingly, his depiction of the poor is more rounded and uncertain than glorified. While Anand has been often accused of mixing propaganda with art, his characters are not larger than life or vehicles of the author's political consciousness. They come from the lowest walk of life, experience hardship, and consequently explore the possibilities open to them. Hence, the political sentiment of Anand's novels arises out of experience and is settled through action; it is not the result of imposed feelings of nationhood infused through religion, commonly accepted to be the characteristic trait of Indians.

Clearly, the intelligentsia is not a homogeneous category. It is comprised of the older guardians of tradition as well as the secular-minded custodians of the nation eager for activism. The latter, in the spirit of social reform, attempt to 'modernize' religion but feel compelled to backtrack as reason and enlightenment must find support either from the colonial regime which amounts to a betrayal of nationalism or from a return to tradition. For the former, the state is perceived almost as an accidental in view of the larger cultural goals of achieving nationhood through a discovery of the past and a celebration of their cultural distinctiveness.

---

[42] In his autobiography, MacNeice recounts Anand's strong feelings against the belief in a spiritual India: 'It was all a mistake, Mulk said, India was *not* spiritual, no Indian had even thought so until fifty years ago.' See Louis MacNeice, *The Strings are False: An Unfinished Autobiography* (London: Faber, 1965), 209.

[43] Isaiah Berlin's analysis of the 'evaporation' of the religion of infantile nationalism after the destruction of the system of capitalism is pertinent to Anand's treatment of nationalism. Berlin, however, considers nationalism to be a logical first step in a true socialist revolution. See Isaiah Berlin, *The Crooked Timber of Humanity: Chapters in the History of Ideas*, ed. Henry Hardy (London: Fontana, 1991), 249.

Constituted by the different perspectives on nationalism employed by the intelligentsia, the nation itself becomes a challenging category, both discursively and historically. It might be appropriate to use the phrase 'nation-space' rather than 'nation-state' in view of the narrative strategies that are devised by constructing upon the 'space of the people'.[44]

## II

It is perhaps to build upon such a nation-space that Rao locates his representation of a traditional village community hierarchically within an orthodox organization of castes. In an earlier part of this chapter, I have drawn attention to the opposition between the ideological movement of the novel and its action, and pointed out that the direction of the 'thought-movement' sometimes works against the literary principles of organization. It would be useful therefore to channel the analysis in terms of two models—the ideological and the novelistic/dramatic. While the author dictates the former, the intrinsic properties of the novel comprise the latter. The tensions posed by the two models characterize Rao's ambivalent treatment of caste, and invite comment on his adoption of Gandhi's views on caste and untouchability. A further schism is evinced within the conflicting elements of Rao's ideology—the Gandhian/national and the brahminical/cultural. It has to be asserted that Gandhi's own views on caste were not completely unambiguous and sacrosanct. The analysis is intended to set up a contradiction between the Gandhian and the brahminic modes of nationalism facilitated through the conflict between the ideologue and the novelist.

Within the novel, the challenge to the national ideal of *ramrajya* comes from the endemic system of caste. Moorthy's initiation of Gandhi's programme of spinning yarn creates disorder in a traditional society of brahmins. Nanjamma, a brahmin, is precise in

---

[44] Homi Bhabha, 'DissemiNation: Time, Narrative and the Margins of the Modern Nation', in id. (ed.), *Nation and Narration* (London: Routledge, 1990), 297–9. Bhabha has targeted the 'real' claims of nationalism by treating the nation's narration as a form of address, as enunciation, which 'cannot be signified without the narrative temporalities of splitting, ambivalence, and vacillation' (298). He speaks of an ambivalence that results from an awareness that the 'modern' nation-space is riven rather than historically constituted.

identifying her *dharma*, and has no wish to spin when there are enough weavers in the village. As for the pariahs, the feeling of being upwardly mobile through close contact with a brahmin, as well as the promise of economic self-sufficiency they have always been denied owing to their status, are clearly the motivating principles: 'Not a pie for this! . . . They would spin and spin and spin, and if that Brahmin boy was to be believed they would have clothes to wear, blankets and shirts and loin-cloths. They said it was all for the Mahatma!' (33). The primary significance of employing the *charkha* was political and lay in boycotting the use of foreign mill-made cloth to promote village industry, but the simple and, indeed, believable, response of the pariahs obstructs the development of such a view. The other instance of inducting brahmins into the national cause is equally resisted by the limitations of caste. Evidently, the practice of spinning introduces discord in the traditional functioning of castes, and has the potential to upset the novel's sphere of national activity. Social reform and the stronghold of caste, at this point in the novel, stand far apart. Significantly, it is Rao who creates the problematic which allows an alternative interpretation of his homogeneous nationalistic model.

In fact, from the very outset, the Gandhian ideas of equality encounter tremendous resistance owing to caste differentiations and the routine system within which the different castes of the village work. Bhatta is disgusted with 'this Gandhi vagabondage' and the intermingling of pariahs and brahmins for which he holds Gandhi responsible: 'He is a Vaisya and he may do what he likes. That does not pollute me. But, Rama-Rama, really if we have to hang the sacred thread over the shoulders of every pariah . . . it's impossible, impossible' (44). His speech recounting the Swami's instructions speaks blatantly for brahminism, and clearly goes against the grain of the novel's Gandhian ideology:

'The Swami is worried over this pariah movement, and he wants to crush it in its seed, before its cactus-roots have spread far and wide. . . . You should speak to your people and organise a brahmin party. Otherwise brahminism is as good as kitchen ashes. The Mahatma is a good man and a simple man. But he is making too much of these carcass-eating pariahs. Today it will be the pariahs, tomorrow it will be the Mohomedans, and the day after the Europeans. . . . We must stop this. The Swami says he will outcaste every brahmin who has touched a pariah. That is the right way to begin' (44–5).

Not even Moorthy can abandon his beliefs, fears, and superstitions related to the brahminical order. He stands 'trembling and undecided' when Lingamma, a pariah, invites him into her hut. As she spreads out a mat for him, Moorthy becomes agitated and confused:

[He] blurts out, 'No, no, no, no,' and he looks this side and that and thinks surely there is a carcass in the back yard, and it's surely being skinned, and he smells the stench of hide and the stench of pickled pigs, and the roof seems to shake, and all the gods and all the manes of heaven seem to cry out against him, and his hands steal mechanically to the holy thread, and holding it, he feels he would like to say, 'Hari-Om, Hari-Om' (105).

Indeed, Moorthy has a genuine dread of intermixing with the pariahs in spite of being the first Gandhian in the village. Within an acknowledgement of the analytic principles introduced at the beginning of this section, the reader's consciousness of Moorthy as a dramatic character is evoked as he is seen facing a major dilemma. The fictive, in this instance identified with caste solidarity, conflicts with the ideological or the nationalistic. Moorthy wonders where his loyalties should lie: the message of Gandhi that has succeeded in making him give up college education and pledge himself to the national cause, or brahminical purity, the corruption of which can 'pollute' his progeny for generations? The given sanctity of brahminism rests uneasily on Moorthy's shoulders as he accepts a tumbler of milk from Lingamma, soon after which he would like to purify himself:

Rangamma says, 'Maybe you'd better change your holy thread,' but Moorthy says, 'Now that I must go there every day, I cannot change my holy thread every day, can I?' and Rangamma says only, 'I shall at least give you a little Ganges water, and you can take a spoonful of it each time you've touched them, can't you?' So Moorthy says, 'As you will,' and taking the Ganges water he feels a fresher breath flowing through him, and lest anyone should ask about his new adventure, he goes to the riverside after dinner to sit and think and pray (107).

Both Moorthy and Rangamma, Gandhian activists of the village, cannot really come to terms with the ethics of social reform which can mobilize the masses towards the achievement of political ends. Moorthy hesitates to enter Rangamma's house in his 'unclean' state; Rangamma is reluctant to usher him in when he is thus 'polluted'. The tensions in the text come to a climax with the narrator's remark: 'After all a brahmin is a brahmin, sister' (107). Surprisingly, Achakka, being a brahmin widow, is shown to have no inhibitions about her own son,

Seenu, visiting the pariahs. While Moorthy's dilemma appears credible, the contradiction in the case of Achakka can only be explained in terms of the constant interplay between the ideological and the dramatic, each of which dictates opposing standpoints.

Gandhi had also realized the impossibility of the venture even as he attempted to create equality between castes for the success of the national movement. While he preached that spirituality could be attained only through 'work and action',[45] he also knew the risk he undertook in breaking the stranglehold of the caste system. Even though the evils of the caste system had been widely recognized by the 1940s, few Indians were willing to abandon the notion of caste altogether since it was a powerful source of social identity, protecting the individual within a specific caste group. The introduction of 'sanskritization'—the emphasis on brahminical or upper caste rituals and practices—into Hinduism was a way of ironing out differences and making the multi-religious society uniform. Gandhian politics capitalized on this Hindu culture for integrating Hindu society, while stressing repeatedly that such an identity would not form itself into a Hindu state.[46] All the same, the national movement turned out to be a mass movement largely because Gandhi hinduized it, although it cannot be denied that by underlining the principles of humanity, he made Hinduism broad based, thereby including the precepts of other religions. While this exercise did ensure the success of the national movement, it was also a miscalculation, resulting in communal clashes.[47]

Gandhi endeavoured to find a solution to the caste system by interpreting the traditional distinction of castes in a less restricted manner that allowed him to be free of addressing it in terms of ritual purity and pollution. His understanding of the *shastras* or scriptures had made him realize that no one *varna* or caste was superior to another in terms of birth. In terms of office, however, a brahmin would be superior to others if he was true to his *dharma* of protecting the weak against the strong, but not if he were to prey upon the other castes. Gandhi's reasoning did not insist upon the coexistence of castes in terms of common celebrations or communal eating that Rao, in his enthusiasm, permits in his vision of a united India.

---

[45] M. K. Gandhi, 'Speech at Y. M. C. A., Madras', 4 Sept. 1927, in *Collected Works*, xxxiv. 451.

[46] Achin Vanaik, *The Painful Transition: Bourgeois Democracy in India* (London: Verso, 1990), 142.        [47] Ibid. 142–3.

The action of the novel takes a turn as soon as the brahmin outcry begins to intrude upon the ideological movement of the text. But the crisis is averted as we find Moorthy suddenly sweeping aside his brahmin faith, and even risking excommunication to embrace the common religion of nationalism. Bhatta, the debunker of Gandhi, is eased out of the text while Narasamma, Moorthy's unhappy mother, dies an untimely death, leaving behind a community that accepts Gandhi in the name of religion. Despite the removal of brahmin antagonists to ensure the validity of the Gandhian/national model, it is the very presence of brahmins, however, that makes nationalism possible, for it is the brahmins—Moorthy, Rangamma, Ratna, and Seenu—who initiate national activity in the village. It is paradoxical that the very caste which debunks nationalism should, at the same time, include those who preach nationalism as a religion. This creates two classes within brahminism: the radical and the orthodox. Although all brahmins are opposed to 'caste pollution', as the novel successfully brings out, it is the radical brahmins who succeed in triumphing over strict orthodoxy. An understanding of Rao's treatment of brahminism thus enables the reader to accept the brahminical at one level even as its reactionary hold is dismissed at another.[48] Significantly, the accommodation of brahminism within the national auspices, while easing dramatic tension, is a feature of nationalist rhetoric. For many nationalists, it was through brahminism that it was possible to reach out to a 'pure' past, owing to its correspondence with purity and 'roots' which were desirable cultural attributes in conceptualizing the nation.[49] The institutions and beliefs of brahminism—caste restrictions, the worship of cows, the Vedic representation of women, the philosophy of Vedanta—have all been evoked in the name of Hinduism by cultural revivalists to act as unifying agents to further the nationalist cause. The representation of brahminic culture as the basis of the national struggle, as seen through the main characters of the novel, is thereby an ideological endeavour to project the brahmins as the true inheritors of civilization.

[48] The division within brahminism anticipates Rama's dismissive gesture in *The Serpent and the Rope* when he says: 'Brahmin is he who knows Brahman, etc. etc.' which is not, in fact, an indication of his condemnation of 'real' brahmins. See Raja Rao, *The Serpent and the Rope* (Delhi: Orient Paperbacks, 1960), 5.

[49] The disclosure that Rao himself is a south Indian brahmin, is perhaps gratuitous in the current analysis since the information tends to personalize national identity. However, it is an important consideration in any discussion of Rao's later novels.

## III

Rao's homogenizing tendency to represent brahmin sentiment in national politics raises questions about the degree of participation of other religious groups and minorities. It has been argued that the traditional dominance of brahminism can be rarely exercised outside ideological parameters. In his study of eighteenth-century India, Christopher Bayly speaks of counter ideologies that existed against caste boundaries and rigid hierarchies, demonstrating how the adaptability of Hinduism, in fact, rendered brahminism almost peripheral in many types of Indian society.[50] The loosening hold of brahminism is seen even within the south Indian community of Karnataka, where the caste system was denounced by Basaveshvara around AD 1100 to introduce a more egalitarian order called Veershaivism.[51] Though the brahmins enjoy a considerable majority in the district, they are outnumbered by the Veershaivites or the commonly known *lingayats*.[52] Given that the brahmins and the *lingayats* observe different modes of worship, common devotion to a local *gram-devata*, as in the case of Kenchamma, appears to be a superimposition.[53] A literary tradition

[50] Christopher A. Bayly, *Indian Society and the Making of the British Empire* (Cambridge: Cambridge University Press, 1988), 157. By the middle of the 18th cent., caste was no longer an immutable 'given' in Indian society in general owing to the rise of a politically powerful 'gentry' distinguished in terms of the capital and property it possessed. These dominant social groups were formed in obvious disregard for caste and religious distinctions. The loosening hegemony of Mughal power in the late 18th cent. further consolidated the position of these small groups so that the rigidity of the 'immutable' caste system that had characterized orientalist India for so long could not be taken as an unqualified assumption any more. The economic and political changes that swept across the country in the declining years of the Mughal empire resulted in new kinds of class compositions that cannot be ignored.

[51] Veershaivism is a 'protestant faith' which does not follow the caste system. Common people following different occupations—farmers, merchants, weavers, pot and basket-makers, tanners, cobblers—are accepted democratically into this faith as equals. In the novel, the people following these occupations are referred to as the low castes. See *Mysore State Gazetteer, Hassan District*, 114.

[52] C. Hayavadana Rao (ed.), *Mysore Gazetteer* (Delhi: Goyal Printers, 1984), v. 904. The census reports of 1924–5 give the population count of the *lingayats* as 84,526 and the brahmins as 20,409.

[53] The worship of a *gram-devata*, or local deity, is significantly free of the dominance of a priestly class. Usually the head of the family performs the priestly rites. The worship of Kenchamma in the novel is, however, governed by attendant priests—Priest Rangappa and the pontifical brahmins, Bhatta and Ramanna. Consequently, there is a pronounced presence of brahminism in so far as the ritual enactment of festivals and discourses is concerned. The religious attitudes of the villagers are standardized into an awe-inspiring brahminism witnessed in the afternoon discussions on Vedanta, in the

such as Rao's, full of religious references to upper-caste Hindus, would tend to be dismissed by the newly educated and self-conscious lower castes as in the Tamil *sudras* attack on the Ramayana.[54] One could also question why Rao should have imposed the worship of a brahmin saint, Sankara, on all of Kanthapura since the birth anniversary of Sankara, or *Sankara Jayanthi*, is observed only by the Smartha brahmins and not by all the castes of a village as depicted in the novel.[55] In fact, even the all-brahmin *agraharas* (brahmin landholdings) with fringe groups of potters, weavers, and low-caste *sudras* cannot act cohesively, let alone have identical ways of worshipping and feasting as Rao describes.[56]

The impossibility of a brahmin/non-brahmin solidarity is also implicit in the psychological and political divide between the two groups. The non-brahmin movement, which in 1921 attained considerable proportions in the Madras Presidency, was a natural and inevitable result of the social and political awakening brought about by the impact of the west.[57] Having no connection with religious issues, it arose as a part of the struggle for sharing power and privileges under the British. In the initial stages, the non-brahmin

recitation of the *Sankara-Vijaya* by old Ramakrishnayya and in the discourses on *maya-vada*. Even the narrator, Rao's storyteller, proudly asserts her brahmin status, and participates in the Vedic recitals. But she is also a gossipy, *puranic* narrator, and her credibility depends on the open quality of her storytelling which must resist brahminic orthodoxy and control.

[54] U. R. Anantha Murthy, 'Is Indian Society Congenial to the Creation of a Classic? A Writer's View', *The Literary Criterion*, 15.2 (1980), 61.

[55] In the course of a visit to the Hassan district of Mysore, a number of *lingayats* and brahmins were interviewed to evaluate particular modes of worship. L. S. Shashidhara from Chikmagalur maintained that the *lingayats* had gradually emerged as the more powerful social group whose religious practices were customarily less complicated and elaborate than those of the brahmins. Shashidhara also emphasized that the *lingayats* promised an alternative and relatively less orthodox way of life. It is ironic, however, that the *lingayats* now have almost as rigid an hierarchy as the caste system. L. S. Shashidhara, personal interview, 11 Nov. 1989. In another interview with Vishnu Gowda of Kenchamma Hoskere *taluq*, it was learnt that *lingayats* generally have their own gurus and priests called *viraktas* and *jangamas* who give religious and spiritual guidance. Unlike the brahmins, the *lingayats* do not perform *yajnas* (sacrifices) and annual *shraddhas* (ceremonies performed in honour of one's ancestors), having instead more simplified ceremonies. Some of their doctrines have even been borrowed from the Muslims. Vishnu Gowda, personal interview, 3 Jan. 1991.

[56] Romila Thapar, personal interview, 30 Nov. 1990.

[57] David Arnold, *The Congress in Tamilnad: Nationalist Politics in South India, 1919–1937* (Columbia, Mo.: South Asia Books, 1977), 5; and Christopher Baker, *The Politics of South India, 1920–1937* (Cambridge: Cambridge University Press, 1976), pp. x–xi.

movement was not anti-brahmin in nature; its main aim was 'the improvement of non-brahmin communities in the governance of the country and the administration of all activities'.[58] Soon, feelings of rancour and malice became inevitable and the consequent social rift tended to divert popular attention away from the primary question of national unity on which the success of the national struggle depended. It is evident that the enterprise of establishing a core brahminic culture does not allow Rao to represent the dissatisfaction of large classes of non-brahmins.

In the case of one group—the Muslims—the ideological undertones in the novel are even more clearly apparent, as Hindu antipathy for Muslims is allowed to obstruct the author's larger purposes of depicting the equal participation of all Indians in the freedom struggle. Significantly, the villain of the novel is a Muslim—Badè Khan, the policeman. Badè Khan is made to suffer for being a Muslim: 'Being a Mohomedan he could stay neither in the Potters' street nor in the Sudra Street, and you don't of course expect him to live in the Brahmin Street' (24). In other words, he is beneath even the potters and the *sudras* in social status. Though the villagers' fear stems from his role as a policeman, their distrust is accentuated and legitimized by an innate suspicion of Muslims, fostered perhaps by the imperial policy of divide and rule.

Rao's alignment with this tradition of Hindu cultural nationalism introduces a marked contradiction with his Gandhian loyalties. Gandhi had always insisted that the Congress was not predominantly Hindu: it had a Muslim president and four Muslims on its fifteen-member working committee.[59] He had also maintained that Hindus and Muslims were not the followers of two separate faiths, and that conversion to Islam had not altered, in any way, the nationality of Indian Muslims. 'I believe with my whole soul,' said Gandhi, 'that the God of the Qur'an is also the God of the Gita.'[60] It was perhaps because of his positive experience with Muslim traders in South Africa that Gandhi worked tirelessly throughout his Indian experiments to join Hindus and Muslims in national undertakings. In view

---

[58] Rao Bahadur B. Muniswami Naidu, 'Speech at the Non-Brahmin Federation on 5 Oct. 1929', cited in Krishna M. V. Rao and G. S. Halappa, *History of the Freedom Movement in Karnataka*, 2 vols. (Bangalore: Government of Mysore Press, 1962), ii. 26.

[59] Rajmohan Gandhi, *Eight Lives: A Study of the Hindu-Muslim Encounter* (Albany: State University of New York Press, 1986), 154.  [60] Ibid.

of Gandhi's integrative programme for the Muslims, Rao does not make a blatant case for Hindu brahmins, even though there is an implicit rejection of Muslims. But, on the other hand, he also subscribes to only those elements in Gandhian ideology that complement his argument, thereby betraying a cultural and religious bias.

Later writings of the proponents of Hinduism, the extreme Hindu right, were to consolidate their own hegemony by evoking a 'grand and ancient religious tradition' which would 'unify' and 'discipline' into a 'single entity' 'its own cultural practices, its own political needs, and its own leaders'.[61] Needless to say, the Muslims would have little significance in their histories.


## IV


As the novel draws to a close, we witness the emergence of socialist politics.[62] Although the novel throws up occasional references to 'the country of the hammer and sickle', the implication comes through more fully in Moorthy's letter to Ratna:

'Since I am out of prison, I met this Satyagrahi and that, and we discussed many a problem, and they all say the Mahatma is a noble person, a saint, but the English will know how to cheat him, and he will let himself be cheated. Have faith in your enemy, he says, have faith in him and convert him. But the world of men is hard to move, and once in motion it is wrong to stop till the goal is reached. . . . And I have come to realize bit by bit, and bit by bit, when I was in prison, that as long as there will be iron gates and barbed wires round the Skeffington Coffee Estate, and city cars that can roll up the Bebbur Mound, and gas-lights and coolie cars, there will always be pariahs and poverty. . . . The youths here say they will change it. Jawaharlal will change it. You know Jawaharlal is like a Bharatha to the Mahatma, and he, too, is for non-violence and he, too, is a Satyagrahi, but he says in Swaraj there shall be neither the rich nor the poor. And he calls himself an "equal-distributionist", and I am with him and his men' (256–7).

---

[61] Gyanendra Pandey, 'The Civilized and the Barbarian: The "New" Politics of Late Twentieth Century India and the World', in id. (ed.), *Hindus and Others: The Question of Identity in India Today* (New Delhi: Viking, 1993), 7.

[62] It is possible that Rao was swayed by socialist ideas in the 1930s in view of his later association with young socialists and their underground activities during the Quit India movement of 1942, and the representation of the seductive quality of Kirillov's Marxist philosophy in *Comrade Kirillov*. See Raja Rao, *Comrade Kirillov* (Delhi: Orient Paperbacks, 1976).

By 1934, there was discernibly a new way of thinking among many of Gandhi's followers. Nehru had returned from Europe in 1927 after representing the Indian National Congress at the Brussels Congress of the League Against Imperialism, and was convinced through his recent contact with socialist leaders in Europe that India's regeneration could come about only through some form of socialism, adapted though it might be to conditions in India. In fact, a number of Congress members who had ceased to believe in the efficacy of non-violence and *satyagraha* saw socialism as a radical alternative to Gandhian politics. These younger men and women had grown impatient with the slow and halting manner in which their elder leaders were conducting the fight for freedom. The formation of a socialist party was initiated in jails during 1930–1 and 1932–4 by groups of Congress volunteers who were disillusioned with Gandhian ideology.[63] The notion that freedom could not be defined in political terms alone but must have a socio-economic content began increasingly to be associated with Nehru who became the undisputed leader of the younger generation of Congressmen. For Nehru, a commitment to socialism was the only 'way of ending the poverty, the vast unemployment, the degradation and the subjection of the Indian people'.[64] It was during this period that Nehru's views came steadily into conflict with those of Gandhi. He became critical of Gandhi's condemnation of large-scale industrialization, and was cynical of his policy of trusteeship which advocated the humane aspect of authority to which the labourers were unquestioningly to submit. Undoubtedly, Gandhi's role in building the consciousness of the masses was enormous and Nehru had no intention of dispensing with it. His intention, instead, was to relate nationalism and political freedom as represented by the Congress with socialism and 'continue these two outlooks and make them an organic whole'.[65]

For the reader of Rao's novel, the fascinating quality of Gandhism and the establishment of an identity within Gandhian politics receives a setback with Moorthy's disenchantment of Gandhi.[66] Association

[63] Chandra *et al.*, *India's Struggle for Independence*, 304.

[64] Jawaharlal Nehru, *Selected Works of Jawaharlal Nehru, 1903–46*, ed. S. Gopal, 15 vols. (New Delhi: Orient Longman, 1972–82), vii. 181.

[65] Ibid. 61. See also Chandra *et al.*, *India's Struggle for Independence*, 300.

[66] Moorthy's gravitation towards Nehruvian politics is linked with the Gandhi–Irwin pact which is mentioned towards the end of the novel. After a series of discussions

with other boys in prison has taught him to look beyond the spiritual, the non-violent, and the renunciatory. By turning towards more radical politics, he grows in stature, and moves beyond the cultural space in which we have so far been accustomed to seeing him. His conversion establishes a parallel with history and, in effect, a departure from the regenerative nature of the *puranic* narrative. It also indicates Rao's attraction for Marxism, at least in so far as it can be accommodated within Gandhi's utopian refrain of the meek inheriting the earth.

Moorthy's defection, however, has little effect on the immutable nature of Indian culture represented in *Kanthapura*. In spite of the challenge from socialism, Rao reinstates the sanctity of his Gandhi-*purana* by abandoning Moorthy towards the end of the novel, thereby maintaining the *dharmic* inevitability of Gandhism. In an interview, Rao himself explains away Moorthy's deviation as a confusion experienced even by Nehru:

Moorthy was a young man who felt dissatisfied after he suffered a defeat. His faith in Gandhi was shaken for a moment. But the novel does project the Mahatma as the chief inspiration. At one time, Nehru was also dissatisfied with Gandhi's way of struggle. But if Nehru had not been a true Gandhian, India would not have been in the state we are today. At best you can say that Moorthy was a deviating Gandhian. Nehru too was a deviating Gandhian.[67]

Apparently, it is Rao's intention to show Gandhi without flaws. Any deviation from Gandhi's policies and ideologies is sidelined to the extent that even Moorthy, the protagonist, is given up in the end in order to keep a competing socialism at bay which has the potential of impairing a cultural nationalist discourse.

As a heroic character, Moorthy possesses all the traits of a mahatma-martyr. Yet his departure is contrary to the expectations the reader builds of his character and his particular role in history. For Rao's nationalist ideology leads one to expect Moorthy's martyr-

---

with Lord Irwin in 1931, Gandhi accepted a truce, called off Civil Disobedience, and agreed to attend the Round Table Conference in London as the sole representative of the Indian National Congress. The conference, which concentrated on the problem of the Indian minorities rather than on the transfer of power to India, was a great disappointment to the Indian nationalists. The Mahatma was criticized by Nehru for having 'sold' his country, and consequently, many young socialists turned away from Gandhi.

[67] Shiva Niranjan, 'An Interview with Raja Rao', in K. N. Sinha (ed.), *Indian Writing in English* (New Delhi: Heritage, 1979), 23.

dom to secure the underpinnings of the novel within a timeless religious ethos. That Rao writes into the novel the hero's defection from its prevailing ideology is a remarkable testimony to his loyalty to 'history' in the usual sense of the term. Moorthy's departure thus creates an inconsistency with the cyclical nature of the narrative, and even suggests an alternative history. However, the contradiction inherent in Moorthy's millenarian turn to socialism is straightened by a return to Gandhi's sainthood. So strong is the tendency in the later part of the novel to uphold the Gandhian–nationalist model that Rao does not permit Gandhi's halo to slip even in Moorthy's letter to Ratna where the analogy with the Rama myth is explicitly enumerated: Moorthy believes Nehru to be like a Bharatha to the Mahatma. The grandmother takes up this refrain and mentions how 'brother Bharatha will go to meet them with the worshipped sandal of the Master on his head' (257).[68] In other words, despite the possibility of a clash between the socialists and the nationalists, Rao subsumes the former within Gandhism as a concession to the invocation of a traditional Indian culture where Gandhi alone can be 'the chief inspiration'.

## V

*Kanthapura* is a remarkable success in spite of Rao's selective interpretation, not simply because the countrymen hunger for the kind of cultural identity Rao fashions, but also because the genre used by the author has an engaging immediacy. As in the case of language, the oral narration and its writing into a fiction imparts both a sense of unreality and authenticity. The double-edged quality of the narration allows the interplay of both dismissal and acceptance so that fiction becomes a site in which fact is tested. The dual nature of the representation is acceptable precisely because the governing structure of orality, in spite of being seductive, is believed to be harmless.

In many ways, the oral and the written dovetail into each other in the construction of a 'true' history for the purposes of national

[68] Bharatha, Rama's step-brother, had ruled Ayodhya in place of his exiled brother by symbolically placing Rama's sandals on the throne. Just as Bharatha waited for Rama to bring back the abducted Sita, and then faithfully handed the kingdom over to his able leadership, Nehru, as the young Bharatha, cannot have any discord with Gandhi.

integration, taking Rao even beyond Gandhi's own frequent contra-dictions and paradoxes in the making of *ramrajya*. For Rao is inter-ested more in evoking an identity from India's timeless and enduring past culture, than from a dynamic present defined ambiguously in terms of Gandhi's confused and often contradictory views. It cannot be denied, for instance, that Gandhi's rather ambivalent attitude towards caste prevented him from being the unimpeachable champion of the untouchables he is commonly believed and depicted to be. While Gandhi sought passionately to free them of all their social disabilities, he staunchly opposed Ambedkar, the advocate of the untouchables, when it came to granting them reservation status in the electorate, as conceded to the Muslims. A bitter Ambedkar had to accept Gandhi's resolute stand in the face of his fast unto death, and it was many years after Gandhi's death in 1948 that Ambedkar was able to have his way.

Gandhi was interested, perhaps, less in caste reformation than in the success of the freedom movement in which the unification of castes had a definite contribution. In so far as the propaganda for the removal of untouchability nudged the movement, it was encour-aged. But when the pressure from the untouchables threatened to rival the national movement itself, Gandhi saw no point in abetting them further. In Rao, on the other hand, the reader's view of Gandhi as a force in regenerating village society is shaped to a large extent by the idolatry he receives from the untouchables in the novel who unques-tioningly comply and fall in willingly with the proposals Moorthy outlines for them. Rao, thus, succeeds in presenting a unified India that could scarcely be attained even under the auspices of Gandhi's national integration programme.

Gandhi's politics were, by no means, as unambiguous and clear as in Rao's interpretation of them. Even within the concept of *swaraj*, an undisputed objective for all nationalists, there existed rivalries and tensions. Rival factions treated the issue of freedom in quite different ways, and were, therefore, oblivious to Gandhi's appeal. Social reform which was part of Gandhi's doctrine was inimical to the extremist wing of the nationalists. Gandhi's assassin, Godse, a brah-min-Hindu nationalist who belonged to the Hindu Mahasabha, was opposed to Gandhi even though the two had a similar end in view. Both Gandhi and Godse were staunch nationalists, austere, and abstemious, yet the nations they imagined were distinct. While Gandhi was hostile towards custodian brahmins, Godse defended the superior position of the high castes who now stood the risk of being swamped by the sectarian currents rampant among freedom fighters.[69] For Godse, Hindu revivalism alone could safeguard the high traditions of India and preserve its cultural distinctiveness. Gandhi was, therefore, considered a traitor in his compromises with Muslims, while his principles of non-violence were taken as signs of feminine cowardice.[70]

Rao's own brand of nationalism is a rather curious mixture: on the one hand, Gandhi's responsibility for the betterment of the downtrodden is appreciated, and the hostility both to imperial powers and the immediate society of India is maintained; on the other, the glories of a brahmin past and its potential in promoting solidarity are equally endorsed. This makes *Kanthapura* a text that combines cultural chauvinism with a selective spiritual interpretation of Gandhian politics that harks back to Tilak's revival of the Shivaji festival or Bipin Chandra Pal's invocation of Krishna. Rao overrides important differences and builds up the pressure of communal consciousness to the extent that only seven families fail to join in the protest. To quote Charles Larson:

Raja Rao's implication by the end of the story is quite clear: symbolically, Kanthapura is all of India. If all of India were as united as these villagers, if the caste system could break down as quickly as it did here, independence would come tomorrow, for, after all, it is the forces brought in from outside that eventually lead to destruction. Kanthapura today, India tomorrow.[71]

Moorthy's eloquent desire to build 'a thousand-pillared temple, a temple more firm than any that hath yet been builded . . . in dream and in life' (170) evidently cannot be realized in a society with ingrained caste differences. His vision of an India that 'will live in a temple of our making' (170) betrays, clearly, the author's idealization of an imagined India which can only be accomplished in a world of make-believe.

In the interests of the nation-state, Gandhi, too, had depoliticized caste as he did with other social and economic issues relating to the Hindu–Muslim divide or the position of women. His politics,

[69] Fox, *Gandhian Utopia*, 222.

[70] Ashis Nandy, *At the Edge of Psychology: Essays in Politics and Culture* (Delhi: Oxford University Press, 1980), 78.

[71] Charles R. Larson, *The Novel in the Third World* (Washington, DC: Inscape, 1976), 137.

further, were not free from spiritual principles, even though he laid great stress on action as part of one's *dharma*. Yet he was far from being a revivalist. Although he objected to superficial Europeanization, he refused to accept that the only alternative was 'a complete reversion to the ancient Aryan tradition'.[72] On the contrary, he insisted that Hindu society and Hindu religion itself had to change with changing circumstances. For Rao, however, the activist is subsumed, to a large extent, in the inevitable triumph of the Hindu *dharma* which advocates the victory of Good over Evil. The conquest of the Good, a motif which lends an epic dimension to the story, is implicit in a spiritual/religious sense even though the rebellion results in the destruction of the village and the exodus of its inhabitants. The broader governing theme of spiritual victory expands the local context, and includes not only all of India but the spatial mythology built around it as well.

In the context of this transference, I find it suitable to mention Naipaul's disapproval of the fundamental ontological belief reposed in a placid India. In *India: A Wounded Civilization*, Naipaul quotes from Prakash Tandon's Punjabi trilogy and Jaya Prakash Narayan's speeches to show how Gandhi's concept of *swaraj* could be transformed into *ramrajya*, enabling a translation of the political end of self-rule into a religious principle that envisions the rule of the mythological god-king, Rama.[73] It may be inferred that the self-government following imperialism would be the rule of god on earth since it is relatively easy for those who are familiar with the Ramayana to see the two terms conjointly. By itself, the rhetoric of freedom and *swaraj* might be intriguing, but within the cultural context, it has enormous significance. Tandon, in his trilogy, recounts the mysterious implications of nationalism which are reported to be perplexing until the politicians begin to talk in 'familiar analogies':

[They talked about] the Kal Yug, [whereupon] we saw what they meant. Had it not been prophesied that there were seven eras in India's life and history: there had been a Sat Yug, the era of truth, justice, and prosperity; and then there was to be a Kal Yug, an era of falsehood or demoralization, of slavery and poverty. . . . These homely analogies, illustrated by legend and history, registered easily, but not so easily the conclusion to which they were

[72] M. K. Gandhi, 'Unity in Variety', 11 Aug. 1927, *Young India*, in *Collected Works*, xxxiv. 315.
[73] V. S. Naipaul, *India: A Wounded Civilization* (London: André Deutsch, 1977), 143–8.

linked. . . . We could not see how the British were to blame for Kal Yug, which had been foretold so long ago. . . . Gandhi rechristened India Bharat Mata, a name that evoked nostalgic memories, and associated with Gao Mata, the mother cow. . . . Gradually a new picture began to build in our minds, of India coming out of the Kal Yug into a new era of freedom and plenty, Ram Rajya.[74]

While ordinary people found it difficult to blame the British for what they believed to be destiny, the use of 'homely analogies' facilitated comprehension. In the same way, the interchangeability of *swaraj* with *ramrajya* in Gandhi's early nationalist politics exposes the contribution of the immemorial in the reification of the immediate. Almost three decades after independence, Jaya Prakash Narayan used the idioms and familiar analogies of the political campaigners Tandon speaks of, but in the changed context of the imposition of the Emergency (1975) in India:

The youth, the peasants, the working class, all with one voice must declare that we will not allow fascism to raise its head in our country. We will not have dictatorship in our country. . . . This is not Bangladesh. This is not Pakistan. This is Bharat. We have our ancient tradition. Thousands of years ago we had small village republics. That sort of history is behind us. There were village panchayats in virtually every village. In the times of the Mauryas, Gupta, the Pathan, the Mughals, the Peshwas, we had our Panchayats. The British deliberately broke this tradition in order to strengthen their hold on the country. This ancient tradition was in Bangladesh and in Pakistan, but they seem to have given it up. But our leaders sought a reawakening. Gandhiji always said that *Swaraj* means *Ramraj*. Swaraj means that every village will have its own rule. Every village, every mohalla and town will manage its own affairs.[75]

Narayan's straightforward appeal against Indira Gandhi's 'fascist' rule is qualified by a less direct invocation of the past—the ancient tradition of Bharat (India) and its rich repository of self-governing villages. He draws attention to the eighteenth-century Maratha warriors, the Muslims reigning around AD 320–600, and then to the Mauryas, a further 500 years back into history. What needs to be emphasized in this speech is the resilience of India despite invasions, chaos, dynasties, and wars, for India has maintained her pure spirit and her democratic form of government through her little republics.

[74] Prakash Tandon, *Punjabi Century, 1857–1947* (London: Chatto and Windus, 1961), 120–1.     [75] Cited in Naipaul, *Wounded Civilization*, 143–4.

She has always possessed democracy, and the current crisis can be overcome simply by rediscovering her soul.[76] Narayan, then, takes recourse to Gandhi and his belief in village structures that would usher in *ramrajya*, a 'modern attempt at recreating a golden age in the past'.[77] In effect, Gandhi becomes part of the soul of India and her permanency.

The instance of Jaya Prakash Narayan's speech is brought up as an analogy to Rao's construction of national identity. The speech was delivered in 1975, long after Gandhi's *ramrajya* as a political instrument had lost its efficacy. The unchanging character of India, nevertheless, continues to be a potent vehicle and includes even Gandhi as a part of its 'truth', as though he was not the creation of particular circumstances but an eternal symbol to be employed even after the British had long since departed.[78] Needless to say, the history and sociology of Indian villages that both Rao and Jaya Prakash Narayan take as their specific domain are far removed from the clichés of rural innocence in which they are depicted. As Gyanendra Pandey has pointed out, the very notion of uncontested and predetermined 'national' cultures comes from the 'compradore' character of India's political leadership that lends special strength to Hindu accounts which often bring up the India of real villages and real culture against the assumed sense of impoverished history.[79] It is to instances of village unrest that I now turn, so as to sharpen the contrast with nationalist constructions.

[76] Naipaul, *Wounded Civilization*, 144–5.

[77] Madhav Deshpande, 'History, Change and Permanence: A Classical Indian Perspective', in Gopal Krishna (ed.), *Contributions to South Asian Studies* (Delhi: Oxford University Press, 1979), i. 11. For an interesting study of the ways in which the present attempts to project itself into the past, see Deshpande, 1–28.

[78] Naipaul, *Wounded Civilization*, 145.

[79] See Gyanendra Pandey, 'Modes of History Writing: New Hindu History of Ayodhya', *Economic and Political Weekly*, 29.25 (1994), 1525; and 'The Civilized and the Barbarian', in id. (ed.), *Hindus and Others*, 8.

Part II

'Fragments' of the Nation

# 3   Peasant Uprisings and Fictional Strategies

What is at once striking about *Kanthapura* is why Rao thinks he needs history in the writing of a novel, and why he favours a particular interpretation of historical events. The answers to these questions issue from the analysis in the previous chapters. History not only lends credibility to the depiction of political events but also allows a respectable interchange between past and present for interpreting current politics. Widely interpreted, history can also include poetry, mythology, or cosmology, as traced from the early narrative traditions of the *puranas*. *Kanthapura* is a syncretic compound of material which is both historically valid and questionable. It is interesting that Rao sees the fabulous as part of the venture of putting together an historical narrative. Of course, it can be alleged that history in this popular form can, at best, have only a rather flimsy relationship with *itihaas* (thus-it-was). I am interested, on the other hand, in seeing how far the dimensions of fictionalized history— implying both fiction as history as in the context of the novel, and history as fiction as in the broad framework I have adopted—can succeed in creating nationalist consciousness.

In this chapter, I move from a comparative analysis of ideological positions to the consideration of historical political action. More specifically, the translation of historical events into the narrative action of the novel is seen against historical representations of peasant movements in the late nineteenth and early twentieth centuries. In terms of the novel, I review the situation of the coolies at the Skeffington Coffee Estate and their lack of enterprise in an exploitative situation until the advent of Gandhi when they are inspired into participating in the national programme. In contrast, accounts of instances of subaltern insurgency in several parts of India, and within Karnataka itself, are cited to emphasize the local nature of peasant rebellion and the equivocal and plural quality of Gandhi's appeal. The contrast is intended to underscore the ideological representation

of history and the role of the nationalist intelligentsia in the construction of national identity. As I stressed earlier, the comparison of
a nationalist–bourgeois ideology and subaltern history, by no means,
favours one truth over another. Alternative histories are brought in
only to pose a series of interruptions in one's conceptualization of a
homogeneous cultural identity, and significantly, to show the difficulties of translating ideology into history within the national struggle.


I


Roughly, *Kanthapura* has two societies: the people in the village and
the coolies at the Skeffington Coffee Estate. While village life is
characterized by harmonious agrarian traditions, the coffee estate is
rampantly corrupt owing to excessive proletarianization and exploitation of labour by the resident Englishmen. All but two coolies are
illiterate as against the people of the village who have a definite
hierarchy of literacy. Some of the villagers read newspapers, books,
and scriptures which are used for the edification of the rest through a
disseminating hierarchy of information. Not surprisingly, it is the
people of the village who first hear of Gandhi and the foreign rule.
Their contact with some of the coolies from the estate helps com-
municate Gandhi's ideas which are absorbed in the same religious
way by the coolies as they have been by the villagers. While an
excessively personalized Gandhian appeal, mediated through
Moorthy, may be acceptable within the precincts of the serene village
model, the exploitation at the coffee estate creates an altogether
different expectation. As the story unfolds, we discover that the white
men's domination over several generations has caused scarcely a stir
among the coolies. Even though some of them join the Congress
Committee eventually, their participation is not motivated by the
presence of white slave-drivers but engineered by Moorthy who
appears to be the only one fully aware of the harassment of his fellow
'brothers' working in the coffee plantation. Again, it is on the religious dimension of the Mahatma's appeal to picket toddy booths that
their participation is enlisted.

  Unlike the 'permanent' village life, the labourers at the coffee estate
move with the market. They have been lured into the estate with
promises of reward. But once they commence work they are not only
forced into working longer hours for less wages, their women are also

sexually exploited by the white sahib. It is important to establish the oppression of the coolies at this point because their later rebellion for the independence of their country has to be seen within their social and economic exploitation by their masters. The adverse circumstances of the coolies make rebellion inevitable, yet the novel favours a shift to the violation of the traditional social code by the white man, who being a *mleccha* or an outcaste, dares to rape a brahmin girl. Viewed only as brahminic outrage, Rao does not relate their exploitation to the possible arousal of resentment against English rule, especially when the coolies are seen to have a direct relationship of subordination with the English. Being harassed employees, they have reason to join Gandhi out of concerns other than religious. The coolies are shown, on the other hand, to continue to be tied to a life of labour and subservience because of poverty and a resolute belief in fatalism.

Down in the village, too, the people have to bear the burden of taxes: Nanjamma pays revenue as well as Bhatta's interest; Lingayya borrows money from Bhatta at exorbitant rates of interest to pay his debts; the *sudras* also 'always paid revenues due and debts' (15) though their payments are delayed owing to their poverty. It is only after Moorthy's return and his subsequent appeal as a Mahatma that they are stirred into action. Their apathy returns when Moorthy is imprisoned and no longer in their midst. Given to fatalism, they cannot be persuaded into forming a volunteer corps: '"Oh, father, we cannot hope for Ramarajya in these days; we live in Kaliyuga"' (155). The novel shows us quite clearly that the peasants' world view precludes any kind of activism, this being a part of the Hindu belief-system where destiny or ill-luck is accepted as inevitable.

Nevertheless, in view of the revolution Gandhi wrought in the consciousness of the peasantry, Rao does incorporate his political vision in the second half of the novel where Gandhi's programme of Civil Disobedience is worked out largely through, what Moorthy calls, the 'Don't-touch-the-Government' campaign.[1] Moorthy emphasizes the need for a parallel government, and speaks of the taxes that have to be evaded, 'even if the Government attaches the lands' (179), and

---

[1] Gandhi's call for non-cooperation is understood in terms of the 'Don't-Touch-the-Government' campaign implying a pollution by touch. There is a tension here between Gandhi's philosophy and the premises of brahminical purity. A further paradox is that of the equation of the British government with the victimized pariahs whose touch is polluting rather than the more suitable analogy with the victimizing brahmins.

of the picketing of toddy booths. He appeals primarily against using violence for 'the purer we are the greater will be our victory, for the victory we seek is the victory of the heart' (180). Moorthy thus succeeds in arousing the villagers in the true spirit of Gandhi's *satyagraha*:

The Satyagrahi . . . fights by suffering himself. . . . The greater the suffering a satyagrahi goes through, the purer he becomes. As gold is tested in fire, so does a satyagrahi have to go through a fiery ordeal. His only weapon is uncompromising insistence on truth. A true satyagrahi fears nothing and holds fast to truth as he fights.[2]

It is the power of truth and the realization of god within that principle which serves to unite the villagers and push them into rebellion. However, in an atmosphere of tradition and conservatism, we also witness instances of acute village receptivity to the eventful world: regular correspondence with cities is maintained by Moorthy, Bhatta, Seenu, Vasudev, and Rangamma; news travels in through Rangamma's 'Blue paper', and discourses are held on Gandhi's *Autobiography*. Some of the village women have even read a short story by Saradamma called 'The Red Pyre', presumably about *sati*, while others have heard about 'the country of the hammer and sickle' where 'all men are equal—every one equal to every other—and there were neither the rich nor the poor' (47). Their awareness of current affairs on the one hand is at odds with the depiction of the village as remote and timeless on the other, and is perhaps indicative of the dilemma of nationalist thought which compels the nation to assert its modernity, yet take cognizance of its indigenous, pre-modern categories.

It is Gandhi's arrest that stimulates the peasant uprising in Kanthapura. The women fashion themselves into a 'Sevika Sangha' and join the men in toddy picketing. From what has been discussed, it is evident that their rebellion stems not from unrest but from the assault on their sentiments on seeing Gandhi captive. They have been through the experience of Moorthy's imprisonment, and it is not difficult to transfer their anxieties to Gandhi in keeping with the Moorthy–Gandhi–Kenchamma hierarchy. They fight, in effect, for a national sentiment based entirely on religious faith, and their desire for the freedom of their motherland similarly issues from a reverence

---

[2]   M. K. Gandhi, 'Speech at Public Meeting, Bombay', 23 Apr. 1918, in *Collected Works of Mahatma Gandhi, 1884–1948*, 90 vols. (Ahmedabad: Navajivan, 1958–84), xiv. 369.

commanded by deities. Even as they contend with debts and other grievances, nowhere do we see their problems to be part of their motivation to join the struggle. It is much after the commencement of rebellion that we hear of revenue notices 'turning yellow into their hands' (206).

A surprisingly different perspective on peasant politics is offered by historical accounts of the Indian national struggle.[3] In contrast to Rao, we come across a range of motives and reasons other than *dharmic* or nationalistic out of which peasants join the struggle. One such example is that of the Indigo Revolt of 1859–60 in Bengal, which resulted from years of coercive indigo farming. The indigo strikes and disturbances involved hundreds of villagers who refused to pay high rents and grow indigo which brought no fruitful returns. This initiative would have failed if it was not for the pronounced organizational and disciplinary nature of this uprising. Significantly, the rebellion was marked by a complete unity among Hindu and Muslim peasants regardless of any antipathy on the grounds of religion or caste. Other peasant rebellions include the Pabna revolt in 1873 and the agrarian outbreaks in Poona and Ahmednagar in 1875, which pertained largely to the abolition of illegal coercive methods such as forced eviction and the seizure of crops and cattle. What is striking about peasant insurgency in these cases is their convergence on the basic demand for the removal of their immediate injustices and protection of their fundamental rights through the legal state apparatus. Large causes like national liberation and anti-imperialist demands were not part of their objective: the uprising was neither aimed at the system of *zamindari* or landlordship, nor did it have at any juncture a slant against imperialism.[4] The peasants raised no anti-British demands; they used, in fact, the legal system to oppose their immediate landlords. At no stage did the agrarian leaders have anything to do with the British; in fact, the peasants asserted their loyalty to the British by desiring 'to be the *ryots* (peasants) of Her Majesty the Queen and of Her only'.[5] Considering that the *zamindars* were, in effect, agents of the British and appointed by them, the willingness of the peasants to be of service to the Queen reveals their ignorance of colonial implications and the limited nature of their revolt. Again, in so far as the Hindu–Muslim issue was

[3] See e.g. Bipan Chandra et al., *India's Struggle for Independence* (New Delhi: Penguin, 1989), 50–60.           [4] Ibid. 55.           [5] Ibid.

concerned, the peasants showed complete unity in spite of the statistical balance being in favour of the Muslim peasants, though the zamindars were largely Hindu.

Another instance of conflict between the peasants and the moneylenders, in the Deccan (the villages of Sirur), arose not from the evils of colonization but from the practices of coercive moneylenders who compelled the peasants to surrender their land when they were unable to pay land revenue. The Sirur disturbances soon instigated rebellion in other villages—Poona, Ahmednagar, Sholapur, and Satara—where peasants looted and burnt moneylenders' houses and shops for the main purpose of destroying official records containing promissory notes or contracts signed under pressure. That the peasants were hardly motivated by national causes is evident from the marked serenity which followed the agitation, assisted by the Deccan Agriculturists' Relief Act of 1879 which vastly reduced dependence on the moneylenders. The colonial government thus appears to be a sympathetic government for the peasants since the immediate aggression was that of the oppressive *zamindars*. Bipan Chandra corroborates:

They now fought directly for their own demands, centred almost wholly on economic issues, and against their immediate enemies, foreign planters and indigenous *zamindars* and moneylenders. . . . They did not make colonialism their target. Nor was their objective the ending of the system of their subordination and exploitation. They did not aim at 'turning the world upside down'.[6]

It is amply clear that the Indigo agitation, the Pabna agrarian leagues, and the social-boycott movement of the Deccan *ryots*, were abandoned once the motives of rebellion were achieved. These movements arose for a definite purpose, and there is no evidence that their focus of attack was ever the foreign power. With the aim achieved, the rebellion ended.

What needs to be emphasized in these accounts is the modest nature of peasant rebellion and the imperfect understanding of colonialism by the peasantry. The peasant uprising existed only at the level of peasant problems without resentment of colonial rule. The peasants were not acutely aware of the social and political forces behind the movements themselves, even though these instances

[6] Bipan Chandra et al., *India's Struggle for Independence*, 58.

become part of the nation's history in the twentieth century, when the efforts of the modern intelligentsia appropriated peasant discontentment into the national movement.[7] The peasants of Kanthapura, too, are unaware of the implications of colonial rule. It is intriguing what motivates their eagerness 'to drive the British out' (190). Since their unrest is neither generated by local grievances, nor linked ideologically with any social, political, or economic programme relating to colonialism, their rebellion appears to be part of the author's schema, and not a natural initiative for the villagers. It is difficult, therefore, to conceive that they have the ability to envisage a definite programme for a long-term political movement which has behind it the solidarity of a common national struggle.

Later examples of peasant unrest are less distinct from the mass mobilization programmes of the nationalists. While the intelligentsia widely reported and backed the agitations in the indigo districts of Bengal, Pabna, and the Deccan, it was in the peasant struggles of the twentieth century that the appropriation was almost complete. The Bardoli struggle in Gujarat (1927–9) which owed its origin to an enormous increase in the payment of land revenue in fact took impetus from constructive activities which were prevalent in the area even after the Non-Cooperation Movement had been called off. This enabled Congress leaders like Sardar Patel to champion the peasants' cause and take the movement closer to *swaraj*. Again, the 1,500 mile march by the Andhra farmers in 1938, which took over 100 days, had the legislative backing of the Congress. In cases where the workers were employed in British-owned enterprises, the support of the nationalist intelligentsia was much more since the protest could be conveniently alloyed to anti-imperialism.[8] Despite all the ambiguities and confusions, and the manoeuvres of the leadership, nationalist sentiment itself formed a very small part of peasant struggles, although it may be admitted that the national movement certainly provided an environment germane to the cause of the peasants.

But for those peasants, like Rao's, who had little to worry about, the need to join the national movement seems exaggerated. A more plausible representation comes from Anand's ignorant peasantry in *The Sword and the Sickle*, who have no conception whatsoever about the state and its politics. The novel depicts a band of communists

---

[7] Ibid. 60.     [8] Ibid. 212–13.

under the leadership of Count Rampal Singh, who rebel against the running of foreign government activities, and attempt to educate the peasantry of their rights. The Count tells the peasants about the 'big thief, the Sarkar [who is] behind all the small thieves'[9] who have been terrorizing them, but the villagers have no complaints against the *sarkar* or the government. They insist on seeking protection only against the 'small thieves' until the Count realizes 'that to their simple minds the Sarkar was an unalterable fact, a force like the sun, an inevitability, which they never questioned, and that their hatred was concentrated on the petty tyrants, the agents of authority.'[10] The peasants are not geared into thinking beyond their little concerns to the enslavement of their country and ways of freeing it, even though the Count emphasizes that 'liberty consists in the awareness of our slavery and the struggle to abolish this slavery'.[11] Anand attempts to sweep away the nostalgia that always lingers around any representation of village life. He censures even the Count for assuming too much power and getting drunk on his idealism:

[To go] on believing in primitivism and . . . not lay[ing] stress on intelligent organization and solidarity among the workers, betrays not only a lack of confidence in the revolutionary movement of the people, but almost a kind of unconscious contempt and hatred of the masses! . . . The wild dreams of the exalted leaders flourish, and people begin to dream of glory, build up private myths of a revolution, in this world, in the heavens and nowhere in particular![12]

Anand reveals the quality of the minds of not just the ignorant peasants but also the leadership who have assumed the role of revolutionizing the peasantry without raising their levels of consciousness. The Count depends on the gullible nature of the peasants and uses his authority to sway them without affecting their political thinking in any way. Anand's view of the revolution thereby mocks the treatment of the peasants by the elite leaders, and for my purposes, invites comment on Rao's particular representation.

In *Kanthapura*, peasant participation in nationwide political activity depends solely on a religiously mobilized sentiment, amounting to marginalizing the role of social and economic grievances in giving strength to the national movement. Their struggle to 'get rid of the Redman' is motivated only by a pure appeal of nationalism dictated

[9] Mulk Raj Anand, *The Sword and the Sickle* (London: Jonathan Cape, 1942), 258.
[10] Ibid.    [11] Ibid. 314.    [12] Ibid. 338.

by religion, enabling the author to present an ageless and static, depoliticized Indian peasantry which nationalist intellectuals would find attractive—a peasantry that is not threatening in any way, that is not class conscious, but one that homogeneously embodies ancient ideals of duty, commitment, and sacrifice. Closely resembling the Celtic sentiment of Irish nationalism, Rao's representation of the peasantry is an expression of the spiritual strength required to reshape and rebuild antique culture after a long period of eclipsing English influences. If the wider discontentment with imperialism had issued from local resentment, Rao's villagers would have been credible. But Rao limits peasant concerns. As a member of the nationalist intelligentsia, he is interested in depicting the peasants as having simple and romantic ideas about politics. Assisted further by using Gandhi as deity, he marginalizes Gandhi's role in redressing peasant grievances, and confines it within the limits of divine grace, thereby keeping alive the iconography of a saintly agent whose presence and teaching would appear to be the only means of stirring the passivity of the population.

## II

To be sure, Gandhi's saintly qualities will not be disputed by many. All the same, the plural nature of his sainthood and its varied appeal, as discussed by the Subaltern Studies group of historians, have given a new turn to peasant protest, and done much to dispel nationalist ideology. When, in 1921, Gandhi visited Gorakhpur, a district in eastern Uttar Pradesh, the Congressmen and their agents amongst the local elite glorified and projected him as a saint so that the peasants would see him only from a religious perspective and thus worship him. But the peasants had independent interpretations of his message. They participated by locating the image of the Mahatma within the existing patterns of their own popular beliefs which were different from routine Congress interpretations of the Mahatma's glory.[13]

---

[13] Shahid Amin, 'Gandhi as Mahatma: Gorakhpur District, Eastern UP, 1921–2', in Ranajit Guha (ed.), *Subaltern Studies*, 9 vols. (Delhi: Oxford University Press, 1982–97), iii. 1–61. As an instance of the standard manner in which the 'enthusiasm' of peasants was articulated in nationalist accounts, Shahid Amin cites Mahadev Desai's *Day-to-day with Gandhi*: 'It is impossible to put in language the exuberance of love which Gandhiji . . . experienced in Bihar. Our train . . . stopped at all stations and

They disregarded the agents and even rejected the Mahatma's appeal to be non-violent.[14] In fact, the peasants devised their own Gandhi 'not as he really was, but as they had thought him up'.[15] Appropriating their own image of Gandhi, the peasants violently attacked their adversaries in the very manner Gandhi had condemned. Clearly, they were not passive consumers of Gandhi's message, but had very active interpretations of their own concerns and needed only some legitimizing figure on whom to project them. Gandhi's concept of *swaraj* consequently empowered them to realize their own notions of justice and fair play. *Swaraj* itself, was kept deliberately ambiguous by the intelligentsia so that all possible definitions of independent India could be included in that 'polysemic' term.[16] It was an open-ended concept often employed for political expediency, and Gandhi himself was careful to keep the symbol undefined, yet tremendously evocative.

In his recent study on Chauri Chaura, Shahid Amin gives an account of the making of nationalist narratives based on the February 1922 'rioting' in which twenty-three policemen were burnt to death when a police station was set ablaze by the locals of Chotki Dumri.[17] While the 'volunteers' chanted 'Long Live Mahatma Gandhi' in justification of their 'rioting', Gandhi, himself, called off the nation-wide Non-Cooperation movement in condemnation of their undisci-

there was not a single station which was not crowded with hundreds of people at that time. Even women, who never stir out of their homes, did not fail to present themselves so that they could see and hear him. A huge concourse of students would everywhere smother Gandhiji with their enthusiasm. If at some place a sister would take off her coral necklace . . . at some other, *sanyasis* would come and leave their rosaries on his lap.' Shahid Amin also quotes from D. G. Tendulkar's *Mahatma: Life of Mohandas Karamchand Gandhi* to depict the aura of Gandhi's *darshan* in narratives of nationalism: 'Remarkable scenes were witnessed. In a Bihar village when Gandhi and his party were stranded in the train, an old woman came seeking out Gandhi. "Sire, I am now one hundred and four", she said, "and my sight has grown dim. I have visited the various holy places. . . . Just as we had Rama and Krishna as *avatars*, so also Mahatma Gandhi has appeared as an *avatar*, I hear. Until I have seen him death will not appear." This simple faith moved India's millions who greeted him everywhere with the cry, "Mahatma Gandhi-ki-jai". . . . Wherever he went he had to endure the tyranny of love.' Cited in Amin, 3–4.

The role of the subaltern has not been seen outside their adulation of the Mahatma, a 'devotion' the urban intelligentsia and the Congress activists appropriated for political ends. It is an ironic conviction that if it had not been for the intelligentsia, the sentiments of the 'dumb-millions' (as Rao depicts the peasantry) would have remained unchannelled.

[14] Shahid Amin, 'Gandhi as Mahatma: Gorakhpur District, Eastern UP, 1921–2', 7; 48.                              [15] Ibid. 54.       [16] Ibid. 51.
[17] Shahid Amin, *Event, Metaphor, Memory: Chauri Chaura 1922–1992* (Delhi: Oxford University Press, 1996).

plined violence. Even so, Amin notes, Gandhi's account of the event attempts to imperceptibly vindicate and explain the part played by the mob:

I understand that the constables who were so brutally hacked to death had given much provocation. They had even gone back upon the word just given by the Inspector that they would not be molested, but when the procession had passed the stragglers were interfered with and abused by the constables. The former cried out for help. The mob returned. The constables opened fire. The little ammunition they had was exhausted and they retired to the thana for safety.[18]

Five decades later, the history of this very episode becomes 'Chauri Chaura *kand*',[19] recounting the outrage committed on the 'accredited freedom fighters' who were fired at indiscriminately. In a 1972 account of the Chauri Chaura incident described in the 'History of Freedom Struggle in the Gorakhpur District', these men from Chotki Dumri are taken to have assembled at the police station to 'commemorate' the 'martyrdom' of those who were shot dead by the police, in utter disregard of time and place-names. As Amin writes, 'The nationalist telescoping of chronology here reaches its temporal limit. A crowd which lost at least three of its members to the police firing of 4 February is here assembled to protest an incident which is yet to happen!'[20] The account substitutes the alliterative Chauri Chaura, a railway station near Chotki Dumri from where Gandhi's train had passed, for Dumri itself. Gandhi's message of picketing depots of foreign cloth dutifully displaces the actual looting of meat, fish, and liquor. As for those who masterminded the boycott and the picketing, the District History does not so much as mention them. On the other hand, the names of two prominent nationalists, Madan Mohan Malaviya and Moti Lal Nehru—the former whose appeal saved 152 convicted from death penalty, and the latter who played no role in the event—are glorified.[21] In present day 'Chauri Chaura', there exist two memorials: one honours Mahatma Gandhi, Moti Lal Nehru, and Indira Gandhi, and nowhere refers to those of Dumri who were killed, hanged, or convicted; the other is the Chauri Chaura memorial, originally built by the British to commemorate the dead policemen, which has now been 'nationalized' and re-engraved

[18] Ibid. 47.
[19] Scandal or tragedy. *Kand*, in Amin's words, is an 'event/outrage'. See ibid. 156.
[20] Ibid. 55.     [21] Ibid. 56–7.

as a monument to those very policemen.[22] Through close readings, Shahid Amin shows how the Chauri Chaura incident attains national proportions even though it had been condemned and in spite of the peasant volunteers who were turned into 'hooligans' and 'criminals' soon after the event. Years later, this piece of nationalist history does not even remember those who were participants in it. The various kinds of testimony that Amin gathers of the events of February 1922 from local memory creates a wide discrepancy between definitive and remembered history, and makes room for exaggeration, distortion, and evasion. Seen outside cultural constructs, the local accounts show the face of popular nationalism: the unnatural phenomena, the atrocities committed on the policemen, and the acts of looting were all accounted for in the name of *swaraj*. As in the earlier account of Gorakhpur, even celestial apparitions, rumours, and stories were taken to be signs of the coming *swaraj*, and used by the locals to justify their acts. All along, the press recounted Gandhi's aura as a Mahatma, although the villagers frequently 'demanded' to see Gandhi by breaking the disciplinary cordon to have his *darshan* (blessings) if his train happened to pass by their villages. Gandhi, himself, was far from saintly, being often infuriated with such unruly crowds who would not allow him his night's sleep, and, therefore, issued strict instructions and guidelines which had to be instituted prior to his arrival, in order to keep them in check. What Amin shows us, in effect, is an 'enmeshed, intertwined and imbricated web of narratives from every available source' in order to intervene in official records.[23]

While in many ways, one can draw parallels between the peasants of Kanthapura and those of Dumri, there can be no exculpation for Rao in presenting them as a type by homogenizing their responses and marginalizing their personal views in order to manifest the cultural consciousness of the 'pure' peasantry. It is clear towards the end of the novel that Rao's peasants belong to a 'class of survivors' since peasant culture is believed to be a culture of survival.[24] For Rao, it is the peasants who maintain their links with the past through storytelling and memory, and perpetuate the 'right' historical consciousness. Nationalism itself, in spite of being a

[22] Shahid Amin, *Event, Metaphor, Memory: Chauri Chaura 1922–1992*, 198–200.
[23] Ibid. 194.
[24] John Berger, *Into Their Labours* (London: Granta, 1992), p. xiii.

modern movement, 'conquers in the name of putative folk culture' and draws its symbolism from the strength, purity, and vigour embodied in the life of the peasants, the '*volk*'.[25] The folkloric rediscovery of 'the people' and their 'history' is, in fact, crucial to the foundation of a populist cultural renaissance essential for generating national sentiment.

Subaltern history, on the other hand, exposes the inconsistencies between the nationalist archive, popular perception, and local recall, and more particularly, between the motives that Gandhi placed before the peasants and those out of which they actually acted. It may be recalled that the 'nation-space' is riven by the opposition between the pedagogy of nationalism which is governed by homogenizing tendencies and the dynamics of actual peasant politics. In many cases, Gandhi was well aware of these differences and even sought to appropriate the peasants on the basis of their reasons alone. Correspondingly, many villages responded to Gandhi's call for reasons other than nationalistic. As an indirect support to the political no-tax campaign in Ankola *taluq* (a collection of villages), a bad monsoon and a failed harvest combined to make the *ryots* of Hirekurur, Sirsi, and Siddapur in the Dharwar district of Karnataka, also unite in opposing the taxation policy. With the Gandhi–Irwin pact, *satyagraha* and the political no-tax campaign in many parts of south India were suspended, but with Gandhi's assent the agitation in the *taluqs* of Dharwar district was allowed to continue owing to its economic justification. Significantly, this grassroots campaign was suspended after the Diwakar-Smart Agreement in which the Commissioner of the Southern Division promised necessary relief.[26]

Gandhi had involved himself in three significant struggles—at Champaran in Bihar, and at Ahmedabad and Kheda in Gujarat. These were related to specific local issues and were fought for the economic demands of the masses. The Champaran agitation, for instance, sought to release the cultivators from the obligation of growing indigo. In Ahmedabad, Gandhi secured a 35 per cent increase in wages from the mill-owners for the factory workers. Again, he fought for the total remission of land revenue for the Kheda

[25] Ernest Gellner, *Nations and Nationalism* (Oxford: Blackwell, 1983), 57.

[26] R. R. Diwakar, *Karnataka Through the Ages* (Karnataka: Government of Karnataka Press, 1968), 918.

peasants when the crops produced were less than one-fourth of the normal yield. In other words, the agitations and Gandhi's role in fighting for just means in dealing with peasant problems were more localized and economic than widely anti-imperialist. Despite their limited significance, however, these movements had widespread efficacy in the national struggle insofar as the appropriation of peasants was concerned. What Gandhi did was to give the masses, for the first time, a sense of involvement in the nation's destiny. Paradoxically, these model movements also served Gandhi's conception of national politics in which the peasants were mobilized but not allowed to participate; they were part of a nation, yet kept at a distance from the national state.[27] On their part, the peasants contributed to the national movement because of the alleviation of their problems related to debts, taxes, and exploitation. It should be kept in mind, therefore, that the nature of problems they faced were not directly related to colonial rule, unlike in *Kanthapura* where Rao shows peasant insurgency to be a consequence of the 'Redman's' effrontery to the motherland, issuing from a nationalist sentiment that is believed to be shared by all Indians in general.

Spivak has posed an intersection of conventional and nominally radical histories, splitting them open to their limits marked by the effaced figure of the gendered subaltern. In her translation of Mahasweta Devi's 'Douloti the Bountiful', the consolidation of the nation-state, mobilized from collective resistance against the Empire, is shown to be a remarkable contradiction in the face of a heterogeneity of tribes existing in independent India.[28] Mahasweta Devi writes of decolonized India's 'others', the pre-capitalist tribals, who have little or no idea of the cartography of their country or the history that created its boundaries, united as they are only in their collective identity as bonded labour. The multiplicity of Oraons, Mundas, Santals, Lodhas, Kherias, Mahalis, Gonds, and many more, are contained within the states—West Bengal and Bihar— and controlled by brahmins and the Rajput *zamindars*, who are complicit with the contractors and the government. Conspired out of existence in the negotiation between Empire and Nation, bonded labour finally gets a space in the nation-state as Douloti appropriates

[27] Partha Chatterjee, 'Gandhi and the Critique of Civil Society', in Ranajit Guha (ed.), *Subaltern Studies*, 9 vols. (Delhi: Oxford University Press, 1982–97), iii. 194.
[28] Gayatri Spivak, trans. and introd. *Imaginary Maps: Three Stories by Mahasweta Devi* (London and New York: Routledge, 1995), 41; 66.

the map of India spread-eagled in her death.[29] She leaves no room at all for the national flag on the map which the schoolmaster has inscribed in the courtyard of the school in preparation for Independence Day. She becomes the text of the 'ignored Fourth World' in decolonized space, not spoken for among the agendas of nationalism.[30] As we shall examine in greater detail in the following chapter, the subaltern, for Spivak, cannot speak, being pushed as she is by history into class or caste positions. Hereafter, the historian needs to step up his or her 'vigilance' in order to avoid representing in terms of ethnic celebration or revisionist recovery. As Spivak writes, 'the historian must persist in *his* efforts in this awareness, that the subaltern is necessarily the absolute limit of the place where history is narrativised into logic'.[31] The heterogeneous field Spivak speaks for comes only from a persistent critique of essentialism, from establishing multifarious subject-positions to problematize a general view of history, even though in her later translations from Mahasweta Devi, Spivak, answering perhaps to her critics, advances Mahasweta herself as a champion among historians who can conform to the requirements of a postcolonial intellectual.[32]

Rao, in contrast, intends to link different communities on the basis of a common Indian cultural tradition. In spite of showing up the differences between the life at the Skeffington Coffee Estate and the valley below, the representation of common 'Indian' characteristics of the coolies and the villagers tends to diminish that difference. In her description of the coolies at the coffee plantation, the grandmother speaks of a familiar set of cultural characteristics: their superstition, religiosity, caste-functioning, and other forms of conditioning which run parallel to the religious environment of the village. Undoubtedly, the society at the coffee estate have grievances, but like their village brothers and sisters, the belief in *karma* makes them accept their troubles. In view of my analysis, their representation is typical: the nomadic coolies readily join Kenchamma-worship for protection against illness and resistance from temptation. They are shown to accept the lifestyle and idols of Kanthapura even though they come

[29] Gayatri Spivak, 'Woman in Difference: Mahasweta Devi's "Douloti the Bountiful"', *Cultural Critique*, 14 (1989–90), 127–8.

[30] Spivak, *Imaginary Maps*, 202.

[31] Gayatri Spivak, 'Subaltern Studies: Deconstructing Historiography', in *In Other Worlds: Essays in Cultural Politics* (New York and London: Routledge, 1988), 207.

[32] Spivak, *Imaginary Maps*, 197–205.

from the Godavari region which has different traditions and gods. Their living, though described minimally, is nonetheless similar to that of the villagers of Kanthapura: there are the usual marriages, deaths, festivals, and caste dinners. Bhatta becomes their money-lender, and a few are even known to go down to Kanthapura occasionally for devotional singing or *bhajan*. It is evident from their easy adoption of the customs of Kanthapura that they are part of the author's design of building an atmosphere of oneness and uniformity.

An interesting setback to Rao's ideological construction of nationalism is witnessed in the last part of the novel when the reckless bravado initiated by Moorthy is frustrated by the withdrawal of the villagers from rebellion. With the imprisonment of most of the male population of the village, Satamma, who has been an active *satyagrahi*, feels disillusioned with 'truth force': 'she had seen enough and she would go away to the town, and she said she had done nothing and she was not a Gandhi person, and it was all this Moorthy, this Moorthy who had brought all this misery upon us' (225). So long as *satyagraha* is a novel form of worship and Gandhi a new sanctum god, she follows Moorthy willingly. But the moment the revolt touches her smooth existence, she wants to escape liability and wash her hands of the entire episode. It is only when the property and possessions of the villagers are about to be confiscated and auctioned by the Government that a sharp distinction between the two levels—the dramatic and the ideological/national—is most apparent. The villagers can sympathize with the Congress nationalists but cannot offer themselves as active volunteers any longer:

We saw cars go up the Bebbur Mound and the Bel-field and the Tank-field and the Big Field, filled with these pariah-looking coolies, and soldiers were at our doors and policemen in our sanctums, and vessels lay broken on the streets, pickle-pots and gods and winnowing pales. And we say, 'No, no—this will not do, this will not do,' and Ratna says angrily, 'Then you are not for the Mahatma!' and we say, 'We are, we are!—But we have only a loin-cloth wide of land and that is to be sold away, and who will give us a morsel to eat— who?' (229).

For the first time the villagers can see their lands and property slipping away because of their involvement with Gandhi. Their gods have always been merciful—distant deities to be feared and worshipped. This one alone has caused them untold misery. The Bebbur Mound, the Bear's Hill, the Tippur Stream, the plantain plantations, the Kenchamma Hill, and the Devil's field are sacred to them and cannot be given up for Gandhi or for his motive of driving away the 'Redman': '"We are not cattle to leave our homes and our fires and the sacred banks of the Himavathy"' (230). It is simply not enough for the Congress to give them aid; they want to go back to their simple worship of Kenchamma, the centre of their lives, who could be appeased with offerings of saris and bodice-cloths, prostrations and perfumed sweetmeats: 'Mad we were, daughters, mad to follow Moorthy. When did Kenchamma ever refuse our three morsels of rice—or the Himavathy the ten handfuls of water?' (230). The village women are clearly disgruntled, even to the extent of trivializing the *Satyanarayana Puja* that the Congress volunteers want to hold in Kanthapura: 'Of what use all this *Satyanarayana Puja*—and all these Moorthy's prayers—and that widowed Ratna's commands? Prayers never paid Revenue dues. Nor would the rice creep back to the granaries. Nor fire consume Bhatta's promissory notes' (230).

This is the first open acknowledgement of discontentment in a novel where religion has defined every aspect of life. But even here they are not allowed a full-throated protest for suddenly the discontented are depicted to be paralysed with fear:

But some strange fever rushed up from the feet, it rushed up and with it our hair stood on end and our ears grew hot and something powerful shook us from head to foot, like Shamoo when the goddess had taken hold of him; and on that beating, bursting day. . . such a terror took hold of us, that . . . we rushed back home, trembling and gasping with the anger of the gods . . . Moorthy forgive us! Mahatma forgive us! Kenchamma forgive us! (230–1).

When compared with the women's earlier reaction to the auctioning of their lands, Rao's authorial voice in this passage can be seen underlying the grandmother's narration. The setback to his pure story of sacrifice is normalized by divine intervention which shakes the village women out of their selfishness. They feel the goddess's wrath jointly as did Shamoo, presumably a villager, rendered incoherent when possessed by the goddess. In a similar crisis in the present, when the village, and, in conjunction, India also is at stake, the goddess intervenes directly and reveals her displeasure at the women's apostasy. Kenchamma's wrath saves the moment: the crisis is diffused, and the women are repentant. The disturbed hierarchy of Moorthy–Gandhi–Kenchamma is also straightened, as the women retreat into the ideological design of the novel. They finally decide to go 'to the end of the pilgrimage' (231) like the 250,000 women of Bombay who, they have been told, bravely bore police beating, not budging until their men were freed. These women have also forsaken their homes and marched through the streets for the sake of 'the Mahatma and the Mother' (221). Even at this stage of rebellion, religion alone has the power to keep the women committed to the task at hand, and soon we hear: '"Only a pariah looks at the teeth of dead cows. What is lost is lost, and we shall never again look upon our fields and harvests"' (232). Rao consciously evokes the psychological atmosphere of sacrifice where material possessions are abandoned for the sake of national solidarity, and men and women give up their lives for religion, homeland, community, and nation. He does not recount the horror and brutality of the freedom movement that involved the deaths of thousands of men and women. Instead he takes a glorified view of the dead subsumed in exhilarating devotion to Gandhi and Mother India. *Kanthapura* remains a 'nice' story despite the destruction of the village and the deaths of many of its inhabitants. What survives the destruction is a spiritual sentiment that transcends material ruin—and that, for the author, is an India which is invincible and the actual 'reality' for its people.

## III

Before we wind up our examination of contrasting Rao's selective interpretation with some accounts of peasant uprising, I would like to briefly focus on the political upsurge in the district of Hassan where the fictional village of Kanthapura is located. The inquiry is intended specifically to position Rao's representation of a Kannada village against other accounts of peasant insurgency in the princely state of Mysore (now Karnataka).

The freedom struggle in the old princely state of Mysore was comparatively less vigorous than in areas which were under direct British rule.[33] Only seven out of the present twenty districts were ruled directly by the British, being part of the Bombay and Madras presidencies.[34] Anti-colonial agitation consequently was more pro-

[33] U. R. Anantha Murthy, 'Kannada II', in H. M. Nayak (ed.), *Gandhiji in Indian Literature* (Mysore: Mysore University Printing Press, 1971), 133.
[34] They were Dharwar, Belgaum, Bijapur, and North Kanara in Bombay; and Bellary, South Kanara, and Coorg in Madras.

nounced in these states than in the princely state of Mysore which comprised ten districts: Bangalore (now two), Mysore, Tumkur, Chitradurga, Kolar, Shimoga, Mandya, Hassan, and Chikmagalur. Congress activities were limited in these districts because it had not permitted any civil disobedience here, or allowed its units to undertake prolonged political agitation. Their representatives had instead undertaken constructive activities like propagating *khadi*, initiating Hindi, and fighting caste oppression.

In contrast, participation in the areas of northern Karnataka was abundant. The sufferings and sacrifices of the peasants of Sirsi, Siddapur, and Ankola in the Satyagraha Campaign of 1930–2 are without parallel. In the district of North Kanara alone, ninety-six *patels* or village-headmen resigned in Sirsi *taluq*, twenty-five in Siddapur, and forty-three out of sixty-three in Ankola. Three lakh palm trees were cut down to prevent the manufacture of toddy. Hundreds of people, including a large number of women, were arrested in almost all parts of the state. Many farmers were evicted from their homes, and many forfeited their lands valued at thousands of rupees.

It is on the strength of the northern, non-princely areas that the landmarks in the history of the Karnataka freedom struggle have been primarily established. Noticeably, the list excludes the princely state of Hassan. It is perhaps to compensate for this exclusion that Moorthy is shown to be in regular communication with the Congress activists in Karwar.[35] It was in Karwar and other districts of North Kanara—Hubli, Mangalore, Sirsi, Siddapur, Honnavar, and Kumta—that the Salt Satyagraha was first introduced. These were areas directly controlled by the British. It could be argued that in locating *Kanthapura* in a semi-autonomous state not under direct British rule, Rao chooses an area which is comparatively untouched by nationalist politics, and consequently more traditional. While this lends support to the way he represents the politics of Kanthapura, it is also contradictory in a novel that purports to be about nationalism.

Hassan's participation in the freedom struggle, significantly, is evinced only after the Quit India Movement of 1942. Picketing of toddy booths was started for the first time in Arsikere on 14 August 1942.[36] Hassan district took up this programme on a large scale

---

[35] Karwar is a town on the west coast of North Kanara, an area of active political rebellion in comparison with the sedate Hassan.

[36] Suryanath U. Kamath, *Quit India Movement in Karnataka* (Bangalore: Lipi Prakashana, 1988), 55.

during the coming weeks which witnessed an intense stir among the students. The 'trouble', however, came from outside and was not generated from within the district. This is indicated by a letter from the District Commissioner of Hassan to the Chief Secretary: the movement was 'not getting the amount of encouragement from the local people that would enable it to survive. The trouble however is that gangs of students have been coming from Tumkur, Bangalore, and Mysore and inciting students in Arsikere and Hassan'.[37] There is, in effect, hardly any evidence of political activity in Hassan district in the 1930s which could have found a context in *Kanthapura* as programmes like boycott of schools, no-tax with reference to shandy toll, hurdles to government work, picketing of liquor shops, felling of toddy trees, or the cutting of telegraph wires were undertaken only in 1942.

The historical inaccuracy makes Rao's narrative predictive: instead of using the future tense common to 'anterior' narratives, Rao employs the simple past or the present continuous, customary in biblical prophecies. Apart from being analogous with the biblical or the romantic traditions of western literature with which educated Indians came into contact, predictive narration also has a strong link with *puranic* stories which include dreams, curses, and prophecies anticipating the future. The novel may then be re-categorized as prophetic history or may even continue in its classification as *puranic* history although it is only from an *ex post facto* availability of historical knowledge that a discussion of the proleptic quality of the novel can be sustained. Rao overrides the narrative voice in his representation of a south Indian village, synthesizing the north and the south, the princely and the non-princely into one province to impart an even flavour to the struggle.[38] The synthesis is a deliberate attempt to make a representational or ideal model of the whole movement, comprising its religious, social, and economic elements. Apparently, Rao was not indifferent to the political activities in the rest of the country which he absorbs prophetically within the context of his own village.

Despite his information of political circumstances in parts of southern India, it has to be remembered that *Kanthapura* was

[37] District Commissioner to Chief Secretary, 20 Aug. 1942, *Confidential Branch File*, 147/42–24, Karnataka State Archives, Bangalore.
[38] An interesting comparison can be made with John of Gaunt's prophecy in *Richard II* which envisions England as an island, subsuming Scotland (and ignoring Wales) before the union of the crowns.

written between 1929 and 1933 when Rao was in France. In a letter to Naik, he confessed to having worked 'in a thirteenth century castle in the French Alps belonging to the Dauphins of France [where he] slept and worked on the novel in the room of the Queen'.[39] It follows that Rao's descriptions of the peasant participation in the Indian struggle for freedom came from his self-reflection on nationalist activity, from information acquired, perhaps from newspapers and books, and from the influence of the Irish he speaks of in the fore-word. His idealism, on the other hand, could have been generated from his readings of Gandhi's autobiography, the Ramayana, and Ananda Coomaraswamy.[40] In Coomaraswamy, particularly, Rao felt that he was 'at last discovering an India that one *felt* but could not have named'.[41] It is from Coomaraswamy's influence that Rao's conception of 'real' India is perhaps shaped, for both Rao and Coomaraswamy carry an inheritance of India which is part of the experience of expatriates.

Significantly, in the foreword to the first edition of the novel, Rao refers to *Kanthapura* as the story of 'my village'. But in the revised New Directions edition, it has been amended to 'a village'. The author's comment accounts for the change: 'The background is my village—Harihalli or Hariharapura, near Kenchamma Hoskere Taluk, Hassan district, but nothing like this drama took place at Harihalli. Hence in my new edition I have corrected the "my" into "a".'[42] The explanation, though retrospectively gathered, allows us to maintain our assessment of Rao's village as an idealized and an historically inaccurate representation even as this ideal village becomes symptomatic of India's other villages which had joined the national movement, judging from the author's alternation from the personal to the general. Evidently, like in the *puranas* and the *Dhar-masastras* (Law Scriptures), Rao employs 'a kind of historical syn-cretism' which could only be 'partly unintentional', being largely a consequence of 'pragmatic considerations',[43] but wholly identifiable with classical Hinduism. He was later to turn history altogether into an amalgam of the philosophical and the spiritual.

[39] Cited in M. K. Naik, *Raja Rao* (New York: Twayne, 1972), 60.
[40] Raja Rao, 'Books Which Have Influenced Me', in M. K. Naik (ed.), *Aspects of Indian Writing in English* (Delhi: Macmillan, 1979), 45–9.    [41] Ibid. 49.
[42] Naik, *Raja Rao*, 60.
[43] Madhav Deshpande, 'History, Change and Permanence', in Gopal Krishna (ed.), *Contributions to South Asian Studies* (Delhi: Oxford University Press, 1979), i. 14.

Rao's presentation of the village as the image of rural consciousness, in sum, is inadequate, since the political upheaval affects the
villagers only within the realm of the spirit. The evacuees simply
begin living in another village, Kashipura, which does not appear to
be very different from Kanthapura.[44] The same routine of feasting,
praying, and searching for qualified bridegrooms goes on: gods,
Upanishads, and Vedanta continue to exercise their hold. Apparently,
in Rao's view, one Indian village cannot vary much from another.
Despite the tensions, most of those who participate in the *satyagraha*
do not go beyond their cultural innocence, enabling Rao to preserve a
cultural purity through mutation. In the end, Rangè Gowda cannot
leave the derelict village without drinking three handfuls of Himavathy water, praying for its protection and thereby rejuvenating a
timeless experience: '"I spat three times to the west and three times
to the south, and I threw a palmful of dust at the sunken wretch, and I
turned away"' (258). While *Kanthapura* is annihilated in the material physical sense, there has definitely been a gain in terms of spiritual
consciousness, embodied in the flooding of the Himavathy on Gauri's
night. Within the cultural context, Rangè Gowda's ritual spitting and
the offering of a handful of dust are a significant part of the mood of
the whole story, and, in Rao's representative cultural context,
undeniably 'real'.

[44] Kashipura is a village in Arkalgud *taluq* of Hassan district.

# 4  Involvement and Resistance
of Women

For a fuller realization of Rao's model of cultural identity, it is important to locate the women of Kanthapura in the freedom movement. The issue of women's participation is here seen in terms of the wider theme of muted peasant unrest dealt with in the previous chapter. In the context of the novel, the contradiction between women's desires and their permitted sphere of participation is revealed by textual inconsistencies which allows us to see how they are marginalized in the essentialist representations of nationalist discourse.

Gandhi's involvement of women in India's struggle for independence invites comparisons and contrasts with the participation of Rao's fictional heroines who join the *satyagraha* in response to Gandhi's call. We see in the novel a reworking of Gandhi's esteem of women in combination with their role in the freedom movement. Despite the sweeping domination of brahminic patriarchy in the novel, it is striking that women—both brahmin and non-brahmin— are permitted equal participation with men in Gandhi's programme. The author goes so far as to allow them to assemble themselves into a 'Sevika Sangha' and discipline themselves as true *satyagrahis*. Though this form of dissent was largely unknown to brahminic culture, the brahmins in the novel suffer the 'outrage' silently. Gandhi's own bent towards the 'commoners' in procuring a national mandate had not made him very popular with pan-Hindu conservatives who till then had possessed unchallenged power. His sympathetic treatment of women, moreover, threatened the stronghold of chauvinist brahminic culture which was contemptuous of his encouragement to women to come forward.[1]

In many ways Gandhi worked against the predominantly patriarchal order and evoked a response in women because the feminine

[1] See Ashis Nandy, *At the Edge of Psychology: Essays in Politics and Culture* (Delhi: Oxford University Press, 1980), 78.

nature of his protest touched their sphere of domesticity: his fasts, penances, and prayers were integral to a cultural ethos common to women where domination over the patriarchal order was exercised by self-penalization.[2] Since women did not have the formal power of taking positions in a dominantly male system, they could subvert authority by penance and fasting, thereby maximizing the hidden potential of Hindu conservatism. For Gandhi, the association with the suppressed woman and her subtle manoeuvre worked even when transferred to the imperialists where both he and his followers used non-violence and pacifism instead of brutal reciprocity for their ends.[3] By using the qualities of femininity to underwrite his principle instrument, passive resistance, he was able to both subvert the dominant views of the anti-imperialist struggle and the nature of the struggle itself.[4] In effect, he gave the protest a moral quality in its emphasis on the virtues of female perseverance. Even though his adversaries insisted that his approach was unmanly and would lead to their eventual disablement, Gandhi's method of resistance was useful in drawing women into the national movement since he revealed through the adoption of non-violence that women were not completely resourceless in spite of being in a situation of complete subordination within the formal structure of patriarchy. It may be inferred here that by referring to self-sacrifice and non-violence as 'manly' virtues, he also subverted the terrain of masculinity apart from turning the traditionally weak into the morally strong.[5]

By advocating equal rights for women in all spheres, Gandhi

[2] Ashis Nandy, At the Edge of Psychology: Essays in Politics and Culture, 73.

[3] Gyanendra Pandey has also spoken of Gandhi's feminization of nationalism which led right-wing organizations to question how Gandhi with his 'feminine' spinning wheel could possibly be considered the 'Father of the Nation'. See Pandey, 'Which of Us Are Hindus?', in id. (ed.), Hindus and Others: The Question of Identity in India Today (New Delhi: Viking, 1993), 264. Gandhi's appeal to spin yarn, it was reasoned, made many 'able-bodied men sit . . . spinning, like women.' See M. K. Gandhi (ed.), 'Not Man's Work?', Young India, 7.24 (1925), 204; and Ketu H. Katrak, 'Indian Nationalism, Gandhian "Satyagraha" and Representations of Female Sexuality', in Andrew Parker, et al. (eds.), Nationalisms and Sexualities (New York and London: Routledge, 1992), 399.

[4] Somnath Zutshi, 'Women, Nation and the Outsider in Contemporary Hindi Cinema', in Tejaswini Niranjana et al. (eds.), Interrogating Modernity: Culture and Colonialism in India (Calcutta: Seagull, 1993), 105.

[5] Ironically, Gandhi's emphasis on non-violence had violent repercussions for women: 'his symbols of female obedience became repressive social instruments even as they helped to create new mechanisms for managing national crisis.' See Parker, et al., 'Introduction', in eid., Nationalisms and Sexualities, 13.

asserted the relevance of women to a non-violent struggle aimed at a just social order. He also maintained that 'to postpone social reform till after the attainment of Swaraj is not to know the meaning of Swaraj',[6] and further that 'when the women in the country have woken up, who can hinder swaraj?'[7] Consequently, the heroic role of women lay in leading the revolution against inequality, abuse, and social injustice, both for themselves and for the other exploited groups in society. Gandhi's programme of national integration worked for the improvement of all—the *harijans* (low-caste untouchables) and the women—to change the course of Indian society.

Gandhi's role for women within the national struggle, however, appears to be limited largely to the domestic sphere: believing men and women to be playing complementary but different roles, he insisted that service to the husband, his family, and the country (in that order) should be accepted as the 'primary duties' of women.[8] But he also argued against the traditional stereotype of the weak and inferior woman, asserting that women were not weak as they had been rendered by custom, because they possessed moral strength, if not the physical strength of men.[9] His severe condemnation of the victimization of Indian women in the forms of purdah, child marriage, dowry, and prostitution served to reinforce the virtues of sacrifice, devotion, and moral strength of Indian womanhood. Yet Gandhi did not visualize a complete revolution or transformation of women's roles; indeed, his writings appear to indicate their immobility within the system regardless of their inner strength. The moral strength that he imputes to women has almost an inborn, genetic complexion which bears little or no relation to generations of exploitation, humiliation, and hardship which is part of women's history.[10] Even as he sought social reform, his gaze remained fixed on the symbology of the mother, so that women entered public life primarily

[6] Charles H. Heimsath, *Indian Nationalism and Hindu Social Reform* (Princeton, NJ: Princeton University Press, 1964), 343.
[7] Pushpa Joshi, *Gandhi On Women: Collection of Mahatma Gandhi's Writings and Speeches on Women* (New Delhi: Centre for Women's Development Studies and Navajivan Trust, 1988), 59.
[8] Karuna Chanana Ahmad, 'Gandhi, Women's Roles and the Freedom Movement', *Occasional Papers on History and Society*, 1st series, no. 19 (New Delhi: Nehru Memorial Museum and Library, 1984), 9. Chanana Ahmad's study of Gandhi's roles for women has been of much use in exploring Gandhi's attitudes.
[9] M. K. Gandhi, *Women and Social Injustice* (Ahmedabad: Navajivan, 1942), 196.
[10] Chanana Ahmad, 'Gandhi, Women's Roles and the Freedom Movement', 10.

to play maternal roles. His image of the Indian woman remained an essentialized one, an unchanging and passive picture of womanhood who undoubtedly possessed freedom, but 'functioned within relatively narrow parameters and well defined boundaries'.[11] Moreover, by limiting women's roles only within the boundaries delineated by the patriarchal system, he broke down the family resistance of his women associates with the assurance that women would not step outside their traditional household roles. While for himself he altogether relinquished 'the desire for children and wealth', for women he advocated the performance of primary duties since it was not possible to do justice to both the public and the domestic.[12]

In general, his attitude to the area of women's participation in the freedom movement can be seen at three, often contradictory, levels.[13] Women who bore the responsibilities of a family such as the care of children and the aged were to fulfil only their primary duties which were not to be given up for the sake of the national movement. Yet a second group included women from whom he hoped for a sacrifice of the pleasures of housekeeping and childbearing. If already married, these women were expected to remain celibate for the sake of the national movement. He exhorted Vijaylakshmi Pandit and her husband, for instance, to practise sexual abstinence after their marriage.[14] Thirdly, workers who had dedicated themselves entirely to the struggle for independence were expected to stay single in clear pursuit of their target. Gandhi is known to have disapproved of the marriage of the Kriplanis because it meant the loss of a devoted worker. Thus, while he was trying to safeguard traditional gender roles, he could not always avoid rupturing this model.

We notice that Gandhi's roles for women are dictated by different circumstances and levels of participation. In general, he allocated issues like prohibition to the women's domain since they were the principle victims in this area: 'Only those women who have drunkards as their husbands know what havoc the drink devil works in homes that once were orderly and peace-giving.'[15] Since women from all

---

[11] Madhu Kishwar, 'Gandhi on Women', *Economic and Political Weekly*, 20.40 (1985), 1692.

[12] M. K. Gandhi, *An Autobiography: Or, the Story of My Experiments with Truth*, trans. Mahadev Desai (Ahmedabad: Navajivan, 1927), 173.

[13] Chanana Ahmad, 'Gandhi, Women's Roles and the Freedom Movement', 13; 18.

[14] M. K. Gandhi, 'Letter to Narandas Gandhi', 27 Nov. 1930, in *Collected Works of Mahatma Gandhi, 1884–1948*, 90 vols. (Ahmedabad: Navajivan, 1927), xliv. 353.

[15] M. K. Gandhi, 'To the Women of India', *Young India*, 12.15 (1930), 121.

classes suffered from the excessive drinking of men, the inclusion of toddy-picketing within the national movement could gain momentum only if turned over to women. But whatever the degree of their recruitment, their participation was defined by and formed within the national movement. Gandhi did not conceive of any clear object-ives to mobilize women in the long run just as he did not question caste hierarchy in India while denouncing untouchability. His pro-gramme did not envisage overturning the traditional and social cir-cumstances concerning women. Perhaps the involvement of women in the national struggle was a strategic tactic, one not intended to empower them at all. By deferring women's demands to until after the revolution, Gandhi not only disavowed that 'nationalisms are from the outset constituted in gender power, but, as the lessons of international history portend, women who are not empowered to organize during the struggle will not be empowered to organize after the struggle'.[16] Gandhi's moral outlook, thereby, had scarcely any outcome for women since it aimed at improving neither 'their relation to the outer world of production' nor 'the inner world of family, sexuality and reproduction'.[17]

In *Kanthapura*, the involvement of the village women in political activity cannot simply be seen at the level of participation depicted in the novel. Though Rao offers a political perspective that can ideologically assemble a diverse Indian society into a harmonious entity, the intrusion of his own political interests as well as his position within the brahminic intelligentsia has also to be consid-ered. Correspondingly, the three primary female characters in

[16] Anne McClintock, '"No Longer in a Future Heaven"': Women and Nationalism in South Africa', *Transition*, 51 (1991), 122. See also Nayereh Tohidi, 'Gender and Islamic Fundamentalism: Feminist Politics in Iran', in Chandra Talpade Mohanty, *et al.* (eds.), *Third World Women and the Politics of Feminism* (Bloomington and Indiana-polis: Indiana University Press, 1991), 260. Tohidi's essay reinforces the argument that any anti-imperialist revolution which does not transform the position of third-world women is inadequate: 'Alone, a women's movement can never transform the founda-tions of sexism and sexual oppression. Neither can a revolution which seeks to trans-form class relationships meet its goals if it does not incorporate the question of women's oppression. Specific demands of women must be incorporated into the national anti-imperialist movement and class struggle right from the beginning. *The women's question should not be relegated to the days after the revolution*—as has been, unfortunately, the tendency of many left and revolutionary movements. Cases such as the Algerian and Iranian revolutions have proven that the success of a nation-alist or even a socialist revolution does not automatically lead to liberation for women.'

[17] M. Kishwar, 'Gandhi on Women', *Economic and Political Weekly*, 20.40 (5 Oct. 1985), 1699.

*Kanthapura*—Rangamma, Ratna, and of course, Achakka—are brahmin widows, and come from a social strata recognized by the author. Rangamma and Ratna are the heroines and the natural leaders of the village women. By having a narrator who, like them, is a brahmin widow, the author is able to invite sympathetic comment on the involvement of the other two in the uprising. Significantly, both Rangamma and Ratna have had husbands, so they have not always been entirely in control of their sexuality even though at the present moment in the narration, they are widows. Thus, marriage, an institution of social control, especially over female sexuality, is not discounted. Having been married, they can also qualify as 'nation-mothers', even though they have no children of their own. At the same time, being widows, they can be granted a certain amount of freedom. More importantly, as widows, they allow Rao to produce the type of woman who could keep apart the dichotomies of the material (temptress) and the spiritual (mother) since they cannot be symbols of desire for their representation would then begin to militate against the powerful, religious, but sexless mother-image the nationalists were creating.[18]

In Hindu discourse, women have been represented as Mother and Nurturer, yet her protectors have always been men. In appropriating Hindu tradition, nationalist discourse similarly capitalizes on the symbol of Mother India. Others have commented on the status of women as 'Container' or 'Vehicle' in the nationalist discourse, as 'the repository of Indian (Hindu) tradition, the essence, the "inner" side, the spirituality and greatness of Hindu civilization.'[19] The pointers are towards the traditional, upper-caste Hindu woman who is represented as sacrificing and passive, eternally giving. In Hindu nationalist discourse, woman has also been represented as 'Property': *'The Hindu is being worsted everywhere—in his own country and in foreign lands. His women are being raped.'*[20] One of Raja Rao's

---

[18] Gandhi's own polarized view of women, especially his resistance to women as sexual temptation and his consequent vow of sexual abstinence, may be seen within the paradigm of the Vedic woman created by 19th-cent. nationalists.

[19] Pandey, 'Which of us are Hindus?', 260. Pandey also quotes from Swami Shraddhanand, an Arya Samaj reformer and militant nationalist in the1920s, on the status of women in Hindu discourse: 'Every child of the Matri-Bhumi (Motherland) may daily bow before the Mother and renew *his* pledge to restore *her* to the ancient pinnacle of glory from which she has fallen!' The child, Pandey ironically notes, is apparently male. See Pandey, 259.

[20] Quoted from a leaflet circulated in Bhagalpur during the sectarian violence of Oct.–Nov. 1989. See ibid. 260.

short stories, 'The Cow of the Barricades', also deals with the mother symbology adducing striking parallels with the cow since both are sacred to Hindus.[21] Conventionally, the cow as a 'symbol of motherhood, of largesse, a source of the vital products milk and ghee'[22] establishes links between the mother and Mother India within the dominant Hindu tradition which esteems the cow as such. But while the cow is always a symbol of purity, the woman can remain pure only within the spiritual dimension of nationalist discourse. She is also evil, sexual, and irrational, and thus polluted, and must be turned into a mother by the denial of feminine eroticism so that she can remain within the great cultural tradition defining the nation. The cow, on the other hand, can never be made impure, only martyred as in Rao's story. Significantly, the employment of the cow, a symbol of worship among Hindus, does not allow her to be a mother to non-Hindus.

The link between woman-as-mother and Mother India serves the important function of staking claim to the land of one's birth which has been forcibly controlled by foreigners and foreign historiographers. As the expanding metaphor of the mother widens beyond its local significance as Goddess Kenchamma, the nation also gets united by 'ties of territoriality.'[23] In terms of the novel form, the attainment of national consciousness also accomplishes the writing of the nation's history. Another good example would be Bankim's early nationalist text, *Anandamath*, in which the link between the land and the mother becomes apparent when Mohendra Singha is told: 'We call our land our mother; but for her, we have neither mother, father, brother, nor friend. We have neither wife nor son nor house nor home. We have her alone, cool with delightful winds, rich with harvests . . .'[24] The Earth Mother is here her people's granary. The symbolic relationship between woman and the nation thus comes from giving her the various identities of Mother, Nurturer, Container, and Property, all of which can be claimed.

[21] Raja Rao, 'The Cow of the Barricades', in *The Cow of the Barricades and Other Stories* (London: Geoffrey Cumberledge, Oxford University Press, 1947), 174–82.
[22] Janet P. Gemmill, 'Raja Rao: Three Tales of Independence', *World Literature Written in English*, 15.1 (1976), 145.
[23] Horace B. Davis, *Toward a Marxist Theory of Nationalism* (New York and London: Monthly Review Press, 1978), 6.
[24] Bankimchandra Chatterjee, *Anandamath* (1882), in *Bankim Rachanavali*, ed. Jogeshchandra Bagal, 3 vols. (Calcutta: Sahitya Samsad, 1953–69), i. 673. My trans.

Within the text, both female activists—Rangamma and Ratna—
are mother figures: Rangamma a surrogate mother for Moorthy
especially after the death of his mother; Ratna also displays concern
for the fasting hero. They are also members of a caste which has
always imposed severe restrictions on its women, especially the
widows. By following Gandhi, however, Rao is able to 'liberate'
this woman from a restrictive life by allotting her more 'space-in-
the-home'.[25] In other words, despite remaining within the four walls
of the household, the home itself would be infiltrated by politics,
enabling women to participate in the national struggle without, in
effect, breaking loose from patriarchal control. Correspondingly, in
so far as their national activity as members of the Sevika Sangha
collides with domestic bliss, they are advised to follow their primary
duties first:

'If we are to help others, we must begin with our husbands,' and she
[Rangamma] tells Satamma, 'Your husband is not against Sevika Sangha.
He only wants to eat in time. . . . Rangamma tells her to be more regular in
cooking, and we all say, 'We should do our duty. If not, it is no use belonging
to the Gandhi group.' Rangamma says, 'That is right, sister,' and we say, 'We
shall not forget our children and our husbands' (152).

Rao's sentiment is part of the nationalistic belief in the 'protection' of
women within the household. In Rangamma's advice to women to
first do their housework, he follows the characteristic nationalist
patriarchy which, while allowing flexibility, nonetheless insisted on
'*differences* between socially approved male and female conduct'.[26] In
a speech at the meeting of textile workers in Ahmedabad, Gandhi,
too, had said:

If the workers find it necessary today to send their wives and children to work
in factories, it is our duty to see that they do not have to. . . . Work is not for
children. Nor is it for women to work in factories. They have plenty of work
in their own homes. They should attend to the bringing up of their children;
they may give peace to the husband when he returns home tired, minister to
him, soothe him if he is angry and do any other work they can staying at
home. . . . If we send them to the factories, who will look after our domestic

[25] Sujata Patel, 'The Construction and Reconstruction of Woman in Gandhi',
*Occasional Papers on History and Society*, 1st series, no. 49 (New Delhi: Nehru
Memorial Museum and Library, 1984), 17.
[26] Partha Chatterjee, 'The Nationalist Resolution of the Women's Question', in
Kumkum Sangari and Sudesh Vaid (eds.), *Recasting Women: Essays in Colonial His-
tory* (New Delhi: Kali for Women, 1989), 247.

and social affairs? If women go out to work, our social life will be ruined and moral standards will decline. . . . I feel convinced that for men and women to go out for work together will mean the fall of both. Do not, therefore, send your women out to work; protect their honour; if you have any manliness in you, it is for you to see that no one casts an evil eye on them.[27]

When encountering what appear to be issues relating to honour and fidelity, affected by his narrow middle-class moral values, Gandhi emphasizes the need for women to stay at home and practise their spinning within its confines. As Sujata Patel has discussed, the pledge of *swadeshi*[28] is thus metamorphosed from its political underpinnings to a religious and moral issue and holds within itself the protection of Indian womanhood as a *dharma*. The defence of this honour, in turn, becomes *Ishwarbhakti* or devotion to God.[29]

Both Gandhi and Rao are unmindful of the familiar sight of women workers in rural areas who work hand in hand with men in fields and plantations.[30] Such women would be surprised at the 'traditional', accepted sphere of women's participation floated by nationalists. The image of women Gandhi develops is that of physical frailty and innate strength: 'the non-violent movement is to enable the weakest human beings to vindicate their dignity.'[31] Hence, at the formation of the Congress in *Kanthapura*, Rangamma is elected a representative because 'the Congress is for the weak and the lowly' (110). Gandhi's ideas pertaining to the second group of women—the more nationalistic and celibate—are also woven into the lives of Rangamma and Ratna. Since neither woman has a husband or children, they adjust well within the Gandhian parameters of chastity and abstinence. Like Gandhi, Rao also creates categories of women—those who owe their services first to the home, and those who have no familial responsibilities and can therefore serve the nation. He is thus able to maintain the privileged position of marriage and the woman's role as a devoted wife and sacrificing mother from the ancient models of upper-caste Hindu women which conform to the contemporary urban, middle-class Hindu society. It is only this

[27] M. K. Gandhi, 'Speech at Meeting of Mill-Hands, Ahmedabad', 25 Feb. 1920, in *Collected Works*, xvii. 49–50.

[28] Indigenous, especially in terms of the refusal to buy British-made cloth.

[29] Patel, 'Construction and Reconstruction of Woman in Gandhi', 27.

[30] In Pushpa Joshi's collection of Gandhi's writings and speeches on women, it is surprising that Gandhi has not referred once to peasant women. See Joshi, *Gandhi On Women*.

[31] Cited in Patel, 'Construction and Reconstruction of Woman in Gandhi', 31.

class of women who can respond readily to the image of Sita who sacrificed her ostentatious lifestyle to follow her husband, Rama, into exile. Contemporary Indian society, on the other hand, was full of women who could not afford to possess more than one *sari*, and had no clothes or jewellery to give up. They did not need to be persuaded to spin and wear *khadi* since they had no alternative but to wear cheap handlooms. In this regard, both Gandhi and Rao seem to be consciously showing an ideological preference for the urban middle-class women who used foreign cloth, as well as for antiquity in embellishing a modern national struggle.

Within the novel, however, the grandmother's narration gives us occasion to hear women's voices outside the limits demarcated by the author. After a reversal of their roles, Achakka cannot, any longer, be party to Rangamma's advice about having 'space-in-the-home':

But how can we be like we used to be? Now we hear this story and that story, and we say we too shall organise a foreign-cloth boycott like at Sholapur, we too, shall go picketing cigarette shops and toddy shops, and we say our Kanthapura, too, shall fight for the Mother, and we always see the picture of Rani Lakshmi Bai that Rangamma has on the verandah wall, a queen, sweet and young and bejewelled, riding a white horse and looking out across the narrow river and the hills to where the English armies stand (152–3).

Significantly, Rani Lakshmi Bai of Jhansi, who was killed in the 1857 rebellion, is both 'sweet and young and bejewelled' yet valiant, an embodiment of 'female—as opposed to feminist—valour'.[32] She can thus be represented as part of tradition (virtuous), yet imbued with contemporaneity (liberated), seen to possess cultural values, yet able to stand up to the modern. As Sunder Rajan has shown, the Indian discourse of women balances the virtues of homemaking with 'the project of modernization-without-westernization' so that they can serve as 'harmonious symbols of historical continuity rather than as conflictual subjects and sites of conflict'.[33] This model ensures that women do not overreach the specific social and political imperatives for which they are appropriated. In the present context, Achakka's sentiments and aspirations are a challenge to the construction of a feminine identity within the home, advocated by Gandhi and

[32] Ania Loomba, 'Overworlding the "Third World"', *Oxford Literary Review*, 13.1–2 (1991), 167.
[33] Rajeswari Sunder Rajan, *Real and Imagined Women: Gender, Culture, and Post-colonialism* (London: Routledge, 1993), 133; 135.

absorbed by Rao. Here again, we witness a contestation between fiction and history in the discrepancy between the dramatic and the ideological levels of narration: the grandmother separates herself from being merely an oral storyteller and assumes the dimension of a character who is no longer prepared to do what Rangamma advocates. On the contrary, she seeks to dedicate herself to the service of the nation like Lakshmi Bai. Perhaps Achakka is not prepared to make a contribution only in terms of spinning. That tactical move by Gandhi was possibly his way of enlisting women in the national struggle 'without shifting the terrain of their involvement from the household'.[34] Had Gandhi also intended to wage a feminist struggle side by side, on the other hand, he would be compelled to address a simultaneous participation at two interconnected levels: one 'ideological', addressing questions of representation; and the other, a more 'material' level which centres on work, home, family, sexuality, and so on.[35] Achakka, significantly, engages with more than simply the domestic; she feels magnified into Rani Lakshmi Bai, and is possessed by *shakti* or the primal, original power which renders the male principle in the godhead, *purusha*, passive, weak, and inferior.[36] Achakka's exaltation into Lakshmi Bai is even more striking when compared with her 'near-anonymous' characterization in the novel: even though she is the narrator, she is not created to excite curiosity in the reader, which may be part of the author's design to foreground the community rather than the individual.[37]

At the level of *shakti*, the female point of view assumes more significance than Rao is prepared to allow. The women-power grows as it assumes identification with the power of the village protector who is a goddess. The village owes its very origin to Kenchamma's accomplishments, and her legend is used as a choric refrain to ritualize the pattern of events affecting the lives of the villagers. The women believe Kenchamma to be present in each one of them, energizing them onwards. In fact, each of them becomes Kenchamma to the extent that they are unnerved by the fear of their own unnatural

[34] Patel, 'Construction and Reconstruction of Woman in Gandhi', 23.
[35] Chandra Talpade Mohanty, 'Cartographies of Struggle: Third World Women and the Politics of Feminism', in ead. et al., *Third World Women and the Politics of Feminism*, 21.                              [36] Nandy, *Edge of Psychology*, 35.
[37] See Ruth Vanita, '"Ravana shall be Slain and Sita Freed . . .": The Feminine Principle in *Kanthapura*', in Lola Chatterji (ed.), *Woman/Image/Text: Feminist Readings in Literary Texts* (New Delhi: Trianka, 1986), 188.

courage: 'we felt as though we had walked the holy fire' (187). Kenchamma is believed to have 'even settled down among [them]' (8) and that is why the women engage in a similar battle as Kenchamma did to kill the demon. It is Kenchamma's role as a woman, who is incarnated in the village women, that creates a new dimension in the novel, thus releasing their latent strength. In addition, it is Kenchamma's abiding presence in their lives that makes them take to Gandhi easily, not simply because both Kenchamma and Gandhi correlate on the level of sainthood, but, more importantly, because of the 'woman' in Gandhi: '"No, sister, I do not imagine the Mahatma *like a man* or a god, but like the Sahyadri Mountains . . ."' (176). He is not like their husbands, men who beat them up, but like a 'mountain', which serves also to link him with the Kenchamma Hill.[38]

The narration from a female perspective to an audience who, too, are women, adds to the impression of their growing power. An audience of 'sisters', however, does not imply that Rao expects only women to comprise his readership. The categorizing of the audience as female can be, in fact, a tantalizing and irresistible bait to attract male readership, and to increase the 'perlocutionary effect' on the readers, both male and female.[39] The accessibility of the story to female listeners may thus suggest Rao's investment in the seductive appeal of 'voyeurism' to gather listeners. In addition, while men are the excluded audience in the all-female gathering in the text, their presence is unrestricted in the reading of it. The narration, thereby, not only widens the span of the story to a mixed audience, but also raises the threshold of consciousness among women.

The aspect of feared womanhood is associated with matriarchal societies in India where goddesses, and not gods, are given first place.[40] These are areas where *stri-rajya* or the rule of women is predominant, unlike brahminic culture in which the patriarchal social system places

[38] Ruth Vanita, ' "Ravana shall be Slain and Sita Freed . . .": The Feminine Principle in *Kanthapura*', 190. The emphasis in the quotation from the text is Vanita's.

[39] Marie Maclean, *Narrative As Performance: The Baudelairean Experiment* (London: Routledge, 1988), 94.

[40] The matriarchal system has a special significance for Rao. While the evidence of the strength of the women in *Kanthapura* is tacit, *The Cat and Shakespeare* has direct references to female power since Shantha, the heroine, belongs to a matriarchal Nair family. See Raja Rao, *The Cat and Shakespeare: A Tale of Modern India* (Delhi: Orient Paperbacks, 1971).

restrictions upon the female sex.[41] The action of the novel appears to support matriarchal power through Achakka, and that is why the contrast between her narration and Rangamma's dictum is striking. While Rangamma does not envisage any fundamental change in the traditional role of women, Achakka, as the voice of a dominant matriarchy, unconsciously assumes authority and challenges the idea of a rigid division of labour between the sexes. She is impatient to move beyond an auxiliary role in the freedom struggle in the same way as the many women who had urged Gandhi to let them join the famous Dandi march. Gandhi had seen their eagerness as a 'healthy' sign, yet refused them participation with the ambiguous reasoning that they were 'destined' to make a far greater contribution to India's programme for independence in ways other than merely breaking salt laws.[42] In the novel too, the awakening *shakti* is restrained as the power of Kenchamma the mother goddess takes over from Kenchamma the woman. Significantly, the women's magnification into Kenchamma is envisaged only within the limits of the nationalist venture. At their routine level of existence, Kenchamma's red hill can only be an intimidating presence.

But even within the nationalist project, women-power must not be allowed to go unchecked or to become action oriented in spite of the obvious power of the discourse itself. In *Anandamath*, the powerful and destructive goddess Kali, who even tramples upon her spouse Shiva, is turned into Durga, the third of Bankim's three images in the monastery, who represents 'domesticated' power.[43] While Kali might represent unleashed power, her transformation into Durga is controlled by men, or as in Bankim's novel, by the *sanyasi* rebels. She is not allowed to remain an all-powerful woman who tramples upon *purusha*. The use of the woman in conceptualizing a nation thus becomes both fascinating and terrifying, fruitful and disrupting,

[41] Later brahminism differs from that of the Vedic period when most religious rites and ceremonies were open to women who had the same privileges of participation as men. It was later that the lawgivers opposed literacy in women and their right to study the Vedas. They declared women to be impure and hence unfit to receive education. Women were generally condemned, the prominent exceptions being the legendary husband-worshipping, devoted, and uncomplaining Sita or Savitri.

[42] Gandhi, 'To the Women of India', 121.

[43] Zutshi, 'Women, Nation and the Outsider', 100–1. Zutshi calls Kali the 'independent, uncontrolled woman, seductive, destructive, the woman who upends traditions and rules; the-woman-on-top, in fact.' Significantly, Kali bites her tongue in shame for having Shiva under her feet, and thereby represents the 'classic sign of social control internalized.'

because while a transformatory model can dispel a disappointing history and posit an India free from foreign representation, it also presupposes a changed social order. On the one hand, territorial identification is made by mobilizing representations and memories of a mythical past, timeless and resistant to change, and on the other, these very images '[militate] against the restlessness of modernity.'[44] Consequently, just as Gandhi's programme for women complemented their household roles which, to an extent, seemed to give them a sense of mission within their prosaic existence, Rao also secures their participation within limits so as to not upset the traditional Hindu image of the Indian woman, thereby freezing third-world women in time, space, and history. As Mohanty puts it, 'it is Indian middle-class men who are key players in the emergence of "the women question" within Indian nationalist struggles.'[45]

There is another section of women who have not been dealt with in a novel concerning peasant uprising—the peasant women at the coffee estate. Though the women at the plantation have smaller earnings than those of men, and live in fear of sexual exploitation, the 'Sevika Sangha' is formed only at the initiative of the brahmin women in the village. Parallels can be drawn with the feudal oppression of the Nizam and the Hindu landlords in the Telengana area of Hyderabad state (1948–51).[46] The basic feature in the life of the Telengana peasants was a continued feudal exploitation in the form of taxes and forced labour. For women, in particular, exploitation took the forms of concubinage, sexual assaults, and *adi bapa* where a young girl from a bonded family was made to accompany the bride to her husband's home and thereby provide sexual gratification to the master among other services. But the analogy cannot be maintained entirely because the Telengana women's exploitation led to an energetic and aggressive struggle for higher wages, moderate rates of interest on various loans, and, more than anything else, for the possession of land. With such a background, it was not surprising to see women drawn into political movements, aided especially by the Communist Party in Andhra which served as the base for the Telengana Struggle. For the women who moved eagerly into the struggle,

[44] Zutshi, 'Women, Nation and the Outsider', 135–6.
[45] Mohanty, 'Cartographies of Struggle', 20.
[46] Vasantha Kannabiran and K. Lalitha, 'That Magic Time', in Sangari and Vaid (eds.), *Recasting Women*, 180–203.

it was a possible opening in a world in which they had always been helpless and 'invisible'.[47]

The acute political awareness of the Telengana women's struggle offers a striking contrast to *Kanthapura* where hierarchies are dissolved and class agitations are suppressed in loyalty to the nation. It is odd that the novel shows us the anti-toddy campaign, but no particular basis in the women's experience that justifies their agitation. There are no instances of harassment of women by drunk husbands that would induce them to picket toddy groves. Rao consciously takes the thread of the story further and further away from the actual and lived experiences of the villagers by deepening the emphasis on Gandhi's religious philosophy, and attempts to dehistoricize their struggle so that women are not permitted to seize nationalism as a possible opening to let them out of their suppression. While the national movement could have prescribed a new dimension for women's lives, that of greater independence—interpreted as a kind of *swaraj*—within both domestic and public living, the Kanthapura women achieve little in altering the private domain. *Swaraj*, for them, remains loaded with religious significances. Towards the end of the novel, after having undergone initiation, we hear the women saying plaintively: 'Men will come from the city, after all, to protect us!' (231). Although they feel that despite their losses, they have gained something, 'an abundance like the Himavathy on Gauri's night' (255), their awakening is confined to a spiritual upliftment which claims legitimacy from the vision of the Mahatma: 'They say Rangamma is all for the Mahatma. We are all for the Mahatma. Pariah Rachanna's wife, Rachi, and Seethamma and Timmamma are all for the Mahatma' (257). While Moorthy moves away from Gandhi, the women remain within the timeless metaphysics generated by the author, content with reinforcing their faith in the *dharmic* ideal of the triumph of Good over Evil.

Surprisingly, while the Telengana revolt is known to have been 'the best period' for the women, it turns out that even theirs was 'a vision betrayed', for the women did not, in effect, 'make' history because they were 'judged and assessed' continually within 'the code of the private domain'.[48] And so the 'magic time' quality of the Telengana struggle and of *Kanthapura* does cohere in at least one way: the women retreat into their traditional lifestyles. The hegemonic project

[47] Ibid. 182.     [48] Ibid. 194–6.

of nationalism in both cases turns women into 'active agents in the nationalist project—complicit in the framing of its hegemonic strategies as much as . . . resistant to them because of their subordination under the new forms of patriarchy'.[49] In a recent essay, R. Radhakrishnan relates the absence of any form of politicization in the women's question to the easy manner with which they were spoken for and appropriated by the discourse of nationalism.[50] But on the other hand, to take women's politics away from 'the ideological presuppositions of so called gender-neutral methodologies' is to limit the thrust of all such 'single subject-positional politics' unless the women's question is conceptualized as a historical and political inevitability.[51] It is here that the categories of 'problematic' and 'thematic' in a nation-state, which Partha Chatterjee describes in *Nationalist Thought and the Colonial World*, can be invoked: in his terms, the Vedic Hindu woman would be the reverse of the orientalist problematic, the construction of which eliminates the possibility of the nation's thematic agenda or, in what is our concern here, the state of the subaltern as woman. And it is precisely because the problematic is fashioned by the nationalist intelligentsia, for whom 'progress', 'reason', and 'modernity' are imbibed from western nationalisms so that history and ideology in their own context are disjunct, that the nation-state thwarts the possibility of representing its people fully. It is thus that the women's question cannot be either liberated from or resolved within nationalist accounts.[52]

The issue here concerns how women were, in fact, conceptualized and imagined in the national movement. Within Gandhi's politics, women assumed a dimension they had never been given before. But although it is true that the motives for social regeneration in his rather contradictory attitudes were not too far removed from his ideological commitment, it was the national struggle that primarily motivated him to mobilize women. Rao uses Gandhi's premises to come out with a similar representation. Like Gandhi, he casts his

[49] Partha Chatterjee, *The Nation and its Fragments: Colonial and Postcolonial Histories* (Delhi: Oxford University Press, 1994), 147–8.

[50] R. Radhakrishnan, 'Nationalism, Gender, and the Narrative of Identity', in Parker, *et. al.*, *Nationalisms and Sexualities*, 80.

[51] Kumkum Sangari and Sudesh Vaid, 'Introduction', in eds., *Recasting Women*, 2–3. See also ibid. 79.

[52] For a discussion of the women's question and its ghettoization within the politics of nationalism, see Radhakrishnan, 'Nationalism, Gender, and the Narrative of Identity', 77–95.

women in a nationalistic framework but does not connect the nationalist sentiment with their social consciousness as peasants. In effect,
their ideological role in the novel, as also evinced in the Telengana
struggle, is constantly in conflict with the old feudal assumptions
which define them culturally and condition them socially. It is because
Rao employs them as mere symbols in a rhetoric of nationalism that
he fails to see how trapped they are within a predominant patriarchy,
thereby diminishing their role altogether.

In terms of such notions of nationalism, Spivak offers a cautionary
note against the appropriation of the subaltern by elite approaches.
She comes up against the voicelessness of the gendered subaltern in
building up the possibility of the recovery of the subaltern's site of
desire. The reason why subaltern identity cannot be recovered is to do
with the critic's own elite placement as an interventionist and the
inadequacy of working nativism as an alternative.[53] For who can tell
whether the nativist demands for nationality, ethnic self-consciousness, mythology, or cultural distinctiveness, as yet unrelated to modes
of self-conceptualization within their own culture, are not imbricated
with western categories of nationalism or even shades of imperialism.
This is a position from which the historians of the Subaltern School
also stand critiqued since their claims to be writing subaltern history

[53] Gayatri Spivak, 'The Rani of Sirmur', in Francis Barker *et al.*, *Europe and Its
Others: Proceedings of the Essex Conference on the Sociology of Literature*, 2 vols.
(Colchester: University of Essex, 1985), i. 140–7. Despite undergoing a historical
critique of her own position as the investigating person, Spivak attempts to open up
a space for the Rani of Sirmur. The Rani's narrative of emergence can lie only within
the archive installed by Company officials. She becomes one with the 'uninscribed
earth' of Sirmur that must be 'worlded' with epistemic violence by the 'alien agent
of "true" history'. Even in the act of *sati*, or sanctioned suicide, she is constituted
between 'patriarchal subject-formation and imperialist object-constitution'. Where on
the one hand, *sati* had been discussed in the *Dharmasastras* to be an act of self-
immolation willingly embraced by the woman who would be *sati*, thus making it an
emancipatory decision, on the other hand, to be dissuaded by the British to be victim of
a cruel practice that had to be put to an end, was equally a decision of free will. Yet, as
Spivak writes, 'Within the two contending versions of freedom, the constitution of the
female subject *in life* was thoroughly undermined.' This is so because her choice to live
would be a transgression of the Hindu patriarchy on the one hand and a submission to
the discourse of imperialism on the other. To examine the Rani from the subject-
position of the critic is to also lose her in First World theories of 'hegemonic "feminism"'. That is why, perhaps, Spivak falls incessantly into the 'confessional mode',
defining the locus of her position in her essays. See, for instance, Gayatri Spivak,
'Who Claims Alterity?', in Barbara Kruger and Phil Mariani (eds.), *Remaking History*
(Seattle: Bay Press, 1989), 276; and Gayatri Spivak, 'Asked to Talk About Myself . . .',
*Third Text*, 19 (1992), 9–18.

would tend to be dismissed as a 'myth of origins', and whose positions as interventionists would become loaded with benevolence. Nonetheless, it is important to bring deconstructionist studies to bear on historical representations in order to highlight the falsification or partial representation of 'historical reality'.

It may be argued, however, that even as poststructuralist methodology gives us direction towards greater self-awareness in speaking for the disenfranchised subaltern, any critique of imperialism or nationalism, as the case may be, does not leave much space from where to speak. On the other hand, to fall upon 'third worldism' or native purism is not to get out of the double-bind victimizing representationality or to reach the 'last philosophical discourse.'[54] A 'conscientious ethnography' that celebrates nativism has also to consider that 'the pure native is *not* some necessarily benevolent and good para-human creature, who is there to give us evidence that we must always trust'.[55] To embrace 'third-worldist' notions of the self or bring back the 'native informant syndrome' is to engage in a new sort of orientalism or neocolonialism in the endeavour to generate political potency.[56] But then, it can be contested equally hotly that deconstruction itself might be interpreted as neocolonialist hegemony in which the third world is disquietingly theorized into silence. The assertion that the retrieval of native voices or third-worldism is tainted may be a case of the interpreter silencing the subaltern, deferring in his or her own writing an investigation of the history of native agency.[57] Significantly, while the Telengana women's struggle and its consequences, in many ways, go hand in hand with Spivak's claim that the subaltern cannot speak, the assertion by the Telengana women that their resistance was not entirely futile resists

---

[54] Richard Rorty, 'Two Meanings of "Logocentrism": A Reply to Norris', in Reed Way Dasenbrock (ed.), *Redrawing the Lines: Analytic Philosophy, Deconstruction, and Literary Theory* (Minneapolis: University of Minnesota Press, 1989), 204.

[55] Maria Koundoura, 'Naming Gayatri Spivak' (interview), *Stanford Humanities Review*, 1 (1989), 93.

[56] Ibid. 84. For Spivak's definition of 'native informant', see Gayatri Spivak, 'Imperialism and Sexual Difference', *Oxford Literary Review*, 8.1–2 (1986), 225.

[57] By citing the powerful example of *sati*, Spivak, for instance, risks overlooking the presence of other realities and other myths. Not only does she limit hearing enunciative voices by her sweeping use of deconstruction, she paradoxically builds up woman as *sati* to the exclusion of her other roles and articulations. Moreover, as Loomba points out, the Rani was later discovered not to have committed *sati*. While Loomba does not celebrate the Rani's survival widely, she does intervene in Spivak's 'easy conclusions'. See Loomba, 'Overworlding the "Third World"', 185.

such an interpretation. Contrary to Spivak, the history of such struggles, especially in their specificity, cannot be shrugged off as a nostalgia for lost origins.

In terms of the above problematic, *Kanthapura* can also be seen as a text politically motivated by the repressive and resistant tensions of the era, bound as it is with the national movement. Even though Rao is highly selective in his encoding of the conditions which motivate the national struggle, our study can attempt to understand the writer's work, however conditioned by its middle-class origins, as part of an active struggle to establish national identity. In the interests of arousing a people, and shaping historical consciousness, *Kanthapura* must be seen within the genre of historical fiction emerging in India at that time. While *Kanthapura*, as a landmark of this genre, stretches the credulity of modern readers, it can be legitimized within the circumstances of the freedom struggle in which the desire to recover a lost past would have imparted an amazing degree of flexibility in the acceptance of mythical history. Apart from the political circumstances in which the genre evolved, the pre-existing narrative traditions—predominantly *puranic*—contributed to the tendency of situating narratives removed from the present. Since the existing traditions of *itihaas* did not attach particular significance to the presentation of facts, writers of historical fiction deviated easily from accuracy and verification. The predominant characteristic in such works is thus not so much their correspondence with what we believe to be the realm of reality, as their functionality in representing a glorified vision of India. This explains the excessively personalized view of Gandhi, and the emphasis on the man rather than the movement.

Rabindranath Tagore has encapsulated the 'true aesthetic experience of history' in terms of a cultural tradition within which the value of fabulation cannot be underestimated:

If, per chance, a great man, a maker of history, is living in our midst, we cannot perceive him and the larger span of history simultaneously through our fragmented vision . . . . In order to see such men not as individuals but as a part of history we have to stand back, place them in time so that we see them along with the enormous stage where they were protagonists.

This distancing from our ordinary lives is important. While we are whiling away our time in our fixed jobs, in laughter and tears, eating and sleeping, in the broad thoroughfares of the world the chariot of time is being driven by men larger than us. This realization gives us a momentary release from our circumscribed existence. This is the true aesthetic experience of history.[58]

Tagore's Nietzschean idealism defines history as a 'larger than life' enterprise and enables a legitimation of the particular character of Rao's historical fiction in projecting an experience that demands a suspension of disbelief. The mythicization of contemporary events thus serves an important function, that of transcending the ordinariness of existence and reaching a plane hitherto inaccessible to ordinary mortals.

It is not surprising, therefore, that Rao's account is believed to be credible and true. As Narasimhaiah has said:

I don't know how village life gets expressed in our regional languages but I do know I can't cite another authentic account of village life among novels written in the English language. Precisely the factors which may have served as a stimulus to writing in one like Raja Rao who knows his village, if any writer knows it, from the inside.[59]

In a similar vein, Naik believes that '[*Kanthapura* is] unique in Indo-Anglian fiction, perhaps the only successful attempt to probe the depths to which the nationalistic uprising penetrated, showing how, even in the remote villages, the new patriotic upsurge fused completely with traditional religious faith, thus rediscovering the Indian soul'.[60] To the extent that the novel convincingly constructs what are commonly believed to be the mythological qualities of the Indian 'soul', Rao's experiment is a remarkable success. His employment of a number of highly successful and innovative literary techniques stretches the regional and local dimensions of a small village to embrace the totality of India, and that totality guarantees its credibility.

[58] Cited in Meenakshi Mukherjee, *Realism and Reality: The Novel and Society in India* (Delhi: Oxford University Press, 1985), 57–8.
[59] C. D. Narasimhaiah, *Raja Rao*, (New Delhi: Arnold-Heinemann, 1968), 39–40.
[60] M. K. Naik, *Raja Rao* (New York: Twayne, 1972), 64.

Part III

# Repositioning of National Identity

# 5 The Future of a Vision

I move now to a more speculative part of the book which examines the trajectory of Rao's later fiction in terms of the earlier analysis of *Kanthapura*. While *Kanthapura* is contextualized in the history of the period, the ensuing analysis does not intend to pursue a similar exercise in the main, partly because the bulk of his fiction is written long after the achievement of independence, and partly since Rao's concern as an artist becomes more metaphysical and personal. It is possible, however, for the metaphysical to be seen as an extreme dimension of the nationalistic: having moved away from the political circumstances of the 1930s and the 1940s, Rao's metaphysical concerns are an assertion of the persistence of a fundamental Hindu tradition in a period of internal dislocation following independence, as also an anchor for personal dilemma. These are some of the issues that need to be mentioned in any consideration of Rao's later fiction comprising *The Serpent and the Rope* (1960), *The Cat and Shakespeare* (1965), *Comrade Kirillov* (1976), and *The Chessmaster and His Moves* (1988). The content of this chapter is ideological since it intends to raise questions related to the body of Rao's later fiction and to speculate on the development of his vision and its inherent contradictions through a brief internal study.

## I

Before turning to consider Raja Rao's vision of India, it should be mentioned that the publication of his novel, *The Serpent and the Rope*, followed *Kanthapura* by more than two decades. Rao described his lack of creativity to be a result of turning to metaphysics.[1] In *Kanthapura* itself, spirituality and religion had been used to define political/historical phenomena. By the time *The Serpent and the Rope*

---

[1] M. K. Naik, *Raja Rao* (New York: Twayne, 1972), 23.

was published, the motives of the struggle for independence and the accompanying Gandhian ideology had become more or less diffused and decentred. If in *Kanthapura* Rao's dehistoricizing of contemporary events held a predominantly historical novel within the romantic mode, history is abandoned altogether to fashion India as an idea or a metaphysic in *The Serpent and the Rope*. The metaphysic of India substitutes for the politics of the nation-state and creates a new identity removed from the recent turmoil of imperial possession and the consequent freedom struggle. As a story, *The Serpent and the Rope* has the usual features of post-colonial writing in which independent intuition and logic, and an emphasis on psychological problems, are the governing themes since the writer no longer bears the responsibility of maintaining national identity.[2] Correspondingly, the communal consciousness and the quality of shared experience present in the earlier novel are missing in the latter as we notice the detachment of the characters from all kinds of social responsibility. Rama's yearning for Truth is abstract and undefined, lacking the historical contextualization of the pilgrimage-metaphor of *Kanthapura* that had been concretized through Gandhi's Salt March.

However, despite the changed historical circumstances of the Indian nationalist project, the modernization programmes which accompany the formation of the nation-state and the resultant clash with the 'authentic', pre-industrialized past provokes a new defence of tradition and might provide an explanation to Rao's treatment of larger cultural themes. As Bruce King says, 'there will be cycles of nationalism followed by more internationalism, followed by more nationalism'.[3] The postcolonial period in India is one in which identities are redefined in a manner similar and yet different from the way they had been fashioned in periods of intense nationalism. The difference arises not simply as a result of the end of colonialism,

---

[2] 'Postcolonial', here, refers both to the 'historical break' signifying the end of colonial rule and to an 'ideological orientation' which carries the implication of some form of continuing resistance as well as oppression, but not freedom from the weight of neocolonial tendencies. For an understanding of 'postcolonial' in the way in which I use the term, see Harish Trivedi, 'India and Post-colonial Discourse', in Harish Trivedi and Meenakshi Mukherjee (eds.), *Interrogating Post-colonialism: Theory, Text and Context* (Shimla: Indian Institute of Advanced Study, 1996), 235–6; and Ella Shohat, 'Notes on the "Post-Colonial"', *Social Text*, 31–2 (1992), 107.

[3] Bruce King, *The New English Literatures: Cultural Nationalism in a Changing World* (London and Basingstoke: Macmillan, 1980), 44–5.

but also as a resistance to what Nandy calls 'the second colonization' which survives nationalism.[4] Postcolonialism, in many ways, thus witnesses a replay of the earlier preoccupation with tradition, this time in order to combat the legacy of neocolonialism. With India's freedom secured, national self-consciousness was also subverted within the same culture in a different way.

During the nationalist phase, Rao undoubtedly uses the iconographic significance of Gandhi to fashion the Indian elite's self-identity by depicting Indian culture through populist modes. In his later novels, on the other hand, his themes become related to high Hinduism, an early concern, of course, but one which lay outside the area of nationalist politics. While Hindu revivalism was witnessed even in the early decades of the national movement, by the late 1920s, there was a discernible bent towards strengthening Hindu interests, arising mainly as a reaction to a growing insecurity among Hindus resulting from Gandhi's fair and equitable doctrines regarding minorities, and the attempts of the British to win over Muslims politically.[5] Gandhi, as we know, anti-intellectualized the dominant religious core of India by de-brahminizing Hindu culture.[6] Although his spiritual interpretations of the Indian past and its sacred texts often came close of those of the brahmin intellectuals, he was a prominent dissenter of brahminism, believing traditional brahminism to have outlived its utility.[7] He did not disclaim Hindu spirituality but instead reinterpreted and mobilized it for the non-brahminic periphery. Thus the absolute value of the Vedas and the Upanishads were substituted, to a large extent, by the Bhagavad Gita. Gandhi was also responsible for introducing politics into the Hindu *dharma*, thereby bringing

---

[4] Ashis Nandy, *The Intimate Enemy: Loss and Recovery of Self under Colonialism* (Delhi: Oxford University Press, 1983), p. xi.

[5] Richard G. Fox, *Gandhian Utopia: Experiments with Culture* (Boston: Beacon, 1989), 217.

[6] Ashis Nandy, *At the Edge of Psychology: Essays in Politics and Culture* (Delhi: Oxford University Press, 1980), 49; 72.

[7] Despite obvious differences, the Hindu cultural tradition corresponds with Gandhian philosophy to a large extent. The emphasis on the orientalist opposition between the spiritual, traditional east and the materialist, modern west is shared both by Gandhi and the revivalists. The consequent need for spiritual revolution and personal regeneration is also common to both sides, especially in the conflict with socialism and the issues of class-conflict. The difference, however, lies in their response to the ideal of 'unity in diversity': while the Hindu revivalists emphasize the absorptive nature of Hinduism, and the forcible eviction of the threatening dissenters, Gandhi treats unity in terms of a single identity—both nationally and in terms of a single god—who is not necessarily Hindu.

together what had always existed separately at a ruthless, 'amoral' political level of *arthashastra* (the science of politics) with the quite traditionally separate religious cultural centre comprising the concepts of brahminism.[8] However, while the very 'loose' nature of Hinduism allowed Gandhi to protest on the one hand, it also permitted the brahminical elite, on the other, to assimilate his structure of dissent within their orthodoxies. Nonetheless, Gandhi's belief that the meek would inherit the earth challenged brahminical patriarchy, which, while tolerant of ideological dissent, was vulnerable in the face of a public ethic that diminished its importance.

I see Raja Rao as an intellectual caught within the insecurity resulting from a repudiation of metaphysics during the nationalist phase. In his post-independence writing, in comparison, there appears to be a self-conscious return to a system of Hindu ethics which is inconsistent with the broad democratic principles on which the freedom struggle was based. For the brahminic elites, the continuity of tradition could not be ensured in any other way. Of course, the writer's consciousness is controlled to a large extent by his individual ethics, which, too, can be assimilated within the post-colonial problematic as being part of the confrontation between modern western history and traditional oriental wisdom. Although the former lacks 'authenticity' and the latter 'history', the historical and the personal have to unite in the mythicized category 'India' if the writer is to succeed in convincing both his audience and himself of the cultural superiority of the east. Raja Rao, as a postcolonial brahminic elite, can be situated both within the wider historical context of post-Gandhism as well as in a more narrowly personal and psychological bind which relates to his expatriation.

Rao's vision of India attains maturity and fulfilment with *The Serpent and the Rope* which explores the opposition between the east and the west, enacted through Rama and Madeleine. Rama works on his doctoral dissertation in France on the Albigensian heresy in the Middle Ages while his wife, Madeleine, is engaged in research on the Holy Grail, a central myth in European thought. Believing India to be the genesis of European civilization, they attempt to trace western myths and phenomena to Indian philosophy. Both, however, are engaged in a deeper quest—a spiritual definition of the self—which overwhelms even their academic pursuits. Rama,

[8] See Nandy, *Edge of Psychology*, 48–9.

identified with Parsifal, seeks to explore the purity of the Albigensian Cathars, and their relation to the features of Buddhism and Jainism. Madeleine, on a different plane, desires to achieve a perfect state of being, quite like the Cathars, by disavowing Catholicism and embracing Buddhism, which she hopes to arrive at through self-denial and a rejection of everyday materiality.

Though Madeleine's quest to reach a state of Buddhism is quite definitely 'Indian', Rama has little faith in her penance—'Madeleine's kingdom was not my world; her . . . Buddhist pigeons were not of my understanding.'[9] Her desire for perfection contradicts Rama's conviction in the paradoxical nature of the world and its beings: while the mind pursues Truth, the body yearns for all sorts of pleasures. In other words, Rama accepts the inevitable coexistence of a physical plane of living (illusion) with a quest for metaphysical idealism (reality), and the limits that the former imposes on the latter. Madeleine's Manichaean mysticism, on the other hand, tends to separate the two realms of existence: she believes that the world is the actual reality and that transcendentalism lies in dismissing the very real aspirations of the body. Unlike Rama, she cannot accept the simultaneous presence of the serpent and the rope, typifying the coexistence of the real and the unreal, which is the essence of *advaita vedanta* Rama is wedded to.[10] For Rama, the denial of the flesh, in fact, affirms its existence: 'Just the same way when she talks of Buddhism I feel the word *dukka* almost with the entrails dropping into my hand, whereas for her it is mere sorrow. *Dukka* is the very tragedy of creation, the sorrow of the sorrow that *sorrow is*.'[11] Clearly, Rama's perception of '*dukka*' is intuitive, an emotion he experiences almost physically. Madeleine lacks that inward sense of reality, and stands outside the system of recognition that Rama has internalized. She is, from Rama's standpoint, representative of a western intellectual tradition as opposed to an intuitive Indian one. For Rama, 'the impossible is the reality',[12] and that reality lies in 'the formless form

[9] Raja Rao, *The Serpent and the Rope* (Delhi: Orient Paperbacks, 1960), 385.
[10] The world, according to Rama, appears to be *maya* or illusion until the recognition of reality through true knowledge of the self (*atman*), and an intellectual apprehension of Brahman or the godhead is attained. The rope always appears to be a serpent to the ignorant who have not, as yet, seen Brahman. It is only the recognition of Truth that clears the mind of illusions or superimpositions whereupon appearance becomes reality. This is the philosophy of Sankara's *advaita vedanta*. Rao's own lineage has been traced to Sankara (AD 8).   [11] Rao, *Serpent and the Rope*, 80.
[12] Ibid. 168.

of Truth',[13] in brahminism, a complex synthesis of Hindu traditions modelled over thousands of generations. Correspondingly, he perceives Madeleine's desire for perfection in Buddhist austerities to be a European's understanding of an Indian system: 'her attraction towards, and eventual commitment to, a great Eastern religion based on intangible mystery, is in fact the purest demonstration of her Catholicism and European classicism.'[14] While intuition is not the privilege of the east alone, Rama's proud inheritance wills the reader to draw a line between a purely Indian experience, which does not permit foreign intrusion, and its supposed comprehension by a European. His apprehension of reality, thereby, must be interpreted within his own categories, which, from Madeleine's perspective, may be defined as 'romance'. As Rama sees it, the description of what is 'real' can only be settled with an understanding of its connotations in both the east and the west.[15] It should be observed, however, that Rama's intuition is not simply a comprehension which necessarily accompanies an insider; it is a metaphysical internalization which makes '*dukka*' substantially real and almost a concrete universal.

While Rama's epistemological understanding of the east might claim superiority in the realization of Truth, his separation from Madeleine cannot be seen entirely within essentialist dichotomies of east and west. Their divorce may also be perceived from the narrower vantage point of orthodox brahminism which diminished Buddhism as a living belief in India. Buddhism has been the cardinal deviation from Hinduism since it opposes the brahmins' sacrificial system and caste rules, an opposition which no devout Hindu can tolerate.[16] The relationship between Madeleine and Rama might not have suffered had she continued being a Catholic, and thereby remained true to her *dharma*.[17] Although Hindu chauvinists have repeatedly absorbed the separate existence and beliefs of the

[13] Rao, *Serpent and the Rope*, 403.

[14] Alastair Niven, *Truth Within Fiction: A Study of Raja Rao's 'The Serpent and The Rope'* (Calcutta: Writers Workshop, 1987), 16.

[15] The demand that Rao be tested on his own ground evokes the argument of Ch. 1, of the particular nature of the Indian reality which Rao offers in contrast to the western parameters of the 'real'.

[16] Theodora Foster Carroll, *Women, Religion, and Development in the Third World* (New York: Praeger, 1983), 89.

[17] In the Gita, Krishna instructs the warrior Arjuna: 'Better is one's own *dharma* which one may be able to fulfil but imperfectly, than the *dharma* of others which is more easily accomplished. Better is death in the fulfilment of one's own *dharma*. To adopt the dharma of others is perilous.'

Untouchables and the Muslims, not to speak of the Buddhists and the Jains, into an assimilative Hinduism in the interest of unity,[18] the model no longer works for Rao since he appropriates a more aggressive Hindu 'nationalism' in a changed political situation in which 'deviants' must either be subordinated or removed.

The symbolic opposition to Madeleine is represented through Savithri who alone recognizes Rama's Self in her being, and thereby responds to him in the same way as Maitreyi did to the sage Yagnavalkya, Rama's Upanishadic ancestor. Rama is drawn to Savithri because she corresponds to the perfect Hindu wife who 'weds her [husband's] gods' as Rama had once tried to wed Madeleine's and failed.[19] It may be questioned why Rama's own desire to embrace Madeleine's gods is not taken as a breach of his Hindu *dharma*. In fact, Rao's hero alternatingly takes the positions of a universalist and a chauvinist which is not surprising considering his physical placement in Europe. The ceaseless connections he seeks to establish between his station abroad and the landscape and myths of his country, dictated by the twin themes of illusion and reality, are both an attempt to reduce the gap between the two as well as a retreat into roots. Myths, both indigenous and foreign—the Tristan and Isolde myth which corresponds with the love saga of Krishna and Radha, the myths relating to Satyavan and Savithri, and Abelard and Eloise—are evoked perhaps in nostalgia or to effect, in Bruce King's terms, a linkage between the 'national' and the 'international'. While the novel records the story of the rift between Rama and Madeleine

---

[18] As Atal Behari Vajpayee said in 1961: 'The Muslims or Christians did not come from outside India. Their ancestors were Hindus. By changing religion one does not change one's nationality or culture.' Cited in Bruce D. Graham, *Hindu Nationalism and Indian Politics: The Origins and Development of the Bharatiya Jana Sangh* (Cambridge: Cambridge University Press, 1990), 96.

[19] For Rao, the devotion of the wife alone fulfils her husband. He wants his woman to be Parvati, Shiva's spouse, whose absorption into the male can recover for the man a state of primordial formlessness. Shiva symbolizes 'essence' in passivity; it is Shakti, the female principle, who animates the essence and gives it form. In each cosmic cycle, Shiva is believed to come out of his meditation and absorb Shakti, thereby annihilating the world and generating a new phase of creation. At a metaphorical level, Rama (and later, Sivarama in *The Chessmaster and His Moves*) aspires for such a union with woman that can banish the world and its chaos and bring him to the discovery of *Shivoham* or the realization of oneness with God. See Uma Parmeswaran, 'Siva and Shakti in Raja Rao's Novels', *World Literature Today*, 62 (1988), 574–7. S. Nagarajan has also explained the male and female principles in terms of *purusha* meaning the Lord of Creation, and *Prakrati* or the woman. See S. Nagarajan, 'An Indian Novel', *Sewanee Review*, 72 (1964), 512–17.

who represent the incompatible 'culturalisms' of the east and the west, the imagined connection between the sacred nature of the Ganges and the Rhône suggests a universal sisterhood as if to culminate in a mythic India. In *Kanthapura*, too, the expanding metaphor, India, had been perfected through the symbolic convergence between Indian rivers. But the universalism effected here is far more difficult to realize since the author's world view precludes outsiders.

It is Savithri who draws Rama out of his confusion and guides him towards Knowledge, which culminates in the guru figures of Rao's later novels.[20] Correspondingly, the epigraph to the novel is quoted from Sri Atmananda Guru: 'Waves are nothing but water. So is the sea.' At a symbolic level, water relates to the past since the ancient Indian rivers have their origins in antiquity and myth, and the continuation of that past into the present. The river Ganges, in particular, becomes a potent symbol of continuity and permanence along with conveying the passing nature of Truth. The subsequent brahminic belief in *Antaranganga* or 'The Ganga/Ganges is within one', strengthened by the conviction that all rivers are Ganges, asserts the common origin of all Indians, and even non-Indians, in brahminism. The connection is strengthened by the metaphor of bridges, which, however, are not crossed.

At another level, the Ganges may be an important organizer of the novel's narrative structure, and in the positioning of the narrative voice. Rama's narration begins as he floats down the Ganges in which his ancestors' ashes have been immersed according to Hindu rites. The permanency of both the river and the narrator's origins are thereby ensured. It is not difficult to relate the first-person narrative voice in the present with the antiquity of the river by the holy city of Benares Rama visits early in the novel. The character of storytelling thus acquires an antique flavour, as in *Kanthapura*, which is part of the continuum of Benares: 'Somewhere on these very banks the Upanishadic Sages, perhaps four, five or six thousand years ago, had discussed the roots of human understanding.'[21] But unlike *Kanthapura*, *The Serpent and the Rope* is distinguished by the nature of its dialogue which corresponds to the Upanishads, the supreme texts of the Hindus:

---

[20] In Hindu philosophy, salvation can only be attained through one's guru who alone can show the path of light.    [21] Rao, *Serpent and the Rope*, 23–4.

'When seeing goes into the make of form and form goes into the make of seeing, as the Great Sage says, "what, pray, do you see?"'

'You see nothing or, if you will, yourself,' answered Savithri, and I wondered at her instant recognition of her own experience.

'Therefore, what is Truth?' I asked. By now we were near Fort Sarrasine at the edge of the plateau of Les Baux, with the whole of La Camargue beneath us.

'Is-ness is the Truth,' she answered.

'And Is-ness is what?'

'Who asks that question?'

'Myself.'

'Who?'

'I.'

'Of whom?'

'No one.'

'Then "I am" is.'

'Rather, I am am.' . . .

'There is no Savithri,' I continued after a while.

'No, there isn't. That I know,'

'There is nothing,' I persisted.

'Yes,' she said. 'Except that in the seeing of the seeing there's a seer.'

'And the seer sees what?'

'Nothing,' she answered.

'When the I is, and where the Nothing is, what is the Nothing but the "I."'

'So, when I see that tree, in that moonlight, that cypress, that pine tree, I see I—I see I—I see I.'

'Yes.'

'That is the Truth,' she said, as we turned and walked back to the village.[22]

Rama's route to truth may be inaccessible and dense, but the tautological word-play is a valid form of debate in traditional Indian rhetoric. The quest for Knowledge and Truth is a Vedic quest since the holy texts of the Vedas are etymologically linked with the word *vid* or 'to know'. Rama's forms and techniques of investigation, then, are in accordance with the Vedic idea of knowing oneself as a necessary prerequisite to knowing Truth. The Upanishads emphasize the self-affirming cycle as well.[23] Like the axioms offered in the Upanishads, Rama's arguments begin by stating an unknown proposition that develops with the help of comparable similes borrowed from

---

[22] Ibid. 130–1.
[23] The Upanishads, in fact, contain the essence of the Vedas, and are sometimes referred to as Vedanta.

nature, and culminate with an assertion of the original statement.[24] The philosophical debate between Rama and Savithri also begins from the abstract premisses of Sankara's *advaita vedanta*, and is then worked out through a systematic dialogue between the two principles, man and woman, to be resolved only when the two unite in an intuitively known, non-dual 'Self'. The dialogue also moves from the unknown to the known. Clearly, Knowledge and Truth pre-exist human intelligence. And so, the reader of Rao's novel has to subscribe to the understanding that non-dualism can be attained only through the recognition of the self-evident truth, not by definition; through eastern 'knowing', not by western 'intellectualizing'. In principle, the aspect of recognition has suggestive affinities with the way one 'knows' literature, in a manner holistic rather than aggregative, which also depends for its efficacy on a kind of assent or belief by the reader. The circling nature of Rama's narrative, technically, then, is suitable to the idealist individualism of his philosophical Sanskritic tradition.[25]

It has to be pointed out, however, that the Upanishadic tradition has no place for the genre of memoirs or autobiography so that the philosophical play or *lila* offers scarcely any space for the circumstantial presence of Fort Sarrasine, Les Baux, and La Camargue. The return from the elevated to the mundane creates a tension between the metaphysical and the dramatic. The intrusion of the local and the historical upon the timelessness of traditional Hindu discourse disrupts the metaphysics of the novel as the reader is jerked back from the Upanishadic representation of Indian philosophy to a consideration of Rama's physical presence in France. However, the French environment can be accounted for if one accepts the intuitive 'Indian' option of reading, and assimilates France within the philosophy of *advaita* which acknowledges the coexistence of the real and the unreal. The reader's perception must therefore be modified to accommodate the local and the time-bound within the metaphysical and the timeless. This raises two interrelated questions: is the metaphysical representation of India the only alternative for an expatriate; or, is the French element in the narration an indication of Rao's universalism, of the generative power of India since 'somewhere, the Rhône must know the mysteries of Mother Ganga'?[26] The answer is related to

---

[24] Paul Sharrad, *Raja Rao and Cultural Tradition* (New Delhi: Sterling, 1987), 157.
[25] Ibid. 158.    [26] Rao, *Serpent and the Rope*, 245.

Hindu solipsism and its aggressive champions for whom the departure from metaphysics is inconceivable, both in terms of a disintegration of national identity following independence, and their personal isolation from their country. In the circumstances, Rao/Rama creates his own metaphysics from the knowledge of his illustrious ancestors which, consequently, becomes increasingly personal. Paradoxically, it is the distance and neutrality afforded by expatriation that permits his 'identity' to flourish and continue unreservedly.

## II

It is in *The Cat and Shakespeare*, Rao's subsequent novel, that the resolution of Rama's Upanishadic quest for Truth is attained. Rao uses the celebrated theory of *marjara-nyaya* or the cat-hold theory of Ramanuja to indicate the path of absolute surrender to Brahman.[27] The cat-figure exists simultaneously on the metaphysical, the philosophical, and even the literal planes of the novel as a guide to the perceptive reader to uncover illusion and illuminate the real. It is intriguing why Rao uses Ramanuja's rival philosophy of *bhakti yoga* or devotion to God, when *The Serpent and the Rope* is quite obviously based on Sankara's *jnana yoga* which does not allow the infiltration of devotion in its intellectual apprehension of Brahman. It has been argued by many that the two great teachers expounded different philosophies, and that Ramanuja vigorously opposed the doctrines of Sankara.[28] Ramanuja did not believe in *maya* or illusion, and thereby respected human faculties more than Sankara could permit in his assertion of human susceptibility to illusion. Ramanuja also argued that Sankara was not a reliable interpreter of the Upanishads. While it is true that Sankara later admitted grudgingly to the common inability to make a distinction between the real and its illusion, Rao's defection to *bhakti yoga* marks a disregard of a widely accepted difference acknowledged among intellectuals. In this light, may we take Rao's monolithic model as evidence of the strength of his desire to syncretize and unify in the name of Indianness actual

[27] Brahman is a term signifying the Ultimate Reality or the Absolute. Beyond definition, Brahman symbolizes the union of male and female principles and is hence neuter.
[28] W. S. Urquhart, *Vedanta and Modern Thought* (Delhi: Gyan Publishers, 1986), 58–9.

Indian traditions which were quite opposed?[29] If so, why cannot Madeleine's Buddhism be subsumed within Hinduism on the same principle as the consolidation of the philosophies of Sankara and Ramanuja?

Like the earlier novel, the narrative in *The Cat and Shakespeare* is an exercise in uncovering reality through the many-layered dialogue based on Sankara's *advaita vedanta*. The essence of the Upanishadic discourse lies in an unquestioning acceptance of the teaching, and requires a complete belief in the system of knowledge. An Upanishadic narrative underscores the sacral nature of the relationship of the guru and the *shishya* or disciple, which works on the assumption that the guru is the divine repository of knowledge, being thus invested by the gods themselves. It is therefore part of the *shishya's* religious duties to make his guru his god.[30] In fact, the narrative structures of both *The Cat and Shakespeare* and *Comrade Kirillov* accommodate the guru-figures—Govindan Nair and Kirillov—who overwhelm their disciples, also the narrators, and admit them into new worlds. *The Cat and Shakespeare* concludes with an unambiguous celebration of an intense religious experience in which Ramakrishna Pai, the narrator hero, for the first time, recognizes reality—*tat tvam asi* or 'that art thou'.[31] Kirillov, on the other hand, is a quite different guru who makes Marxism his metaphysics, and is intellectually as convincing in his system as Nair is in Vedanta. *Comrade Kirillov*, however, makes a complete volte-face towards the end when the guru is discovered to be a Vedantin despite his loyalty to the Party, enabling the narrator, R, to hold back from politics despite his apparently 'false' guru.

The guru-*shishya* relationship in the Hindu system underwrites the relationship between the author and the reader. The essential prerequisites of a *shishya*—recognition and acquiescence to a supreme authority—ultimately link up with the role of the reader who is expected to possess these features to appreciate the teaching of the author/guru. The reader, accordingly, has to be equipped to submit to both the author's superior cultural knowledge of India, and to his

[29] The philosophies of dualism and non-dualism, though opposed, take their origins from the philosophy of the Upanishads.

[30] Translated, Upanishads mean 'to sit near'. The Upanishadic tradition necessitates that the reader/initiate should sit close to the author/teacher in order to learn of Truth.

[31] 'Chandogya Upanisad', in *The Principal Upanisads*, trans. and ed. S. Radhakrishnan (London: Allen and Unwin, 1953), vi. 8. 458.

divine attributes. The author, on his part, illuminates the journey from ignorance to light, treating literature as *sadhana*—as a devotion, not a profession.[32] For Rao, 'unless word becomes *mantra* no writer is a writer, and no reader a reader'.[33] The novel must then be read as a prayer, or a religious chant. It is clear that Rao does not care for the reading public or indeed for the clarity of communication, since the reader must be an initiate with a cultural inheritance. Moreover, the surrender to the superior intellect of the guru implies the abandonment of the reader's critical judgement as well. This is undoubtedly founded on quite different premises from those informing both the western novel and western society.

While the nature of the relationship between the author/guru and the reader/disciple underlines the monist systems of both Sankara and Ramanuja, the prospect of witnessing the disciple's relation to a Marxist guru, Kirillov, within the implication of surrender to the Party is intriguing. Being a *sadhak* or devotee, the reader is expected to have a pre-existing knowledge that the Marxist is really a crypto-Vedantin, and that his journey is mapped out in advance. Rao gives an insight into the misguided Marxist largely by juxtaposing Kirillov's faith in the Party's dogma against the contradictory run of history. Being a good Marxist, Kirillov respects Stalin's injunction to Indian Marxists to suspend agitation until the victory of the allies. In retrospect, we know that the Marxists were wrong, and that India's independence was, in fact, facilitated through the Quit India Movement of 1942. To disprove Marxism by a pure appeal to history, however, amounts to using an illegitimate form of irony at the expense of the character. To call upon history, furthermore, is to be inconsistent with the timeless philosophical principles Rao purports to be using.

Since the metaphysical cannot coexist with the material, the fascination that Marxism exercises for Rao is intriguing. As early as *Kanthapura*, Rao records Moorthy's conversion to socialism even though the change is attributed to his confusion. Later, in *Kirillov*, the author's choice of the hero as a kind of later Moorthy, again questions his appreciation of Marxism within the quintessence of Indian spirituality. It is true that at a point Rao had joined the socialists in India. He also edited *Whither India?* which includes an essay on socialism by Jaya Prakash Narayan, a committed Marxist of

---

[32] S. V. Vasu, 'Raja Rao: Face to Face', *Illustrated Weekly of India* (1964), 44.
[33] Raja Rao, 'The Writer and the Word', *The Literary Criterion*, 7.1 (1965), 78.

the 1930s.[34] It can be debated that Rao's fascination for Marxism must necessarily have grappled with Indian spirituality if his novels are anything to go by as evidence. Yet the deviant heroes are either abandoned like Moorthy who threatens the ideological unity of *Kanthapura*, or depicted to be misguided and confused like Kirillov. As Rao says: 'I am interested in authenticity. One should be authentic. . . . It is to those who are not authentic that misery comes.'[35] Such 'authenticity' in Rao's works is double-edged since the victory of Vedanta appears to be adulterated with a sincere appreciation of Marxism. The final triumph, needless to add, lies in the spiritual, identified with Brahman.

Spiritualism, it must now be evident, has been the largest denominator of the Hindu way of life, and its expediency in ideological formations is significant, both before and after independence. In the late nineteenth and early twentieth centuries, Hindu traditionalists like Vivekananda, Aurobindo Ghose, and Annie Besant sought to stimulate national pride through the Ramakrishna mission school of Vedantism, the culturally assertive neo-Hinduism, and the Theosophical Society.[36] The Theosophists, in particular, endeavoured to revitalize the original caste system which had gradually become diffused and splintered. They emphasized the need for a change from the physical to the astral to attain a release from the mundane. The Theosophical Society gained currency among the intellectuals since its western guardianship legitimized traditional Hindu metaphysical values of the union of the self (*atman*) with Brahman, although at a vulgar level.[37] Significantly, the Vedantic union between *atman* and *brahman* has been appropriated more recently by the Hindu right wing in supporting the issue of Ram Janmabhoomi, or the tussle regarding the birthplace of Rama in Ayodhya.[38] The exclusivity of Rama as god is at the same time linked with the pluralistic character of

---

[34] Jaya Prakash Narayan, 'Socialism: A System of Social Organisation', in Raja Rao and Iqbal Singh (eds.), *Whither India?* (Baroda: Padmaja Publications, 1948), 71–95.

[35] Cited in Sharrad, *Raja Rao and Cultural Tradition*, 125.

[36] We notice that Hindu scriptural authority occupied a pride of place, and scriptural support had to be sought both for maintaining tradition as well as in deviating from it. Social reformers like Raja Rammohan Roy, Ishwarchandra Vidyasagar, and Dayanand made endless forays into the scriptures to initiate reform movements in India.

[37] Suresht Renjen Bald, *Novelists and Political Consciousness: Literary Expressions of Indian Nationalism, 1919–1947* (Delhi: Chanakya, 1982), 10–12.

[38] See Introduction, n. 46.

Hinduism so that he both embodies common reverence and subsumes ideological difference, or, in other words, 'the notion of an inner desire that corresponds to and realizes itself in a universal feeling'.[39] The same principle is employed in *Kanthapura* where the pluralism of India is synthesized in the homogeneous worship of Kenchamma.

In post-independence societies, much use is made of the belief that religion is the only solution in a world going increasingly over to modernity and social change. In order to consolidate a Hindu identity, the revivalist Virat Hindu Samaj, for instance, often called for a reinterpretation of the Inner Spirit of Hinduism. Another Hindu organization, the Rashtriya Swayamsevak Sangh (commonly known as the RSS), declared spiritual knowledge to be a divine trust given to Hindus by Destiny. For Golwalkar, material life and consumerism were crude western tools, having scarcely any solidity when compared with Hindu cultural essentials.[40] The denunciation of socialism as 'western' had always been part of the rhetoric of those who advocated an 'Indianization' of democracy: 'The RSS is not opposed to socialism as an egalitarian philosophy, but to the materialistic aspect of it which does not accord with our culture or our ethos, or the essential values of life we believe in.'[41] Apparently, the national development towards a future Hindu utopia could be guaranteed only through a revolution of the individual spirit, which was of primary importance when compared to the redistribution of wealth and property. In effect, current-day 'Hindutva', or the aggressive idea of Hindu nationhood, disguised as cultural uniformity, conceals the desire of the Hindu upper-class elite to exclude the masses from enjoying the democratic benefits of the new political nation. In one stroke, the dictum—'we are all Hindus'—discredits the 'struggle for new political emergence of the lower caste, tribal and Muslim masses' by its outwardly reasonable formulation.[42] The threat posed by the Muslim minority

---

[39] Pradip Kumar Datta, 'VHP's Ram: The Hindutva Movement in Ayodhya', in Gyanendra Pandey (ed.), *Hindus and Others: The Question of Identity in India Today* (New Delhi: Viking, 1993), 49.

[40] M. S. Golwalkar, *Bunch of Thoughts* (Bangalore: Vikrama Prakashan Chamarajpet, 1966), 1–10.

[41] Nana Deshmukh, *RSS, Victim of Slander* (New Delhi: Vision Books, 1979), 16. See also H. V. Seshadri, *Hindu Renaissance Under Way* (Bangalore: Jagarana Prakashana, 1984). Seshadri laments the havoc caused by the 'Missionary–Muslim–Marxist combine' to Hindu identity and national cultural integration.

[42] G. Aloysius, 'Trajectory of Hindutva', *Economic and Political Weekly*, 29.24 (1994), 1451.

is insignificant compared to the 'threat to the upper caste vested interests' from the 'egalitarian and pluralistic aspirations of the masses within formal democracy'.[43] From this viewpoint, the author's message of spirituality in *Kirillov*, is obviously part of his intention to prevent class structures from splitting up traditional Hindu solidarity and the related upper-class interests:

India is too powerful and too deep in an Indian to allow him to lead an alien life. She loves her children too much—and as long as Lord Siva is in Kailash and the holy Ganges flows from His hair; Indians will not betray their land— for the mother is bigger than all politics, all economics, all castes, all philosophies. India is of every Indian—of which Comrade Kirillov is only one![44]

India, as Rao sees it, is greater than all philosophies and histories.[45] Such a formulation has the all-too-familiar ring of the nationalist rhetoric, characterized on the one hand by evoking the sentiment of Mother India, and on the other by a select interpretation of its very plurality.

On the reader's part, compliance should come easily since the addresser is the guru. The corresponding Upanishadic form of narrative in both *The Cat and Shakespeare* and *Comrade Kirillov* is thus appropriate for describing a spiritual and timeless reality in which western notions of plot and character have scarcely any validity. There are hardly any incidents at the level of plot; the dramatic potential of the characters is also diminished by Vedantic philosophy. Though Kirillov exists outside the author's metaphysics, the turn of the narrative to diary entries indicates a tighter control over the character, for it is through the diary kept by Kirillov's wife that we get an insight into Kirillov the Vedantin. Further limitations are imposed upon the development of the characters by the use of 'I', not only in *Comrade Kirillov*, where Rao admits to being the narrator, but also in *The Cat and Shakespeare*, where the author's perspective is internalized through Ramakrishna Pai, whose name is mentioned only twice in the entire narrative, indicating the primacy of the author's interests over those of the character's.

---

[43] G. Aloysius, 'Trajectory of Hindutva', 1452.

[44] Raja Rao, *Comrade Kirillov* (Delhi: Orient Paperbacks, 1976), 1.

[45] Rao's attack on Communism as alien to the very soil of India could have sprung from his alarm at the 1958 election of a Communist government in Kerala state, next door to Karnataka.

In the journey towards knowledge, Rao's last and most recent novel, *The Chessmaster and His Moves*, identifies the guru as the chessmaster who sweeps away the disciple's incomprehension and raises the individual from the temporal to the Absolute, the *It*. Correspondingly, the enlightened narrator speaks of the idealized linguistics of Indian primary sounds, particularly *sunya*, or zero, in which all numbers have their origin, and to which all numbers return:

'There is a primary language . . . as there are formal numbers, some structure of our thinking that naturally understands ten instead of twenty, of root words instead of a word for every object that the chinese tried to paint and failed. Indeed there must be primary sounds, like particles in our nuclear universe, which act and react according to as yet unknown laws.'[46]

The 'structure' of thinking which Sivarama, the protagonist, speaks of has to be both intuitively comprehended and naturally communicated. This can be possible in the 'language of the gods' alone, for it is only when the language is eternal and unchanging that the comprehension of the word by the hearer/reader will correspond precisely to the effect desired by the speaker/author.[47] In other words, the extreme solipsistic individualism of the speaker can be reproduced in the hearer, quite unlike the reader/writer relationship in western forms taken to its extreme in deconstruction. It is thus that Sivarama attempts to go back to the eternal and the unchanging to establish a true communication with his hearers, which he feels the Chinese have failed to do. This poses the question why the learned brahmin falls prey to a common western misconception of the notion of Chinese characters. However, the poetic compression of the English language succeeds in creating a tightly organized rhythm and structure suitable for Sivarama's philosophical disquisitions. Again, Rao's continued use of the English language is mystifying within his concepts of high Hinduism since English is nowadays considered to be a means of attenuating 'fundamentalist nationalistic, demands for Hindi or regional language study—translated into a revival of "Hindutva"'.[48]

As in *The Serpent and the Rope*, the idealistic metaphysical speculations of a philosophically organized dialogue often have a

---

[46] Raja Rao, *The Chessmaster and His Moves* (New Delhi: Vision Books, 1988), 33. [47] Rao, 'Writer and the Word', 77.
[48] Rajeswari Sunder Rajan, 'Fixing English: Nation, Language, Subject', in ead. (ed.), *The Lie of the Land: English Literary Studies in India* (Delhi: Oxford University Press, 1992), 28.

repetitive quality of the syntax—'ten-twenty', 'words-word', 'act-react'—which enables Sivarama to create the impression of continuity and eternity as in the *puranas*. At the same time, it also introduces slackness and a common level of consciousness. Yet there are profound silences in the book which break conversation and are in keeping with the profundity of the thought. For the moment Sivarama is interrupted, the continuity of his dialogue comes to a halt, and he finds it difficult to resume speech. Partly the result of a stammer, the silence may also arise from the inability to convey 'pure sound' or *sunya*, the inexpressible, through the *puranic*. The silence comes at a point when he is asked to recount the story of Nachiketas who holds a dialogue with the god of Death on the nature of the Absolute. It recurs when he is asked to explain Brahman. In other words, the absence of language conveys that Brahman, whose recognition is intuitive and internal, cannot be explained through words. It is also possible that the novel, at the *puranic* level, is simply not adequate to carry the burden of metaphysics.

The author largely circumvents the difficulty by favouring the voice of the narrator. On a closer look, it becomes obvious that what appears to be a dialogue is in fact a monologue: the contribution of the listener/reader is minimal owing to the modest acknowledgement of self-ignorance. The reader's response is determined entirely by the control exercised by the narrator's position in the text. The conversations between Sivarama and Jaya, for example, are closed units of composition which are not allowed to generate the dynamics of the situation. The story, thereby, records little progress by way of linearity since a new conversation goes back to the premises of the previous conversation. Thus the liberalization afforded by the novel and, to some extent, by the *puranic* structure, are controlled by the narrator who creates a metaphysical system far tighter than that allowed by a sequential episodic narrative, largely because of the philosophical centre in *sunya*.

The pithy moralizing of the Vedanta furnishes the novel with a significant and new theme concerning India—the quality of being universally 'indian' [sic] which comes from the realization that India is 'no country, it's a metaphor'.[49] This is also the message of *Kanthapura* although the contextualization of the novel within history gives it a geographically defined immediacy. The later metaphorical repre-

---

[49]   Rao, *Chessmaster*, 36.

sentation of India indicates the growing imperialism of the nation-
state as it takes more and more people into its fold: '"There are no
indians. . . . India is no country, I told you. . . . Wheresoever one
dissolves is India—every thought when purely understood is India.
When Camus knows he is Camus, that is, there is no Camus, Camus
becomes an indian."'[50] The quality of being 'indian' does not simply
indicate a neo-nationalism to overcome a devitalized contemporaneity but the assertion of a larger cultural theme, *sunya*, which in its
very namelessness, shapelessness, and timelessness is all-consum-
ing.[51] That alone, for Rao, marks the final attainment for the initi-
ates, and shows the triumph of spirit over matter.

Tracing the trajectory of Rao's vision from *Kanthapura* to *The
Chessmaster*, we can see the evolution of a select Hindu India which
resolves Gandhi's moral concerns in the ideal representation of a
universal, all-embracing 'india'. Gandhi's concern for the little cultures and minorities of India was to become more and more insignificant by establishing links with the world, since Truth and God,
being Hindu cultural essences, are, at the same time, human univer-
sals. In effect, Rao comes very close to advocating a sentiment similar
to Tagore's belief in abandoning national boundaries and political
freedom as a cure to the world's problems.[52] His idea of universalism
finds parallels with Tagore's *Gora* where a juxtaposition of nationalist ideals and contemporary politics is shown to 'violate' the 'fundamental principles of Indianness and Hinduism'.[53] Yet Tagore was
not a revivalist even though his concept of Hinduism before 1905 was
predominantly brahminic. Rao, on the other hand, is willing to build
upon the category of 'India' which is both timeless and universal, yet
unashamedly static and narrow. Along with his sweeping assertions
about the universalist principle contained in India (*The Chessmaster*), we also receive a privileged and prejudiced account of that
very India (*The Serpent and the Rope*): for Rama, 'real' India lies
neither with the northerners who embrace 'extreme modernism with
unholy haste',[54] nor in the 'barbaric' city of Bombay. Brahminic

---

[50] Ibid. 37.    [51] See King, *New English Literatures*, 44; 50.

[52] Rabindranath Tagore, *Nationalism* (London: Macmillan, 1918), 97–130. In a
letter to C. F. Andrews, Tagore wrote: 'What is Swaraj! It is *maya*, it is like a mist that
will vanish, leaving no strain in the radiance of the Eternal.' Cited in Harish Trivedi,
*Colonial Transactions: English Literature and India* (Calcutta: Papyrus, 1993), 73.

[53] See Ashis Nandy, *The Illegitimacy of Nationalism: Rabindranath Tagore and the
Politics of Self* (Delhi: Oxford University Press, 1994), 40.

[54] Rao, *Serpent and the Rope*, 31.

purity, instead, seems to have been better preserved in the south which has not suffered the corruption of foreign invasions. It is ironic that an allowance is made for the Ganges which flows through the north. Again, it is part of Rama's selective Indian identity that the Upanishadic opening lines of the novel are surprisingly dismissive about the aristocracy of brahmins, the possessors of Truth: 'I was born a Brahmin—that is, devoted to Truth and all that. Brahmin is he who knows Brahman, etc. etc.'[55] This can be explained within the context of Rama's metaphysics: what otherwise appears to be bathos or mockery is a brahminic gesture of dismissal of the non-real or illusory brahmins who might be born into the caste but do not necessarily possess Brahman, the godhead.[56] At the very outset, then, the reader is asked to make a distinction between those who are only born brahmins and those who attain Brahman.

Rama's protection of a select and partial cultural category amounts almost to a racist imperialism which can both assume a universal alliance between nations and races and also make India and England into distinguishable and mutually insular concepts. The paradox helps to release him from the double-bind of advocating both codes, while at the same time shields his admiration for Europe from criticism by subsuming Europe within India. Or is it Rao's intention to testify not to the necessity of unity but to the inescapability of hybridity? The confusion may be resolved through the understanding that the expanding India is not a liberalization of his closed system. It is, instead, the assertion of universal supremacy built on Truth which is available only to the select. The universal quality of India does not, in other words, embrace the world, but rather perpetuates an imperialism for all those who submit to 'Indianness'. It is thus that his research on the purity of the Albigensians can be traced to Jainism and Buddhism, two deviant religions which could have belonged to India had they not deviated, just as the Albigensians could have been part of Christianity.

---

[55] Rao, *Serpent and the Rope*, 5.

[56] The novelist is quite fair in his depiction of these lesser brahmins, who are gluttonous, mammonistic, and, in Rama's words, 'like the crows asking for funeral rice-balls'. This class of brahmins may include Bhatta, 'the first brahmin' of Kanthapura, who is believed to have gone to Benares where 'for every hymn and hiccup you get a rupee'. See Rao, *Serpent and the Rope*, 12; and *Kanthapura*, 258.

III

In terms of the philosophy of *advaita vedanta*, the recognition of the west as *maya* and the east as reality is expected to be made by the discerning reader. The difference, of course, is metaphorical, not historical: India, or Truth, can be possessed only by those who recognize the difference between the serpent and the rope. This also explains the difference between Madeleine and Savithri. It can be said, therefore, that Rama's conception of Truth and its configuration within the governing leitmotif of illusion and reality presupposes an ahistorical world view. The enumeration of this cosmic theme together with the stories of the Ramayana, the Mahabharata, and of the Buddha, all filtered through a brahmin's senses, serves to create 'a timeless backdrop'[57] of a mythical land, substantiated by Kathleen Raine in her account of a conversation with Raja Rao in New Delhi:

'India' is a potentiality in us all, a state of being in which all may participate who can attain to it. Thus, paradoxically, the India of the Brahmins, that high and ancient civilisation perfected over millennia in the Indian subcontinent, is at the same time the ultimate universal reality to which all humankind aspires. Not by studying Sanskrit or Pali, by chanting mantras or bathing in India's most sacred river, but wherever humanity attains its highest potential, there India has been discovered: 'India is the kingdom of God, and it is within you. India is wheresoever you see, hear, touch, taste, smell. India is where you dip into yourself, and the eighteen aggregates are dissolved.'[58]

The consolidating metaphor, India, symbolizes the internal world of the spirit that is eternal.

Yet Rama purports to be a historian and a chronicler: 'I am not telling a story here, I am writing the sad and uneven chronicle of a life, my life, with no art or decoration, but with the 'objectivity', the discipline of the 'historical sciences', for by taste and tradition I am only a historian.'[59] The history he narrates is an account of his life which corresponds to timeless metaphysics. The possession of India by his all-knowing Self can only be a very arrogant, personalized view:

India was a continuity I felt, not in time but in space; as a cloud that stands over a plain might say, 'Here I am and I pour'—and goes on pouring. The

[57] Paul Sharrad, 'Aspects of Mythic Form and Style in Raja Rao's *The Serpent and the Rope*', *Journal of Indian Writing in English*, 12.2 (1984), 87.
[58] Kathleen Raine, 'On the Serpent and the Rope', *World Literature Today*, 62 (1988), 603.          [59] Rao, *Serpent and the Rope*, 231.

waters of that rain have fertilized our minds and hearts, and being without time they are ever present. It is perhaps in this sense that India is outside history.[60]

Since history appears to be inadequate to narrate his timeless 'India', Rama chooses to universalize a narrative that history is unable to control. It is in this sense that India, for him, is ahistorical. Further, the consciousness of having to project an integrated entity called India results in the narrator's/author's view of history. In his desire, thus, to effect an intellectual renaissance issuing from an elite cultural revival, Rama, as a historian, can only be a persuasive but not a credible narrator. It is finally in the acknowledgement and coalescence of a personal brahmin identity with the larger Brahman identity of a collective ideal called India that Rama/Rao is satisfied: 'Where . . . does . . . history stop, and where do you begin?'[61] This collective ideal holds within itself 'the historian's attempt to invest the events of the world with meaning, the individual's quest for continuity and integrated being, and the yogin/saint's exercise to exhaust the authority of temporal reality'.[62] For a western reader, however, his history is dubious, and can be credible only from a mythical, and by his definition, 'Indian' perspective which would be more romantic than real.

While Rama's India lies outside history, the Hindu right wing in India have brought their monolithic India well within the compass of history. In the last decade or so, the metaphysical nature of the religious accounts of India has been completely refashioned to produce a history of Ayodhya which in the India psyche had always existed on the psychological rather than on the literal plane. By giving a historical account of events, right-wing 'historians' now claim to have reached the truth, to a geographical certainty about the exact location of the Hindu god Rama's birthplace. In many ways, the rewriting of Hindu history is similar to the early experiments in history-writing where myth and meaning were inseparable. But in its very claims to historicity, which it paradoxically dehistoricizes by allowing for 'no change or development in the character, position, interests, behaviour . . . of its several protagonists,'[63] it is removed

---

[60] Rao, *Serpent and the Rope*, 247.    [61] Ibid. 196.

[62] Sharrad, *Raja Rao and Cultural Tradition*, 76.

[63] Gyanendra Pandey, 'Modes of History Writing: New Hindu History of Ayodhya', *Economic and Political Weekly*, 29.25 (1994), 1523.

from the 'factual'. The writing of such histories, fashioned out of myth, is an interesting case of fiction conforming to fact.

With such an ideal, it is perplexing why Rao writes a novel at all instead of a metaphysical or a philosophical treatise. David McCutchion criticizes the very form of the narrative, questioning its right to be a novel when it lacks plot and characterization which are the central concerns of a western novel.[64] Yet *The Serpent and the Rope* can be read as a novel: the story of Rama, his separation from his European wife, and his symbolic marriage with Savithri are indeed signs of a plot. Some critics have read it as a novel with a philosophical theme.[65] The problem arises in yoking the novelistic to the metaphysical, for the western novel form, however indigenized, has the potential to ruin Rao's project. A deep and abiding concern with timeless Indian metaphysics is bound to be antithetical to the linear progression of a novel, and betray Rao into inconsistency.

From the point of view of the author, the novel form does ensure a wide readership, and constructions of identities would be meaningless in terms of the audience if worked out entirely in philosophical treatises. The coexistence of the western novel and eastern wisdom is also compatible with the dichotomy he presents. In addition, what is lacking by way of a local narrator is made up, to an extent, by the written mode, enabling the print medium to disseminate the writer's word. The novel can therefore be significant in terms of the formation of historical consciousness in the postcolonial phase. As for the audience outside India, it is again the novel which would be read to reveal what 'real' India is. However, as one critic has put it:

The Indian elite have nowadays changed their strategy. They are now vigorously pursuing the policy of Indianisation. . . . They would have loved it . . . if Time had stopped on the banks of the sacred Ganges. One may delude oneself into the belief that in turning to ancient India we are trying to discover our roots.[66]

Rao is clearly among those who continue to see India from a perspective located in antiquity. His purposes for positing such an India are equally evident. The urge to evoke an ancient cultural and

---

[64] David McCutchion, 'The Novel as Sastra', in Meenakshi Mukherjee (ed.), *Considerations* (New Delhi: Allied Publishers, 1977), 92.

[65] See, for instance, C. D. Narasimhaiah, *Raja Rao* (New Delhi: Arnold-Heinemann, 1968).

[66] R. B. Patankar, 'The Three Alternatives', *The Literary Criterion*, 19.1 (1984), 55–6.

spiritual tradition that disregards historical mutation centres on an ideal which is an inverted tradition foisted on the present. In effect, Rao's vision permits, though it does not necessarily entail, an unchanging perspective of India built by the orientalists. Within Said's terms, Rao's metaphysical stereotypes may not be part of the orientalist categories of a fecund orient, but the homogeneous nature of his construction allows us to view the metaphysical and the orientalist at one level. Rao's identification with Indian culture as the spiritual centre of the world personalizes and reiterates the classical orientalist representation of the orient as pantheistic, spiritual, and primitive. By contrasting Indian civilization with the products of western Enlightenment—Darwinism, Marxism, Social Realism, Positivism, Reductionism, Existentialism, Pragmatism, Imperialism—Rao seeks to inspire certain absolute and essentialist characteristics of the east which are identifiable with theism, spiritualism, idealism, humanism, and civilization itself. So monolithic is his idealized representation of India that it cannot permit fragmentation by any form of western intervention, be it Madeleine's 'heresy' or Kirillov's Marxism.

In addition, the neglect of plot, dramatic interest, and characterization can be taken as signifying the 'oriental', abstract, 'inscrutable', and the *puranic* which would be gratifying to both the Indian and the western readers looking for the exotic or the 'real' India. The reader's discovery of this India is facilitated by the author's translation of Sanskrit quotations in the text.[67] In view of Rao's audience and his depiction of the 'real' India, it would not be incorrect to say that Rao himself seems to be within the heart of an orientalist tradition worked out in reverse.[68] He is, to a certain extent, himself the 'other', being an expatriate. So is his protagonist, Rama, who lives in France while he advocates Indianness. Rao has striven to nourish his vision of India and to keep it alive all through his existence outside his country, and it is, perhaps, the expatriate soul that prescribes the construction of a particular model. One can see the reproduction of such themes in the many 'festivals of India' abroad. While Rao's mode of operation may be appropriate to the

[67] Incidentally, the passages in European languages are left untranslated, so that their accessibility is limited to either the western reader or the educated Indian one.
[68] Sadik Jalal al-'Azm, 'Orientalism and Orientalism in Reverse', *Khamsin*, 8 (1981), 5–26. Jalal al-'Azm warns the 'orientals' against being tempted to apply the ready-made structures and ontological biases of orientalism against themselves.

mentality of the diaspora positioned in the western academic world, his prejudices and convictions nevertheless approximate to orientalist constructions. His view of India, as we have seen, begins to reproduce the ideology produced by the colonial power almost as a collaborative venture so that his attempt at proving the ontological superiority of the oriental mind becomes very similar to the way the orientalists sought to prove the opposite. Despite all Rao's attempts to build a pristine identity issuing from indigenous idioms, he cannot abandon the correspondence he evokes with the orientalist problematic. The conservative belief in an ageless indigenous tradition—the brahminic— as an authentic and Indian cult tradition confirms his spiritual leanings debated in the analysis of *Kanthapura*. Rao's faith in this tradition also demonstrates that Indians themselves have accepted a history of their society and religion which was devised by the west.

# 6    Fixity and Resistance

> There was an extra festival on the calendar, a new myth to celebrate, because a nation which had never previously existed was about to win its freedom, catapulting us into a world which, although it had five thousand years of history, although it had invented the game of chess and traded with Middle Kingdom Egypt, was nevertheless quite imaginary; into a mythical land, a country which would never exist except by the efforts of a phenomenal collective will—except in a dream we all agreed to dream; it was a mass fantasy. . . and would periodically need the sanctification and renewal which can only be provided by rituals of blood.
>
> Salman Rushdie, *Midnight's Children*
> (New York: Avon, 1980), 129–30.

## I

From the study of Raja Rao's historical fiction to an analysis of his later writing, we have moved from a model which positions national identity staunchly through innovative experiment with language and myth to a metaphysical recreation of India. As we have seen, the rise of modern Indian literature in English developed simultaneously with nationalist and political ideologies. It was a new literature, the output of the elite, in which the pressures of colonization and the stresses and strains of the national movement resulted in a kind of fiction characterized by the coexistence of western forms of writing and indigenous themes. Although Victorian rhetoric or the eighteenth-century novelistic traditions did much to influence this writing, nationalist fiction was basically drawn towards a representation of the lost past through an emphasis on traditional culture. This was a paradox that continues even today in most Indian writing in English. Rao's *Kanthapura* is also part of that endeavour to take the reader back to rural roots believed to be the true repository of Indian culture. *Kanthapura* is indeed conceived as a text for those of us who have moved away from our true identity. As I have shown, the nostalgia for tradition appears to issue from an awareness of the difficulty of building a nation from India's various languages and religions. Nonetheless, Raja Rao has succeeded in creating an 'Indian' novel through the sophisticated portrayal of local culture. In his attempt to build a national community, Rao becomes part of the nationalist intelligentsia of the country.

*Kanthapura* displays none of the critical attitudes to the new nation as seen in their various ways in Soyinka's *A Dance of the Forests*, Naipaul's *The Mimic Men*, or Anantha Murthy's *Samskara*.[1] On the other hand, the novel offers folk culture to an elite readership who read and write in the English language. Rao hopes to build a national culture in which the readership comprising literate people in the cities can develop a recognition of a putative Indian tradition that exists in its villages. *Kanthapura* is thereby an important text in the evocation of the solidarity that is presumed to exist between all classes of people in the fight for freedom. It is the expression of the realization of this ideal in terms of fiction that closely follows the pattern of many nationalist histories.

An examination of the author's ideological purposes through the employment of contextual evidence and literary principles suggests that nationalism is an urban movement of intellectuals, involving the conception of an idyllic authentic culture of the past presumed to be enjoyed by pre-industrialized, rural groups.[2] I have argued that nationalism relies paradoxically on the 'little' traditions of the countryside for its definitions of authenticity and purity although it is a movement initiated in the cities. The sentiment of nationalism thus builds a sense of solidarity with the peasantry, who appear to have scarcely any role in social change or processes of modernization. The rural ethnic groups, on the contrary, are often in conflict with the culturally 'foreign' elites who occupy important social positions. And even though national movements may finally filter down to the masses through these very elites and intellectuals, the villagers, in many cases, have no real need of nationalism.

The reconstruction of a usable past by writers of both history and fiction appears, within this argument, to be a misrepresentation of

---

[1] Anantha Murthy's attempt at 'demythifying reality' in *Samskara* is well explained in his autobiographical essay, 'Is Indian Society Congenial to the Creation of a Classic?', *The Literary Criterion*, 15.2 (1980), 59–60.

[2] See Bruce King, *The New English Literatures: Cultural Nationalism in a Changing World* (London and Basingstoke: Macmillan, 1980), 43.

actual events for political purposes. For it is arguable that the aspirations of the masses for privileges and socio-economic benefits in the
new political state are frustrated after the attainment of the 'imagined community'. While the existence of self-representations on an
imaginary plane—an ideal that successfully manipulates sizable and
diverse people as in India—is regarded by most intellectuals now to
be the creation of a stereotype which is part of any intellectual
practice to enhance strategically its ideological structure, it does
not preclude us from raising questions about the nature of history-
writing and its approximation to the writing of fictions in nationalist
representations. In the preceding chapters, I have attempted to suggest the relevance of myths to the formation of an historical consciousness in which both the real and the imaginary have a significant
role. Though I have confined myself to India and to the ideology
governing its nationalist movement in the 1930s under Gandhi, I have
tried to place stress on the mythical plot-structure that encompasses
the histories of the national movement, blurring thus the very division
between the genres of history and fiction.[3] Broadening the framework
beyond the context of India, it can be argued that the milieu within
which any historical writer functions will inevitably have an effect on
the style of his or her exposition, as it does in fiction-writing. This
debate draws attention to the truth, if any, in constructions of identity, especially in periods of nation-building.

   We should pause here and consider what constitutes history. Generally speaking, history would mean a truthful rendition of events.
The writing of history would comprise of the occurrence of the event
or situation and the narrativization of it. But since the '*object* of
history is the human *subject* itself',[4] it is worth debating the truth
content of this writing. The historian approaches a human past with
an equally human experience, and so his craft reserves a role for
subjectivity in judging the importance of events and factors particularly when historical encounters have to be designated in historical
language. Further, the distance between the past and the writing of it
problematizes and limits the representation of 'reality'. The impos-

---

   [3] Both Collingwood and White speak of the mythic dimensions of the plot-structure
and the language used by historians. See R. G. Collingwood, *The Idea of History*
(Oxford: Clarendon, 1946), 234–7; and Hayden White, *Tropics of Discourse: Essays
in Cultural Criticism* (Baltimore: Johns Hopkins University Press, 1978).
   [4] Paul Ricoeur, *History and Truth*, 4th edn., trans. and introd. Charles A. Kelbley
(Evanston, Ill.: Northwestern University Press, 1992), 40.

sibility of referring back to the past to test the accuracy of history allows us to say that history remains history 'to the extent that the meaning of it remains confused and entangled'.[5] Any attempt at writing history, at best, can remain only on the level of hope since consciousness always tends to veer towards false consciousness. The point at which history is about to lose its actuality, thus, always evades us.

A strong critique of the truth-value of discourse comes from Hayden White's explanation of the symbiotic relationship between the two modes of history and fiction: 'Viewed simply as verbal artefacts histories and novels are indistinguishable from one another. We cannot easily distinguish between them on formal grounds unless we approach them with specific preconceptions about the kinds of truths that each is supposed to deal in.'[6] The conclusions I seek to draw regarding the common ground covered by history and fiction with particular focus on the disposition of the writer may be substantiated by pursuing White's argument elsewhere where he poses a specific and significant question: 'What wish is enacted, what desire is gratified, by the fantasy that real events are properly represented when they can be shown to display the formal coherency of a story?'[7] It is the historian's desire 'to rank events in the record hierarchically from within a perspective that is culture-specific'[8] that allows the moralizing impulse to temper the realm of real events. White goes on to declare that 'the amount of narrative will be greatest in accounts designed to tell a story, least in those intended to provide an analysis of the events of which it treats'.[9] This would imply that narrative prejudice can alternate between the convincingly objective and the seemingly fantastic, making possible, to an extent, a defence of narrative but also exposing, equally, the contribution of the imagination. In spite of establishing boundaries between literature and history, borrowing is inevitable so that the historian's approach to his

---

[5] Kelbley, 'Introduction', in ibid. p. xiv. Ricoeur has characterized truth both as a 'regulative idea' and as a 'singular' conception in the flux of time. The former unifies our diverse experiences into a system of logic and puts an end to the 'vertigo of variation' that narratives impose on experience, and thus kills actual history. The latter, in its exercise of singularity, however coherent in its conception, cannot dismiss its non-singular, multiple aspects. See ibid. 42–50; 65–8; 73–4.

[6] White, *Tropics of Discourse*, 122.

[7] See Hayden White, *The Content and the Form: Narrative Discourse and Historical Representation* (Baltimore: Johns Hopkins University Press, 1987), 4.

[8] Ibid. 10.       [9] Ibid. 27.

subject will not be entirely objective or value-free. As this book shows, the coherence of any narrative is necessarily the result of an imposition from outside by the literary or historical imagination in the interests of power or manipulation. By radically unsettling the nationalist agenda and examining the 'nation' itself as a work of fiction, it becomes possible to jeopardize the objectivity of history, and legitimize the use of the fictional or even the fantastic. Whatever be the degree of intrusion in a narrative, the inevitability of the presence of the moralizing impulse cannot be denied.

Owing to the constant struggle between the possibility of a happening and its actual occurrence, and between the interpreters of discourse and those who are appropriated and victimized by that very discourse, the presence of any single history becomes contestable. In so far as past experience is lost to us, it can be conceded that the historical knowledge of that past is a process of imaginative recreation as much as it is based on evidence, and further, that what we take as 'truth' depends on the ability of the historian to convince us of the 'reality' of his representation. We can say that what exists is discourse, appearing to us in manifold kinds of writing which stimulates us to accept as real that which is closest to our conception of the real. Thus any amount of stories can be told about any sequence of events, all of which may be equally credible.

By conceiving fiction as imaginary and unreal, and owing to the affinities between fiction and history, history itself may be classified as fiction. Indeed, it is not unusual to find correspondences between the two genres based on the common assumption of the phantasmatic nature of fiction-writing which renders histories unreal. However, this raises the related question whether any historical narrative would correspondingly be deemed truthful if on the other hand, fiction were defined positively as an actual representation of reality. My study of *Kanthapura*, in this regard, is not an attempt to carelessly characterize fiction—and subsequently history—as unreal but in its very recourse to historical events, particularly subaltern history, recognize the validity of the nation's myths especially within a cultural context. It is not simply by contextualizing Rao's novel against a whole set of historical and theoretical questions about historical fiction but by problematizing history itself in relation to nationalist ideology that I am able to bridge the division between the real and the imaginary. Although the demystification of nationalist constructions is facilitated by eliding the distinction between the two genres, such a radical theory of history must consider the historical referents of every discourse since it would be unfair to presume sweepingly that there exists no core of history. As Callinicos notes, 'the truism that any attempt to record events is selective offers no guidance about how to identify the position occupied by empirical evidence in the process of historical inquiry itself'.[10] The emphasis on the selectivity of historical accounts undoubtedly precludes one from dwelling on the existence of empirical evidence or a fixed referent. But were we to do so, we would not be any closer to an exact representation of reality. It would be imprudent, in any case, to assume that such 'empirical evidence' did not exist in the case of fiction. When it comes to fictional histories, and this does not exclude Salman Rushdie's forays into magic realism, the existence of a referent is as strong as that in any work of history. However, it is not fixed, just as it is not in any kind of historical narrative. It is another matter that the referent may move between the real and the merely imagined in works of fiction. But then again, the referent may be equally recalcitrant in works of history. Yet historical discourse is always privileged since the immediate referent here is presumed to be real, not imagined.

How best can one write history then, especially in the context of finding alternatives to western hegemonic traditions? The advantage of an extreme deconstructionist position is of especial relevance to the issue of postcolonial identities particularly in posing challenges to old essentialisms, both nationalist and orientalist. It holds out the possibility of seeing fiction and history together so that their roles as mutually coexistent disciplines would release us from an 'authentic' past offered by proponents of nationalism and at the same time obfuscate the disparity between 'objective' history and 'non-linear' or 'timeless' fictions perpetuated to advance the European subjection of the globe.[11] An acceptance of the features of the European theory of time is part of that inheritance which consigns the historical periods of the conquered into myth and tradition: historical texts coming from the east are often defined as a collection of unsystematic and disorganized archetypes denying linearity while history in the

[10] Alex Callinicos, *Theories and Narratives: Reflections on the Philosophy of History* (Cambridge: Polity, 1995), 76.
[11] See e.g. Robert J. C. Young, *White Mythologies: Writing History and the West* (London: Routledge, 1992), 2. Young, in his defence of poststructuralism, has implicitly distinguished history from truth by arguing that all history, especially Enlightenment history, is only a form of eurocentrism.

west is always considered to be chronological, classificatory, and based on real events. A parallel example to the classification of Indian texts as mythical or traditional is found in the anthropological study of native South Americans whose history is discredited as timeless since the Andean people rely on memory as an atemporal device.[12] On the other hand, the starting point of narratives recounting the history of the west is almost always taken to be the year 1400 as in the work of historical 'synthesizers' like Fernand Braudel and Arnold Toynbee, a time when the world systems which had evolved much earlier had declined and those of Europe had reached ascendancy. In her essay, 'On the Remaking of History', Abu-Lughod has argued that history would be so different if the starting point had been situated in an Asian-based world system, converging on China or the Indian Ocean, when the eurocentric system was hardly able to rival its Asian counterpart.[13] Apart from 'partial testimony' and 'levels of generality' generated by the archivists and the synthesizers respectively, the histories written by the victor almost always convert the weaknesses of the dominated into their own strengths. Abu-Lughod points out that the variables used in the histories recounting the deficiencies of the east turn out inevitably to be the 'mirror images of those used to prove Western superiority': 'The West was technologically advanced; the East was "backward". The West was institutionally developed in business techniques; the East was "irrational" and "particularistic" in its commercial and industrial practices. The West had laissez-faire capitalism; the East was monopolistic and statist.'[14] The west scarcely needed to 'despoil' the east had all these allegations been true. Yet there are hardly any history text books which argue in this vein.

So long as one functions within the discourse of foundationalist history, it is difficult to question and restrict the unproblematized power/knowledge relationship which, according to Said, establishes control and subjection. It is equally contestable to have faith in a system of collective memory called nationalist discourse which is no less foundational. To open up the possibility of identity, one would have to create a '"third space" which enables other positions to

---

[12] Joanne Rappaport, *Politics of Memory: Native Historical Interpretation in the Columbian Andes* (Cambridge: Cambridge University Press, 1990), 12.
[13] Janet Abu-Lughod, 'On the Remaking of History: How to reinvent the Past', in Barbara Kruger and Phil Mariani (eds.), *Remaking History* (Seattle: Bay Press, 1989), 111–29.                                    [14] Ibid. 119.

emerge',[15] or write into the history of the nation-state its many contradictions and ambivalences so that it 'deliberately makes visible, within the very structure of its narrative forms, its own repressive strategies and practices'.[16] We need a practice of writing, in other words, which neither disregards history nor, in its insistence on legitimacy, is completely oblivious of memory. Such a practice would not question how far narratives approximate to what once was reality but consider the adequacy of those representations within the circumstances in which they are generated. In my view, fiction fulfils that necessary criterion.

## II

In any construction of a 'minority discourse' in the colonial context, history is fashioned by employing the Fanonian distinction between

---

[15] Homi Bhabha, 'The Third Space: Interview with Homi Bhabha', in Jonathan Rutherford (ed.), *Identity: Community, Culture, Difference* (London: Lawrence and Wishart, 1990), 211. Bhabha has tried to produce a different identity for both the colonizer and the colonized from that which we have been accustomed to in both imperial and nationalist historiography. For Bhabha, ambivalence characterizes both sides of colonialism: mimicry as imitation is a form of subjugating the native through the imperial episteme of discipline and regulation and, at the same time, an enabling device for the native to subvert and transgress official discourse through the menacing tone of sly civility. In other words, narcissism (the self-as-other and the other-as-self) and aggression (domination and resistance) both serve in making colonialism a very problematic category, and not one in which power and discourse belong completely to the colonizer. It is ironic, however, that in his efforts to mark the bounds of western history, Bhabha ends up showing that the native has a voice only in the splitting of imperial discourse, between the gaps of their enunciation and the site of its address, in the 'excess' and 'slippage' inherent in the replication of their history. Anti-colonial struggles undoubtedly have to trigger off from colonial aggression and are not independent of it, but to assume that indigenous response can be barely gestural—that too so imperceptibly as to go almost unnoticed—is to scarcely give the native voice an existence independent of colonialism which emerges, on the other hand, as something of a reified structure. Here we find Bhabha's conclusions tethering him to the binaries he so wishes to be free of. See Homi Bhabha, 'Of Mimicry and Man', in *The Location of Culture* (London and New York: Routledge, 1990), 86; and 'Sly Civility', ibid. 93–101. As Robert Young has pointed out, Bhabha makes us unsure if the mutation from psychological categories of resistance to revolution happened at the instance of the interpreter than, in fact, in historical time. There would have to be a historical consciousness, however essentialized, in which Bhabha's privileged moments could be contained. See Young, *White Mythologies*, 149–55. Young's concerns, however, are surprising in the face of his own endeavour to dismantle the totalizing category of western history.

[16] Dipesh Chakrabarty, 'Postcoloniality and the Artifice of History: Who Speaks for "Indian" Pasts?', *Representations*, 37 (1992), 23.

tradition and modernity, past and present, and so on. The crux of such a binary antagonism lies in retrieving lost culture which has been deracinated by colonialism. While such a recovery evidently gives a prominent place to history, what can be reviewed, within my argument, is the genre of fiction as a carrier of such history. Even as we are able to comment on the flawed nature of such writing, its presence as fictional history enables it to disqualify itself from assuming the status of the 'real' while giving a voice to the native at the same time. In its very nature as fiction, and by belonging to the genre of the unreal, fiction can become an enabling medium to carry the message and yet be free of essentialism. History's only mode of existence can reside in these fragments. Looking back at Rao's construction of nationalist ideology, we can understand how the intelligentsia overturn the inaccuracies and prejudices of western accounts and create their own notions of their place in the historical process to establish a moral link with the past. Though it has been argued that such representations are mythical and even orientalist, they are nevertheless part of the indigenous writer's strategy of representing 'authentic' national identity. As fictional counter-histories, they can animate and alter received assumptions and, as such, revise history. Such works assume tremendous significance within such an understanding that demands a different standpoint of judgement, emerging from the writer's culture alone. Moreover, despite the drawbacks of such an approach, one cannot lose sight of the significance of myth, memory, symbol, ritual, or tradition in recognizing the power these narratives exercise over space and time. Their strength lies in the coexistence of myth and history over and above professional accounts that choose to separate the two. This is felt substantially in the work of Márquez and Rao, and also in that of the more contemporary Rushdie and Bharati Mukherjee. Although the latter are examples of modernist writers whose literary principles and poetics are quite different from those of Rao, and imply a different notion of identity and politics, their recent works can be used as vantage points from where to arrive at a revaluation of the role of myth in history. The rewriting of history, with a combination of the fabulous and the mythological into the historical, is Márquez's method of arriving at a truthful narrative. As Regina Janes writes:

The well-read reader, properly plumped with information, can distinguish the real from the invented and mark the changes worked on the real. His sense of the difference between an imagined and an actual reality is not blurred, but sharpened. The fictions that are most misleading become those that seem most real and most natural, not those that seem most artificial. Perhaps most important, such a rewriting of the past unmoors our sense of the reasonableness, naturalness, and inevitability of such a history. It has occurred, but must it continue to do so?[17]

That is why, perhaps, many intellectuals see the true meaning of 'Indianness' or 'Columbianness' in such 'real' and 'natural' histories. And that is probably why Márquez pronounces the need to tell his story 'before the historians have time to arrive'.[18] In the same way, instead of centring on stereotypical opposites, Abu-Lughod proposes a 're-*storia*' in which the reasons for the fall of the east become more important than those for the rise of the west: 'Something real is going on out there, and a knowledge of the past may be helpful to us in our efforts to 'read' it, interpret it, and possibly even to deal with it.'[19] Thus, in many ways, the indigenous writers are trying to do justice to their misrepresented histories through self-representation. For them, as for Márquez, western history-writing has cut them off from their past by deeming them a nation of savages in order to justify conquest. A denial of this kind of knowledge about the past can be an extremely effective means of destroying indigenous knowledge about the present because indigenous identities do have the power to give a voice to the oppressed, and the capacity to spur and simulate realities.

It becomes important in this regard to bridge the gap between the interpreter and the subaltern, urging theory to intersect history, yet remain conscious of the divergences between the two. A belief in the truth-content of historical narrative along with a scepticism of its possible falsity might suggest a way of displacing categories without giving up the possibility of a subaltern history. Spivak is helpful in accounting for the validity of any such possible representation of reality in so far as it is evaluated from the point of view of the writer and his or her audience. She has advanced the argument that while history will always seem more 'real' than fiction, what emerges as 'truth' will be seen from and conceived by the subject-position that the author, reader, teacher, subaltern,

---

[17] Regina Janes, 'Past Possession in Latin America', *Salmagundi*, 68–9 (1985–6), 300.
[18] Gabriel García Márquez, *Los Funerales de la Mamá Grande*, cited in Rappaport, *Politics of Memory*, 1.    [19] Abu-Lughod, 'On the Remaking of History', 127.

or the historian occupies.[20] Thus she moves between various subject-positions, marking 'the place of that other that can be neither excluded nor recuperated.'[21] Though Spivak's subject-positions are incompatible with grouped identities or shared assumptions defining cultural traditions which underlie any nationalist fiction-writing, she provokes the reader to entertain that literature and history are discursive constructions, history being a narrative brought forth by the medium of language which reports events.

A defence of the fictional possibilities of historical representations can be offered by positing an essentialist position along with building up an awareness of the disadvantages of such a position. If we start from the presupposition that no representation can take place without essentialism, we are able to speak for the subaltern and at the same time dissolve structures of patriarchy. Although 'naming' would amount to venturing into essentialist categories, it would also inter-vene in undermining positions altogether since it is in the very act of naming that it is possible to locate the ever-slipping moment of truth.[22] And although establishing a representative position would privilege one reading over another, a reminder of the hazards inherent in this exercise would always restrain one's conclusions. For this reason, it might be productive to explain why history was categorized under certain names rather than explain away historical labelling under the pretext of finding an answering voice. With this in mind, and as discussed in Chapters 3 and 4, the relationship between theory

[20] Gayatri Spivak, 'A Literary Representation of the Subaltern: A Woman's Text from the Third World', in *In Other Worlds: Essays in Cultural Politics* (London and New York: Routledge, 1988).

[21] Spivak, 'Translator's Foreword to "Draupadi" by Mahasweta Devi', in *In Other Worlds*, 180. Particularly relevant to the issue of subject-positions is her essay, 'A Literary Representation of the Subaltern' in which Spivak engages in a series of 'interruptions' between 'elite methodologies and subaltern material' (241). Under the assignment of any position, she claims, lie a number of 'I'-slots or subject-positions, all of which may be undermined in a deconstructive reading. Spivak fore-closes and marginalizes Mahasweta Devi's narrative 'Stanadayani' (Breast-Giver) as an allegory of postcolonial India in which the indigenous elite, the post-war rich, the diaspora, have oppressed the subaltern. The author's own reading does not satisfy Spivak since Mahasweta Devi's interpretation speaks less of the acute loneliness of the subaltern in the attempt to allegorize her as a 'seme for Mother India' (246). Such a position all too readily gobbles up the nationalist myth of the Hindu Mother Goddess and excludes the subaltern. That is why Spivak takes cognizance of the subaltern as gendered subject, and not as class or caste subject.

[22] Maria Koundoura, 'Naming Gayatri Spivak' (interview), *Stanford Humanities Review*, 1 (1989), 85; 86.

and practice can be brought to crisis so that the very project of elite representation is challenged without decentring the dominant signifying systems, effected through negotiation with the 'structures of phallocentrism' which are enabling, not annihilating.[23]

Alert and vigilant, the postcolonial critic can avoid the dangers of orientalism and its reverse, or of building 'phantom history'.[24] The Subaltern Studies collective have spoken of a humanist concern in representing a subaltern consciousness which may not be different from what Spivak advocates to be the role of an intellectual—that of a learning beyond the privilege of an elite education. Guha himself admits that the history of insurgency 'excludes the rebel as the conscious subject of his own history' and appropriates instead an '*abstraction* called Worker-and-Peasant, *an ideal rather than the real historical personality of the insurgent*'.[25] Interpreted thus, subaltern consciousness can never be recovered completely, and remains in the grip of, and subordinate to, the elite. There may even be shades of complicity with imperialism, and a 'sanctioned ignorance' of the 'epistemic violence' that completely effaces the subaltern.[26] An inconsistent situation, undoubtedly, where the singularity of the essentializing impulse is counterposed against the critical force of deconstruction. This brings up the interesting division between the subaltern voice and the project of reading or between the third-world sexed subject and high feminism, between the teacher of literature and the historian, as also between the defenders of literary theory and the champions of nationalism. At the heart of these contradictions peculiar to postcolonial studies lie unresolved 'disciplinary policing strategies' where one methodology restricts the other, calling the other neo-colonialist.[27]

[23] Gayatri Spivak, *The Post-Colonial Critic: Interviews, Strategies, Dialogues*, ed. Sarah Harasym (New York and London: Routledge, 1990), 45; 139; 147.

[24] Rey Chow, *Writing Diaspora: Tactics of Intervention in Contemporary Cultural Studies* (Bloomington and Indianapolis: Indiana University Press, 1993), 37.

[25] Ranajit Guha, 'The Prose of Counter-Insurgency', in Ranajit Guha and Gayatri Chakravorty Spivak (eds.), *Selected Subaltern Studies* (Oxford: Oxford University Press, 1988), 77.

[26] Gayatri Spivak, 'Subaltern Studies: Deconstructing Historiography', in *In Other Worlds: Essays in Cultural Politics* (London and New York: Routledge, 1988), 209. This essay is particularly useful for an understanding of Spivak's concept of 'strategic essentialism' which she advocates to counter the 'benevolence' of elite approaches in representing the subaltern.

[27] Stephen Slemon, 'The Scramble for Post-Colonialism', in Chris Tiffin and Alan Lawson (eds.), *Describing Empire: Post-Colonialism and Textuality* (London: Routledge, 1994), 29.

The question then arises: can identities ever be fixed? In studying history as hermeneutics, Robert Young raises the question of the 'position of enunciation' possible for the historian to claim in the context of writing:

From Sartre to Foucault history has repeatedly emerged as a contradictory concept, both totalizing and detotalizing, essentialist and non-essentialist. Such contradictions can be productive: the attempt to reject historicism absolutely results either in an utter particularism or in a surreptitious return to historicism in a different form. Only an understanding that recognizes that an irresolvable tension works within the historical schema itself will be in a position to make its contradictory claims productive.[28]

Thus, the 'phantasm' that is history 'will always involve a form of historicism, but a historicism that cannot be sustained.'[29] The line dividing reality from representation is very fine indeed. It is unsettling as well as politically limiting to move around the unresolved issues addressed both from an essentialist and an anti-essentialist view. The point is to negotiate between the complexities arising from both. It is true that scepticism has undoubtedly made redundant the position of the historian since truth has become relative. While relativism has decentred essentialist notions of happenings and error-free truth-claims, it must be conceded that some amount of belief has to be extended to our value-judgements in order to make them conclusive if not absolute. If one was to centre on the idea of a *possibility* of truths about the past, this notion would at least make truth worth struggling for.[30] It may also be admitted that the act of naming may not necessarily be essentialist. Taking the instance of Confucius's concept of *zhengming*, or 'the rectification of names', Rey Chow has proposed a different connotation implicit in naming: 'Instead of causing the reality to disappear, naming is the way to make a certain reality "proper", that is, to make it real.'[31] A defence of naming would however imply that a particular signifier and its corresponding meaning be tied closely together, thus making the language in that context transparent. Correspondingly, such exact claims of the signifier to a meaning must demand a theory of language that can be completely enslaved. Yet, since the claim to power is *'no more than a claim'*, naming

[28] Young, *White Mythologies*, 83.    [29] Ibid. 84.
[30] See Joyce Appleby, *et al.*, *Telling the Truth about History* (New York and London: W. W. Norton, 1994), 7.    [31] Chow, *Writing Diaspora*, 104–5.

permits power and recognition up to a point.[32] As Chow points out, such claims often begin to approximate to the truth when raised to the official ideology of the nation as in the case of the Chinese government's ideology inherent in the People's Republic of China.[33] All the more, a programme of 'strategic essentialism' proves to be a pragmatic manoeuvre for maintaining identities without establishing the singularity of historical narrative which would inevitably represent the subaltern with epistemic 'accuracy' and fall prey to an essentializing construct. Such a manoeuvre would tend to mark the departure from a dogmatic world view and usher in an intertextual study of culture.

Returning to Márquez's method of approaching a true sense of history, we could argue that while nationalist ideology might be dysfunctional today, nationalist texts are, nevertheless, important in the assessment of the manner in which a set of shared assumptions necessarily condition history and indeed shape reality. In so far as nationalist representations are accepted as real, they create their own reality. It is with this in mind, perhaps, that there arises among the intelligentsia the need to govern discourse: underlying the control of language lies the belief in the truth-content of words. The way in which Bankim's evocative slogan 'Vande Mataram' was immensely appealing to his audience, becoming thus a battle-cry in the late nineteenth and early twentieth centuries, or the belief in 'Hindutva' in contemporary Indian society that has led to the abandonment of all sanity by fundamentalist Hindus must itself account for the legitimacy of a particular choice of national identity. Thus, what is even more significant than the denomination of common mythic structures to the subjective lens of the writers of both history and fiction is the actual contribution of fiction to history.

In very many ways, the truth-content of such constructs needs to be judged in terms of their coherence and comprehension within their own cultural fields along with bringing the recognition that any discursive practice is riven by prejudices generated by the various claimants of truth. As Foucault would say:

If a proposition, a sentence, a group of signs can be called 'statement', it is not therefore because, one day, someone happened to speak them or put them into some concrete form of writing; it is because the position of the subject can be assigned. To describe a formulation *qua* statement does not consist in

---

[32] Ibid. 105.     [33] Ibid. 107.

analysing the relations between the author and what he says (or wanted to say, or said without wanting to); but in determining what position can and must be occupied by any individual if he is to be the subject of it.[34]

Foucault's definition of 'discursive formation' does not ignore the telling of an event, but speaks of the need of positioning the subject who tells. History, in this sense, would necessarily have wider implications and hidden agendas if freed from the fetishization of the archive or the archaeological work of historiography. It would, if interrogated further, also begin to resemble literature, a possibility which would be thwarted if history were to continue in its regimented orthodoxies. In the bargain, there would be a greater give and take between the 'real' and the 'imaginary', the true and the sanctioned non-true.

It is in the nature of discursive constructions that all utterance constitutes fictionality owing to the use of language. Foucault's claim to have written nothing but fiction, and further that 'it is possible to make fiction work inside of truth'[35] is utterly meaningful when examined in terms of the abstract nature of language. Although this intention is inexplicated in his work and the status of such truth not clarified, what we can derive is the notion of the insidious nature of discourse resulting from the constrictions of language. A scepticism of narrative structures does not render them intrinsically false or misleading; it is only the semantic content of the discursive field that gives any representation this or that meaning. Language plays an important part in all representations especially when seen to be linked to Nietzsche's theory of the will to power within all discourse. Advanced by those who have power, ideology, engendered through language, can become an indicator of truth rather than just a cultural myth. Although it may be alleged that the consideration shown to language is inconsistent with its ability to represent, the reality so conceived must have in its possession some capacity to invoke belief, despite the slipperiness of language, or rather, in my view, particularly owing to the discordance between the signifier and the signified. As seen in Chapter 1, it is owing to the very nature of language that ideologists have grabbed the advantage of representing reality as

[34] Michel Foucault, *The Archaeology of Knowledge*, trans. A. M. Sheridan Smith (London: Routledge, 1992), 95–6.
[35] Cited in Allan Megill, *Prophets of Extremity: Nietzsche, Heidegger, Foucault, Derrida* (Berkeley: University of California Press, 1985), 234; 235.

truth. For if language did signify unambiguously what it represented, there would be no possibility of concealment, falsification,
or confusion.

In *The Order of Things*, Foucault writes, 'The Classical order of
language has now drawn to a close. It has lost its transparency and its
major function in the domain of language.'[36] The relativist concept
of language we recognize now is far from the nineteenth-century
belief in its centrality to truth and meaning. Yet we can persist by
maintaining that language, conceived through language, is the only
reality available to us. Or as Said has said in his interpretation of
Derrida, that on the level of language, 'difference is already differed
and therefore cannot be thought of as a quality or an idea or a
concept having originals and copies'.[37] This claim may be supported
by taking language to be an essential medium for any kind of knowledge which wishes to offer itself in discourse. But this very language,
though deemed inert, always leans towards the one using it as soon as
the user gives expression to his or her thoughts.

Language may also be said to constitute reality because it is the
repository of a people's thoughts, ideas, and memories. Even though
its users consider it a medium they can dominate, representations
unwittingly begin to contain the qualities of truth since language
exposes non-verbal reality in realizable forms.[38] The value which
has been bestowed upon language in this century, owing to its density
and its capacity to 'govern' and 'paralyse', itself gives strength to
language that has been debased and lost. It is a paradox that the self-
same trap of language tantalizingly offers the 'truth of discourse'.[39]
Another compensation of language comes to us in the form of literature. At a time when language was offering itself to be intersected by
knowledge, 'it was also reconstituting itself elsewhere, in an independent form, difficult to access, folded back upon the enigma of its own
origin and existing wholly in reference to the pure act of writing'.[40]
As seen in the context of nationalist discourse, literature becomes
uncircumscribed and assumes boundless proportions, and the 'pure
act of writing', seemingly uncorrupted by philological caprice,
becomes truth itself.

In Nietzschean terms, the conception of fictionalizing history

[36] Michel Foucault, *The Order of Things: An Archaeology of the Human Sciences*,
trans. W. J. T. Mitchell (London: Routledge, 1991), 295.
[37] Edward Said, *The World, the Text, and the Critic* (London: Faber, 1984), 200.
[38] Foucault, *Order of Things*, 297.    [39] Ibid.    [40] Ibid. 300.

conceals the desire to schematize and govern, to impose stable patterns, to the extent demanded by our practical needs. 'Knowledge', says Nietzsche, 'works as an instrument of power. It is therefore obvious that it grows with every increase of power.'[41] Knowledge as a process of interpretation, then, is shaped by its utility which is understood by its believers and proponents to be the absolute truth, and thereby legitimized. Having no faith in absolute truth, Nietzsche explains that those fictions which outlive their utility become known as 'errors' while others attain the rank of unquestioned 'truths' and become part of our language. Embedded in language, we stand the risk of imagining these truths to necessarily mirror reality.

The problem, therefore, consists in not sorting out what truth is, or characterizing every history as an imposition, but in seeing how effects of truth are created within discourses which in themselves possess neither truth nor falsity.[42] In so far as we are able to comment on self-representations based on a usable past, and this is where the relativist interpretation of truth is found wanting, it is important to establish standpoints, however temporary and fragile. For without standpoints, it is not possible to understand and determine the ideologies, convictions, and prejudices of any particular school of narrative. While nationalist representations may be criticized for being fictional—we have argued, after all, that history and fiction have a common agenda/base—there is some virtue in maintaining specific identities. Why shouldn't every age create its own kind of historical truth? This may be another way of addressing and posing the issue of the truth-content of history as multiculturalists have done. Multiculturalism as a movement does not deny a universal and standardized theory of historicism, and at the same time protects specific group identities and alternative models emerging, say, from oral traditions. While maintaining a universal concept of identity, the multiculturalist project promotes liberal pluralism through recognizing the unique identity and authenticity of cultural groups and individuals.

In my analysis of *Kanthapura*, I have attempted to reconstruct and position the 'reality' and power of nationalist representations by

[41] Friedrich Nietzsche, *The Complete Works of Friedrich Nietzsche*, ed. Oscar Levy, trans. WM. A. Haussmann (New York: Gordon, 1974), iii. 751.
[42] Michel Foucault, *Power/Knowledge: Selected Interviews and Other Writings, 1972–1977*, ed. and trans. Colin Gordon, *et. al.* (London: Harvester Wheatsheaf, 1980), 118.

frequent comparisons with other choices and alternatives, both in the present and in the period when the novel was published. The existence of plural realities at least enables us to say that there exist a battle-field of truths. At the same time, there should be an accompanying understanding that such truths are not lying there to be discovered; rather, they play political and economic roles in subservience to power, but are nonetheless essential to the running of society. Further-ing the history/fiction debate, it can be said that in the representation of reality, the novelist may depict his or her image of the 'real' through the use of figurative techniques while the historian's approach is more direct. Nevertheless, the realm of human experience which it is the purpose of both to represent is as real in literature as that alluded to by the historian. In this light, the analysis of any fiction-writer's experiment is not so much the examination of a fiction/history typology in the manner of Hayden White, as it is a study of how culture-specific modes of interpretation interact with political activity at the interface of opposing cultural traditions. A writer's truth will be largely dependent upon books and documents written by members of the dominant society, and equally upon per-sonal reminiscences and oral traditions coloured by the sacred geo-graphy of the land. Writers of both history and fiction would thus be inclined to address the problem from their vantage point as observers of the people of the nation-state, and expand their texts in ways that make them more relevant to the problems at hand.

Although White's idea of the complementarity of fiction and history is attractive for present purposes, it is difficult to employ when arguing against a particular version of history which gets entrenched in the cultural psyche of the people. It would, therefore, be prudent to keep certain distinctions between representations of fiction and history so that the two cannot be sweepingly substituted one for the other. At best, the two depend on each other for a better understanding of reality. An extension of White's position would be extreme deconstruction which too is problematic in settling ques-tions of identity. We can say that a representation would approx-imate to truth in accordance with the capacity of the intellectual to discern the presence of imagination and manoeuvre, of power and hegemony in discursive systems, and to open up discourse by expos-ing its limitations.

Historical fiction, which I have examined, can accordingly be called 'history imagined into fiction' and at the same time, be well-researched, 'a bit of both in both cases'.[43] To quote Spivak, 'The writer acknowledges this by claiming to do research (my fiction is also historical)' while 'the historian might acknowledge this by looking at the mechanics of representation (my history is also fictive)'.[44] The endeavour towards historical imagination in the case of both the historian and the fiction-writer may clear the misconception that only the subaltern can know the subaltern, or only women can know women, and so on, for an ideal representation. Only the self-conscious intellectual, having at hand a series of frames interrupting each other might open up and contextualize different agencies of knowledge as against the representations and fabrications of histories of exclusion, and be free from reworking supposedly pure nativist origins into nationalist discursive structures.

Interestingly, there now exist more works that celebrate fluid identities than those that assert the truth of the 'pure' and the 'indigenous'. A good example is Rushdie's *Midnight's Children* which tells the story of the birth of the nation with its accompanying ruptures and confusions. It is within the metaphor of hybridity and decomposition that his fiction assumes significance. Rushdie treats the authoritative orthodoxy of an older India in a plural fashion, turning accepted 'truths' into new sets of unverifiable facts. This is his way of removing the objective lens of historical representation, of challenging tradition itself by dislodging history through parody and irony.[45] Yet Saleem Sinai, the protagonist of *Midnight's Children*, maintains a close relationship with indigenous models of history, fiction, and cinema which he uses to produce a de-totalizing fragment of his 'memory's truth'.[46] *Midnight's Children* is marked by the representation of an identity and the simultaneous suspicion of that representation. In the end, however, the writer's industrious quest for truth becomes 'factual' by a selective process of assembling reality symbolized through the metaphor of pickling. His history or presentation of facts is preserved in jars and has to be swallowed if it is to have any meaning. It is noteworthy that while his material is given form in their containers, the content undergoes distortion in the process of pickling/ preservation. This is true of both history and fiction.

[43]   Spivak, 'A Literary Representation of the Subaltern', 243–4.

[44]   Ibid. 244.

[45]   See Linda Hutcheon, *The Politics of Postmodernism* (London: Routledge, 1989), 58.

[46]   Salman Rushdie, *Midnight's Children* (New York: Avon, 1980), 253.

Then again, *The Satanic Verses* is replete with intertextuality: the song, 'O, my shoes are Japanese. . . . trousers are English. . . . On my head [is a] red Russian hat; my heart's Indian for all that', is nothing if not an evocation of internationalism even though it is dictated by the pulls of an 'Indian' heart.[47] It takes its origin from the cultural centre, the Bombay film industry, which is also, at the same time, the space for postcolonial migrancy, breaking national frontiers. Another instance of breaking loose from pure tradition is Bharati Mukherjee's immigrant story which, as she views it, 'is replicated in a dozen American cities, [so that] instead of seeing [her] Indianness as a fragile identity to be preserved against obliteration . . . [she sees] it now as a set of fluid identities to be celebrated . . . a metaphor, a particular way of partially comprehending the world.'[48]

Raja Rao is altogether different since his metaphorical representation of India is synchronous with a sort of expanding imperialism in which India plays conqueror. If so, then Rao's experience as a transplanted national has afforded a view in which India can possess the world in its sweep. Referring to Ananda Coomaraswamy, another expatriate, Rao remarks:

India would never be made by our politicians and professors of political science, but by these isolate existences of India, in which India is rememorated, *experienced* and communicated; beyond history, as tradition, as the Truth. Anybody can have the geographic—even the political—India; it matters little; But this India of Coomaraswamy, who will take it away, I ask you, who?[49]

It appears that Rao's years in France and later in America, may have to account for the culturally aggressive definition of India that he has adopted. As a voluntary exile from his country, Rao has a perspective on India that can only be a product of enchantment which is integral to the diaspora:

India is not a country like France is, or like England; India is an idea, a metaphysic. Why go there anyhow, I thought; I was born an exile, and I could continue to be one. My India I carried her wheresoever I went.[50]

[47] Salman Rushdie, *The Satanic Verses* (London: Viking, 1988), 5. See also Afsaneh Najmabadi, 'Interview with Gayatri Spivak', *Social Text*, 9 (1991), 131.
[48] Bharati Mukherjee, *Darkness* (Harmondsworth: Penguin, 1985), 3.
[49] Raja Rao, *The Serpent and the Rope* (Delhi: Orient Paperbacks, 1960), 352.
[50] Ibid. 376.

An experience which cannot be lived is carried along in a tourist's briefcase.[51] The changes in Rao's perspective are thus few and his view fixed and enduring. This is especially evident in the later novels which are strikingly similar to the constructions of the orientalists.

What I am suggesting in this study of the imbrication of history and fiction in the construction of nationalist ideology is the deeply vexed nature of self-representative accounts. Through the analysis of the fictional nature of historical narratives which both evoke suspicion and tantalizingly offer us the 'truth', it can be argued that the construction of a singular identity will always be a site for contestation, especially in view of the theories of postmodernism that have altered the very nature of truth. Despite the fluid notion of identity, the idealization of cultural myths and models is an ongoing process concomitant with the persistence of the demands for an exemplary nationhood. An understanding of the cultural conditions which stimulate those 'truths' should, thus, underline our efforts to demystify reality. The coexistence of the stronghold of tradition and the presence of multifarious critical traditions enables both a recognition of the colonized who has a special tale to tell, and a simultaneous wariness of his or her privileged voice.

[51] As Tarlo has pointed out, people like Gandhi, Nehru, and Coomaraswamy have all discovered their India by leaving it. See Emma Tarlo, *Clothing Matters: Dress and Identity in India* (London: Hurst, 1996), 299.

# Bibliography

*Books*

AHMAD, AIJAZ, *In Theory: Classes, Nations, Literatures* (New Delhi: Oxford University Press, 1993).

ALTHUSSER, LOUIS, *For Marx*, trans. Ben Brewster (London: Verso, 1986).

AMIN, SHAHID, *Event, Metaphor, Memory: Chauri Chaura 1922–1992* (Delhi: Oxford University Press, 1996).

AMIRTHANAYAGAM, GUY (ed.), *Asian and Western Writers in Dialogue: New Cultural Identities* (London and Basingstoke: Macmillan, 1982).

ANAND, MULK RAJ, *Coolie* (1933; London: Bodley Head, 1972).

—— *Untouchable* (London: Wishart, 1935).

—— *The Village* (London: Jonathan Cape, 1939).

—— *Across the Black Waters* (London: Jonathan Cape, 1940).

—— *The Sword and the Sickle* (London: Jonathan Cape, 1942).

—— *Apology for Heroism: An Essay in Search of Faith* (London: Lindsay Drummond, 1946).

—— (ed.), *The Historic Trial of Mahatma Gandhi* (New Delhi: National Council of Educational Research and Training, 1987).

ANANTHA MURTHY, U. R., *Samskara: A Rite for a Dead Man*, 2nd edn., trans. A. K. Ramanujan (Delhi: Oxford University Press, 1978).

ANDERSON, BENEDICT, *Imagined Communities: Reflections of the Origin and Spread of Nationalism* (London: Verso, 1983).

APPADURAI, ARJUN, *Worship and Conflict Under Colonial Rule: A South Indian Case* (Cambridge: Cambridge University Press, 1981).

APPLEBY, JOYCE, HUNT, LYNN, and JACOB, MARGARET, *Telling the Truth about History* (New York and London: W. W. Norton, 1994).

ARNOLD, DAVID, *The Congress in Tamilnad: Nationalist Politics in South India, 1919–1937* (Columbia, Mo.: South Asia Books, 1977).

ASHCROFT, BILL, GRIFFITHS, GARETH, and TIFFIN, HELEN, *The Empire Writes Back: Theory and Practice in Post-Colonial Literatures* (London: Routledge, 1989).

ASHTON, MARTHA BUSH, and CHRISTIE, BRUCE, *Yaksagana: A Dance Drama of India* (New Delhi: Abhinav, 1977).

ATTRIDGE, DEREK, BENNINGTON, GEOFF, and YOUNG, ROBERT (eds.), *Post-Structuralism and the Question of History* (Cambridge: Cambridge University Press, 1987).

BADEN-POWELL, B. H., *The Indian Village Community* (London, New York, and Bombay: Longmans, Green, and Co., 1896).

BAIRD, ROBERT D., *Religion and Law in Independent India* (New Delhi: Manohar, 1993).

BAKER, CHRISTOPHER, *The Politics of South India, 1920–1937* (Cambridge: Cambridge University Press, 1976).

BALD, SURESHT RENJEN, *Novelists and Political Consciousness: Literary Expressions of Indian Nationalism, 1919–1947* (Delhi: Chanakya, 1982).

BARKER, FRANCIS, HULME, PETER, IVERSEN, MARGARET, and LOXLEY, DIANA (eds.), *Europe and its Others: Proceedings of the Essex Conference on the Sociology of Literature*, 2 vols. (Colchester: University of Essex, 1985).

——— HULME, PETER, and IVERSEN, MARGARET (eds.), *Colonial Discourse/ Postcolonial Theory* (Manchester and New York: Manchester University Press, 1994).

BARTHES, ROLAND, *Image, Music, Text*, ed. and trans. Stephen Heath (Glasgow: Fontana, 1977).

BAUMAN, RICHARD, *Verbal Art as Performance* (Massachusetts: Newbury House, 1977).

BAUMAN, ZYGMUNT, *Modernity and the Holocaust* (Cambridge: Polity, 1989).

BAYLY, CHRISTOPHER A., *Rulers, Townsmen and Bazaars: North Indian Society in the Age of British Expansion, 1770–1870* (Cambridge: Cambridge University Press, 1983).

——— *Indian Society and the Making of the British Empire* (Cambridge: Cambridge University Press, 1988).

BENNER, ERICA, *Really Existing Nationalisms: A Post-Communist View from Marx and Engels* (Oxford: Clarendon, 1995).

BERGER, JOHN, *Into Their Labours* (London: Granta, 1992).

BERLIN, ISAIAH, *Vico and Herder: Two Studies in the History of Ideas* (London: Hogarth, 1976).

——— *Russian Thinkers*, ed. Henry Hardy and Aileen Kelly (Harmondsworth: Penguin, 1979).

——— *The Crooked Timber of Humanity: Chapters in the History of Ideas*, ed. Henry Hardy (London: Fontana, 1991).

BHABHA, HOMI (ed.), *Nation and Narration* (London: Routledge, 1990).

——— *The Location of Culture* (London and New York: Routledge, 1994).

BRENNAN, TIMOTHY, *Salman Rushdie and the Third World: Myths of the Nation* (London and Basingstoke: Macmillan, 1989).

BREUILLY, JOHN, *Nationalism and the State*, 2nd edn. (Manchester: Manchester University Press, 1993).

BRYDON, DIANA, and TIFFIN, HELEN, *Decolonising Fictions* (Sydney: Dangaroo, 1993).

CALLINICOS, ALEX, *Theories and Narratives: Reflections on the Philosophy of History* (Cambridge: Polity, 1995).

CAMPA, ROMÁN DE LA, KAPLAN, E. ANN, and SPRINKER, MICHAEL (eds.), *Late Imperial Culture* (London: Verso, 1995).

CARR, DAVID, *Time, Narrative and History* (Bloomington: Indiana University Press, 1986).

CARROLL, THEODORA FOSTER, *Women, Religion, and Development in the Third World* (New York: Praeger, 1983).

'Chandogya Upanisad', in *The Principal Upanisads*, trans. and ed. S. Radhakrishnan, vi. 8 (London: Allen and Unwin, 1953).

CHANDRA, BIPAN, MUKHERJEE, MRIDULA, MUKHERJEE, ADITYA, PANIKKAR, K. N., and MAHAJAN, SUCHETA, *India's Struggle for Independence* (New Delhi: Penguin, 1989).

CHATTERJEE, BANKIMCHANDRA, *Dharmatattva*, ed. Sribrajendranath Bandhopadhyay and Sri Sajanikanta Das (Calcutta: Bangiya Sahitya Parishad, 1888).

—— *Bankim Rachanavali*, ed. Jogeshchandra Bagal, 3 vols. (Calcutta: Sahitya Samsad, 1953–69).

—— *Vividha Prabandha*, ed. Brajendranath Bandhopadhyay and Sri Sajanikanta Das (Calcutta: Bangiya Sahitya Parishad, 1959).

—— *Kamalakanter Daptar*, ed. Sri Shashankshekhar Bagchi (Calcutta: Modern Book Agency, 1962)

—— *Sociological Essays: Utilitarianism and Positivism in Bengal*, trans. and ed. S. N. Mukherjee and Marian Maddern (Calcutta: Rddhi, 1986).

CHATTERJEE, BHABATOSH (ed.), *Bankimchandra Chatterjee: Essays in Perspective* (Delhi: Sahitya Academy, 1994).

CHATTERJEE, PARTHA, *Nationalist Thought and the Colonial World—A Derivative Discourse?* (London: Zed Books, 1986).

—— *The Nation and Its Fragments: Colonial and Postcolonial Histories* (Delhi: Oxford University Press, 1994).

CHENNAKESAVAN, SARASVATI, *A Critical Study of Hinduism* (London: Asia Publishing House, 1974).

CHOW, REY, *Writing Diaspora: Tactics of Intervention in Contemporary Cultural Studies* (Bloomington and Indianapolis: Indiana University Press, 1993).

CLARK, S. H., *Paul Ricoeur* (London and New York: Routledge, 1990).

COHAN, STEVEN, and SHIRES, LINDA M., *Telling Stories: A Theoretical Analysis of Narrative Fiction* (New York: Routledge, 1988).

COLLINGWOOD, R. G., *The Idea of History* (Oxford: Clarendon, 1946).

*Confidential Branch File*, 147/42–24, Karnataka State Archives, Bangalore.

COOMARASWAMY, ANANDA, K., *Christian and Oriental Philosophy of Art* (New Delhi: Munshiram Manoharlal, 1974).

COWASJEE, SAROS (ed.), *Author to Critic: The Letters of Mulk Raj Anand to Saros Cowasjee* (Calcutta: Writers Workshop, 1973).

—— *So Many Freedoms: A Study of the Major Fiction of Mulk Raj Anand* (Delhi: Oxford University Press, 1977).

DAS, ARVIND N., *India Invented: A Nation-in-the-Making* (New Delhi: Mano-har, 1992).

DAS, SISIR KUMAR, *The Artist in Chains: The Life of Bankimchandra Chatterjee* (New Delhi: New Statesman, 1984).

DASENBROCK, REED WAY (ed.), *Redrawing the Lines: Analytic Philosophy, Deconstruction, and Literary Theory* (Minneapolis: University of Minnesota Press, 1989).

DAVIES, A. M., *Strange Destiny: A Biography of Warren Hastings* (New York: G. P. Putnam's Sons, 1935).

DAVIS, HORACE B., *Toward a Marxist Theory of Nationalism* (New York and London: Monthly Review Press, 1978).

DAY, LAL BEHARI, *Govinda Sámanta: Or, The History of a Bengal Ráiyat* (London: Macmillan, 1874).

DESHMUKH, NANA, *RSS, Victim of Slander* (New Delhi: Vision Books, 1979).

*The Bhagavad Gita*, trans. Eliot Deutsch (New York: Holt, Rinehart, and Winston, 1968).

DIRKS, NICHOLAS B., *The Hollow Crown: Ethnohistory of an Indian Kingdom* (Cambridge: Cambridge University Press, 1987).

—— (ed.), *Colonialism and Culture* (Ann Arbor: University of Michigan Press, 1992).

DIWAKAR, R. R., *Karnataka Through the Ages* (Karnataka: Government of Karnataka Press, 1968).

DUNNE, TOM (ed.), *The Writer as Witness: Literature as Historical Evidence* (Cork: Cork University Press, 1987).

ELPHINSTONE, MOUNTSTUART, *The History of India*, 5th edn. (1841; London: John Murray, 1866).

EMERSON, RUPERT, *From Empire to Nation* (Cambridge, Mass.: Harvard University Press, 1960).

ERIKSEN, THOMAS HYLLAND, *Ethnicity and Nationalism: Anthropological Perspectives* (London: Pluto, 1993).

FOUCAULT, MICHEL, *Power/Knowledge: Selected Interviews and Other Writings, 1972–1977*, ed. Colin Gordon, trans. Colin Gordon, Leo Marshall, John Mepham, and Kate Soper (London: Harvester Wheatsheaf, 1980).

—— *The Order of Things: An Archaeology of the Human Sciences*, trans. W. J. T. Mitchell (London: Routledge, 1991).

—— *The Archaeology of Knowledge*, trans. A. M. Sheridan Smith (London: Routledge, 1992).

FOX, RALPH, *The Novel and the People* (London: Cobbett, 1937).

FOX, RICHARD G., *Gandhian Utopia: Experiments with Culture* (Boston: Beacon, 1989).

GALLAGHER, JOHN, JOHNSON, GORDON, and SEAL, ANIL (eds.), *Locality, Province and Nation: Essays on Indian Politics, 1870 to 1940* (Cambridge: Cambridge University Press, 1973).

GANDHI, MOHANDAS KARAMCHAND, *An Autobiography: Or, The Story of My Experiments with Truth*, trans. Mahadev Desai (Ahmedabad: Navajivan, 1927).

—— *Women and Social Injustice* (Ahmedabad: Navajivan, 1942).

—— *Collected Works of Mahatma Gandhi, 1884–1948*, 90 vols. (Ahmedabad: Navajivan, 1958–84).

GANDHI, RAJMOHAN, *Eight Lives: A Study of the Hindu-Muslim Encounter* (Albany: State University of New York Press, 1986).

GELLNER, ERNEST, *Nations and Nationalism* (Oxford: Blackwell, 1983).

GHOSH, AUROBINDO, *The Renaissance in India* (1920), repr. as *The Foundations of Indian Culture and The Renaissance in India* (Pondicherry: Sri Aurobindo Ashram, 1972).

GOVERSMITH, FRANK (ed.), *The Theory of Reading* (Sussex: Harvester Press, 1984).

GOLWALKAR, M. S., *Bunch of Thoughts* (Bangalore: Vikrama Prakashan Chamarajpet, 1966).

GOSSMAN, LIONEL, *Between History and Literature* (Cambridge, Mass.: Harvard University Press, 1990).

GRAHAM, BRUCE D., *Hindu Nationalism and Indian Politics: The Origins and Development of the Bhartiya Jana Sangh* (Cambridge: Cambridge University Press, 1990).

GUHA, RANAJIT, (ed.), *Subaltern Studies: Writings on South Asian History and Society*, 9 vols. (Delhi: Oxford University Press, 1982–97).

—— *An Indian Historiography of India: A Nineteenth-Century Agenda and Its Implications* (Calcutta: K. P. Bagchi, 1988).

—— and SPIVAK, GAYATRI CHAKRAVORTY (eds.), *Selected Subaltern Studies* (Oxford: Oxford University Press, 1988).

HALBFASS, WILHELM, *India and Europe: An Essay in Understanding* (Albany: State University of New York Press, 1988).

HARARI, JOSUE V. (ed.), *Textual Strategies: Perspectives in Post-Structuralist Criticism* (London: Methuen, 1980).

HAVELOCK, ERIC A., *The Muse Learns to Write: Reflections on Orality and Literacy from Antiquity to the Present* (New Haven: Yale University Press, 1986).

HEIMSATH, CHARLES H., *Indian Nationalism and Hindu Social Reform* (Princeton, NJ: Princeton University Press, 1964).

HOBSBAWM, E. J., *Nations and Nationalism Since 1780: Programme, Myth, Reality*, 2nd edn. (Cambridge: Cambridge University Press, 1991).

—— and RANGER, TERENCE (eds.), *The Invention of Tradition* (Cambridge: Cambridge University Press, 1983).

HUTCHEON, LINDA, *The Politics of Postmodernism* (London: Routledge, 1989).

HUTCHINSON, JOHN, and SMITH, ANTHONY D. (eds.), *Nationalism* (Oxford: Oxford University Press, 1994).

INDEN, RONALD, *Imagining India* (Oxford: Basil Blackwell, 1990).

JENKINS, KEITH, *Re-thinking History* (London and New York: Routledge, 1991).

—— *On 'What is History?': From Carr and Elton to Rorty and White* (London and New York: Routledge, 1995).

JHA, RAMA, *Gandhian Thought and Indo-Anglian Novelists* (Delhi: Chanakya Publications, 1983).

JOSHI, PUSHPA, *Gandhi on Women: Collection of Mahatma Gandhi's Writings and Speeches on Women* (New Delhi: Centre for Women's Development Studies and Navajivan, 1988).

JOSHI, SVATI (ed.), *Rethinking English: Essays in Literature, Language, History* (New Delhi: Trianka, 1991).

KACHRU, BRAJ B., *The Indianization of English: The English Language in India* (Delhi: Oxford University Press, 1983).

KAMATH, SURYANATH U., *Quit India Movement in Karnataka* (Bangalore: Lipi Prakashana, 1988).

KAMENKA, EUGENE (ed.), *Nationalism: The Nature and Evolution of an Idea* (London: Edward Arnold, 1976).

KAVIRAJ, SUDIPTA, *The Unhappy Consciousness: Bankimchandra Chattopadhyay [Chatterjee] and the Formation of Nationalist Discourse in India* (Delhi: Oxford University Press, 1995).

KEDOURIE, ELIE, *Nationalism* (London: Hutchinson, 1966).

—— (ed.), *Nationalism in Asia and Africa* (London: Weidenfeld and Nicolson, 1970).

KEER, DHANANJAY, *Veer Savarkar* (1950; Bombay: Popular Prakashan, 1966).

KEJARIWAL, O. P., *The Asiatic Society of Bengal* (Delhi: Oxford University Press, 1988).

KING, BRUCE, *The New English Literatures: Cultural Nationalism in a Changing World* (London and Basingstoke: Macmillan, 1980).

KOHN, HANS, *The Idea of Nationalism: A Study in Its Origins and Background* (New York: Macmillan, 1944).

—— *Nationalism: Its Meaning and History* (New Jersey: D. Van Nostrand Company, 1965).

KOPF, DAVID, *British Orientalism and the Bengal Renaissance: The Dynamics of Indian Modernization, 1773–1835* (Calcutta: Firma K. L. Mukhopadhyay, 1969).

KRUGER, BARBARA, and MARIANI, PHIL (eds.), *Remaking History* (Seattle: Bay Press, 1989).

LARRAIN, JORGE, *Ideology and Cultural Identity: Modernity and the Third World Presence* (Cambridge: Polity, 1994).

LARSON, CHARLES R., *The Novel in the Third World* (Washington, DC: Inscape, 1976).

LORD, ALBERT B., *The Singer of Tales* (New York: Athenum, 1976).

LOWE, LISA, *Critical Terrains: French and British Orientalisms* (Ithaca and London: Cornell University Press, 1991).

MCHALE, BRIAN, *Postmodernist Fiction* (London: Methuen, 1987).

MACLEAN, MARIE, *Narrative As Performance: The Baudelairean Experiment* (London: Routledge, 1988).

MACNEICE, LOUIS, *The Strings are False: An Unfinished Autobiography* (London: Faber, 1965).

*The Mahabharata of Krishna-Dwaipayana Vyasa: Karna Parva*, trans. Pratap Chandra Ray (Calcutta, 1889).

MAHADEVAN, T. M. P., *Outlines of Hinduism* (Bombay: Chetana, 1956).

MAINE, HENRY SUMNER, *Village-Communities in the East and West* (1871; London: John Murray, 1907).

MAJEED, JAVED, *Ungoverned Imaginings: James Mill's 'The History of British India' and Orientalism* (Oxford: Clarendon, 1992).

MATHEW, GEORGE (ed.), *Panchayati Raj in Karnataka Today: Its National Dimensions* (New Delhi: Institute of Social Sciences and Concept Publishing Company, 1986).

MEGILL, ALLAN, *Prophets of Extremity: Nietzsche, Heidegger, Foucault, Derrida* (Berkeley: University of California Press, 1985).

MEMMI, ALBERT, *The Colonizer and the Colonized* (London: Earthscan, 1990).

MILL, JAMES, *The History of British India*, 3 vols. (London: Baldwin, Cradock, and Joy, 1817).

MITCHELL, W. J. T. (ed.), *On Narrative* (Chicago: University of Chicago Press, 1981).

MOHANTY, CHANDRA TALPADE, RUSSO, ANN, and TORRES, LOURDES (eds.), *Third World Women and the Politics of Feminism* (Bloomington and Indianapolis: Indiana University Press, 1991).

MOHANTY, PRAFULLA, *My Village, My Life* (London: Davis-Poynter, 1973).

MUKHERJEE, BHARATI, *Darkness* (Harmondsworth: Penguin, 1985).

MUKHERJEE, MEENAKSHI (ed.), *Considerations* (New Delhi: Allied Publishers, 1977).

—— *Realism and Reality: The Novel and Society in India* (Delhi: Oxford University Press, 1985).

MUKHERJEE, SUJIT, *Towards a Literary History of India* (Simla: Indian Institute of Advanced Study, 1975).

MUTHANNA, I. M., *History of Karnataka* (Mysore: Usha Press, 1962).

*Mysore State Gazetteer, Hassan District* (Bangalore: Government of Mysore, 1971).

NAGARAJAN, K., *Chronicles of Kedaram* (Bombay: Asia, 1961).

NAIK, M. K., *Raja Rao* (New York: Twayne, 1972).

NAIK, M. K. (ed.), *Aspects of Indian Writing in English* (Delhi: Macmillan, 1979)

NAIPAUL, V. S., *The Mimic Men* (London: André Deutsch, 1967).

—— *India: A Wounded Civilization* (London: André Deutsch, 1977).

NANDY, ASHIS, *At the Edge of Psychology: Essays in Politics and Culture* (Delhi: Oxford University Press, 1980).

—— *The Intimate Enemy: Loss and Recovery of Self under Colonialism* (Delhi: Oxford University Press, 1983).

—— *The Illegitimacy of Nationalism: Rabindranath Tagore and the Politics of Self* (Delhi: Oxford University Press, 1994).

NARASIMHAIAH, C. D., *The Writer's Gandhi* (Patiala: Punjabi University, 1967).

—— *Raja Rao* (New Delhi: Arnold-Heinemann, 1968).

—— and SRINATH, C. N., *A Common Poetic for Indian Literatures* (Mysore: Dhvanyaloka, 1984).

NARAYAN, R. K., *The English Teacher* (1946; Mysore: Indian Thought Publications, 1973).

—— *Waiting for the Mahatma* (London: Heinemann, 1979).

NAYAK, H. M., *Kannada Literature—A Decade* (Mysore: Rao and Raghavan, 1967).

—— (ed.), *Gandhiji in Indian Literature* (Mysore: Mysore University Printing Press, 1971).

NEHRU, JAWAHARLAL, *Selected Works of Jawaharlal Nehru, 1903–46*, ed. S. Gopal, 15 vols. (New Delhi: Orient Longman, 1972–82).

NIETZSCHE, FRIEDRICH, *The Complete Works of Friedrich Nietzsche*, ed. Oscar Levy, trans. WM. A. Haussmann, iii (New York: Gordon, 1974).

NIRANJAN, SHIVA, *Raja Rao: Novelist as Sadhaka* (Ghaziabad: Vimal Prakashan, 1985).

NIRANJANA, TEJASWINI, *Siting Translation: History, Post-Structuralism, and the Colonial Context* (Berkeley: University of California Press, 1992).

—— SUDHIR, P., and DHARESHWAR, VIVEK (eds.), *Interrogating Modernity: Culture and Colonialism in India* (Calcutta: Seagull, 1993).

NIVEN, ALASTAIR, *Truth Within Fiction: A Study of Raja Rao's 'The Serpent and The Rope'* (Calcutta: Writers Workshop, 1987).

ONG, WALTER J., *Orality and Literacy: The Technologizing of the Word* (London: Methuen, 1982).

PANDEY, GYANENDRA (ed.), *Hindus and Others: The Question of Identity in India Today* (New Delhi: Viking, 1993).

PAREKH, BHIKHU, *Gandhi's Political Philosophy: A Critical Examination* (London: Macmillan, 1989).

PARKER, ANDREW, RUSSO, MARY, SOMMER, DORIS, and YAEGER, PATRICIA (eds.), *Nationalisms and Sexualities* (New York and London: Routledge, 1992).

PHILIPS, C. H. (ed.), *Historians of India, Pakistan and Ceylon* (London: Oxford University Press, 1961).

PRAKASH, GYAN (ed.), *After Colonialism: Imperial Histories and Postcolonial Displacements* (Princeton, NJ: Princeton University Press, 1995).

RADHAKRISHNAN, R., *Diasporic Meditations: Between Home and Location* (Minneapolis and London: University of Minnesota Press, 1996).

RAO, HAYAVADANA C. (ed.), *Mysore Gazetteer*, v (Delhi: Goyal Printers, 1984).

RAO, K. R., *The Fiction of Raja Rao* (Aurangabad: Parimal Prakashan, 1980).

RAO, KRISHNA M. V., and HALAPPA, G. S., *History of Freedom Movement in Karnataka*, 2 vols. (Bangalore: Government of Mysore Press, 1962).

RAO, RAJA, *Kanthapura* (Delhi: Orient Paperbacks, 1938).

—— *The Cow of the Barricades and Other Stories* (London: Geoffrey Cumberledge, Oxford University Press, 1947).

—— *The Serpent and the Rope* (Delhi: Orient Paperbacks, 1960).

—— *The Policeman and the Rose* (Delhi: Oxford University Press, 1968).

—— *The Cat and Shakespeare: A Tale of Modern India* (Delhi: Orient Paperbacks, 1971).

—— *Comrade Kirillov* (Delhi: Orient Paperbacks, 1976).

—— *The Chessmaster and His Moves* (New Delhi: Vision Books, 1988).

—— *On the Ganga Ghat* (New Delhi: Vision Books, 1989).

—— and SINGH, IQBAL (eds.), *Changing India: An Anthology* (London: George Allen and Unwin, 1939).

—— *Whither India?* (Baroda: Padmaja Publications, 1948).

RAPPAPORT, JOANNE, *Politics of Memory: Native Historical Interpretation in the Columbian Andes* (Cambridge: Cambridge University Press, 1990).

RAYCHAUDHURI, TAPAN, *Europe Reconsidered: Perceptions of the West in Nineteenth Century Bengal* (Delhi: Oxford University Press, 1988).

RICOEUR, PAUL, *History and Truth*, 4th edn., trans. and introd. Charles A. Kelbley (Evanston, Illinois: Northwestern University Press, 1992).

RIMMON-KENAN, SHOLOMITH, *Narrative Fiction: Contemporary Poetics* (London: Methuen, 1983).

ROBB, PETER (ed.), *Society and Ideology: Essays in South Asian History* (Delhi: Oxford University Press, 1993).

—— and TAYLOR, DAVID (eds.), *Rule, Protest, Identity: Aspects of Modern South Asia* (London: Curzon, 1978).

RUSHDIE, SALMAN, *Midnight's Children* (New York: Avon, 1980).

—— *The Satanic Verses* (London: Viking, 1988).

RUTHERFORD, JONATHAN (ed.), *Identity: Community, Culture, Difference* (London: Lawrence and Wishart, 1990).

SAID, EDWARD, *Orientalism* (London: Routledge, 1978).

—— *The World, the Text, and the Critic* (London: Faber, 1984).

—— *Culture and Imperialism* (London: Chatto and Windus, 1993).

SANGARI, KUMKUM, and VAID, SUDESH (eds.), *Recasting Women: Essays in Colonial History* (New Delhi: Kali for Women, 1989).

SARMA, GOBIND PRASAD, *Nationalism in Indo-Anglian Fiction* (New Delhi: Sterling, 1978).

SEAL, ANIL, *The Emergence of Indian Nationalism* (Cambridge: Cambridge University Press, 1968).

SESHADRI, H. V., *Hindu Renaissance Under Way* (Bangalore: Jagarana Prakashana, 1984).

SHANIN, TEODOR, *Peasant and Peasant Societies* (Harmondsworth: Penguin, 1971).

SHARMA, K. K. (ed.), *Perspectives on Raja Rao* (Ghaziabad: Vimal Prakashan, 1980).

SHARMA, SUDARSHAN, *The Influence of Gandhian Ideology on Indo-Anglian Fiction* (New Delhi: Soni, 1982).

SHARRAD, PAUL, *Raja Rao and Cultural Tradition* (New Delhi: Sterling, 1987).

SHETTY, VASANTHA B., *Studies in Karnataka History* (New Delhi: Sterling, 1984).

SINHA, AVADESH K. (ed.), *Alien Voice: Perspectives on Commonwealth Literature* (Lucknow: Print House, 1981).

SINHA, K. N. (ed.), *Indian Writing in English* (New Delhi: Heritage, 1979).

SMITH, ANTHONY D., *Theories of Nationalism* (London: Duckworth, 1983).

—— *National Identity* (Harmondsworth: Penguin, 1991).

SMITH, VINCENT A., *The Early History of India* (Oxford: Clarendon, 1904).

SMITH, WILFRED CANTWELL, *The Meaning and End of Religion* (New York: Mentor, 1964).

SOYINKA, WOLE, *A Dance of the Forests* (London: Oxford University Press, 1963).

SPIVAK, GAYATRI CHAKRAVORTY, *In Other Worlds: Essays in Cultural Politics* (London and New York: Routledge, 1988).

—— *The Post-Colonial Critic: Interviews, Strategies, Dialogues*, ed. Sarah Harasym (London and New York: Routledge, 1990).

—— *Outside in the Teaching Machine* (London and New York: Routledge, 1993).

—— trans. and introd. *Imaginary Maps: Three Stories by Mahasweta Devi* (London and New York: Routledge, 1995).

SRINIVAS, M. N., (ed.), *India's Villages* (Bombay: Asia, 1955).

—— *The Remembered Village* (Delhi: Oxford University Press, 1990).

SULERI, SARA, *The Rhetoric of English India* (Chicago and London: University of Chicago Press, 1992).

SUNDER RAJAN, RAJESWARI (ed.), *The Lie of the Land: English Literary Studies in India* (Delhi: Oxford University Press, 1992).

—— *Real and Imagined Women: Gender, Culture, and Postcolonialism* (London: Routledge, 1993).

TAGORE, RABINDRANATH, *Nationalism* (London: Macmillan, 1918).

TANDON, PRAKASH, *Punjabi Century, 1857–1947* (London: Chatto and Windus, 1961).

TARLO, EMMA, *Clothing Matters: Dress and Identity in India* (London: Hurst, 1996).

THOMAS, NICHOLAS, *Colonialism's Culture: Anthropology, Travel and Government* (Cambridge: Polity, 1994).

TIFFIN, CHRIS, and LAWSON, ALAN (eds.), *Describing Empire: Post-Colonialism and Textuality* (London: Routledge, 1994).

TRIVEDI, HARISH, *Colonial Transactions: English Literature and India* (Calcutta: Papyrus, 1993).

—— and MUKHERJEE, MEENAKSHI (eds.), *Interrogating Post-colonialism: Theory, Text and Context* (Shimla: Indian Institute of Advanced Study, 1996).

TURNER, BRIAN S., *Marx and the End of Orientalism* (London: George Allen and Unwin, 1978).

URQUHART, W. S., *Vedanta and Modern Thought* (Delhi: Gyan Publishers, 1986).

VANAIK, ACHIN, *The Painful Transition: Bourgeois Democracy in India* (London: Verso, 1990).

—— *India in a Changing World: Problems, Limits and Successes of its Foreign Policy* (New Delhi: Orient Longman, 1995).

VANSINA, JAN, *Oral Tradition: A Study in Historical Methodology*, trans. H. M. Wright (Harmondsworth: Penguin, 1961).

VISWANATHAN, GAURI, *Masks of Conquest: Literary Study and British Rule in India* (New York: Columbia University Press, 1989).

WALKER, BENJAMIN, *Hindu World: An Encyclopedic Survey of Hinduism*, 2 vols. (London: Allen and Unwin, 1968).

WHITE, HAYDEN, *Tropics of Discourse: Essays in Cultural Criticism* (Baltimore: Johns Hopkins University Press, 1978).

—— *The Content and the Form: Narrative Discourse and Historical Representation* (Baltimore: Johns Hopkins University Press, 1987).

WILLIAMS, PATRICK, and CHRISMAN, LAURA (eds.), *Colonial Discourse and Post-colonial Theory: A Reader* (Hemel Hampstead: Harvester Wheatsheaf, 1993).

YOUNG, ROBERT J. C., *White Mythologies: Writing History and the West* (London: Routledge, 1992).

—— *Colonial Desire: Hybridity in Theory, Culture and Race* (London: Routledge, 1995).

ZIPES, JACK, *Fairy Tales and the Art of Subversion: The Classical Genre for Children and the Process of Civilization* (New York: Wildman, 1983).

*Articles*

ABDEL-MALEK, ANOUAR, 'Orientalism in Crisis', *Diogenes: An International Review of Philosophy and Humanistic Studies*, 44 (1963), 103–40.

AHMAD, AIJAZ, 'The Politics of Literary Postcoloniality', *Race and Class*, 36.3 (1995), 1–20.

AHMAD, KARUNA CHANANA, 'Gandhi, Women's Roles and the Freedom Movement', *Occasional Papers on History and Society*, 1st series, no. 19 (New Delhi: Nehru Memorial Museum and Library, 1984), 1–24.

ALOYSIUS, G., 'Trajectory of Hindutva', *Economic and Political Weekly*, 29.24 (1994), 1450–2.

ALTER, ROBERT, 'The Novel and the Sense of the Past', *Salmagundi*, 68–9 (1985–6), 91–106.

AMUR, G. S, 'The Kannada Phase', *Journal of Karnataka University (Humanities)*, 10 (1966), 40–52.

ANAND, MULK RAJ, 'The Story of My Experiment with a White Lie', in M. K. Naik, S. K. Desai, and G. S. Amur (eds.), *Critical Essays on Indian Writing in English* (Dharwar: Karnataka University Press, 1968), 21–7.

—— 'Why I Wrote', in K. K. Sharma (ed.), *Indo-English Literature: A Collection of Critical Essays* (Ghaziabad: Vimal Prakashan, 1977), 9–17.

—— 'Variety of Ways: Is There a Shared Tradition in Commonwealth Literature?', in C. D. Narasimhaiah (ed.), *Awakened Conscience: Studies in Commonwealth Literature* (New Delhi: Sterling, 1978), 420–2.

ANANTHA MURTHY, U. R., 'Is Indian Society Congenial To the Creation of a Classic? A Writer's View', *The Literary Criterion*, 15.2 (1980), 54–61.

BAGCHI, JASODHARA, 'Positivism and Nationalism: Womanhood and Crisis in Nationalist Fiction—Bankimchandra's *Anandamath*', *Economic and Political Weekly*, 20.4–5 (1985), 58–62.

BARBER, KARIN, 'Yoruba *Oriki* and Deconstructive Criticism', *Research in African Literatures*, 15.4 (1984), 497–518.

BARTHES, ROLAND, 'Historical Discourse', in Michael Lane (ed.), *Structuralism: A Reader* (London: Jonathan Cape, 1970), 145–55.

BHABHA, HOMI K., 'Difference, Discrimination and the Discourse of Colonialism', in Francis Barker, Peter Hulme, Margaret Iversen, and Diana Loxley (eds.), *The Politics of Theory* (Colchester: University of Essex, 1983), 194–211.

BRENNAN, TIM, 'Cosmopolitans and Celebrities', *Race and Class*, 31.1 (1989), 1–19.

CHAKRABARTY, DIPESH, 'Postcoloniality and the Artifice of History: Who Speaks for "Indian" Pasts?', *Representations*, 37 (1992), 1–26.

CHAUDHARY, SHREESH, 'Indianness in Indian Writing in English: Towards a Descriptive Approach', *Journal of Indian Writing in English*, 18.2 (1990), 55–65.

CUNNINGHAM, VALENTINE, 'Nosing Out the Indian Reality', *Times Literary Supplement* (15 May 1981), 20.

DAS, ARVIND N., 'Changel: Three Centuries of an Indian Village', *The Journal of Peasant Studies*, 15.1 (1987), 3–59.

DERRIDA, JACQUES, 'Cogito and the History of Madness', in *Writing and Difference*, trans. Alan Bass (London: Routledge, 1990), 31–63.

DESHPANDE, MADHAV, 'History, Change and Permanence: A Classical Indian Perspective', in Gopal Krishna (ed.), *Contributions to South Asian Studies*, i (Delhi: Oxford University Press, 1979), 1–28.

DEWEY, CLIVE, 'Images of the Village Community: A Study in Anglo-Indian Ideology', *Modern Asian Studies*, 6 (1972), 291–328.

DHARESHWAR, VIVEK, 'Marxism, Location Politics, and the Possibility of Critique', *Public Culture*, 6 (1993), 1–14.

DIRLIK, ARIF, 'Culturalism as Hegemonic Ideology', *Cultural Critique*, 6 (1987), 13–50.

DUMONT, LOUIS, 'The "Village Community" from Munro to Maine', *Contributions to Indian Sociology*, 9 (1966), 67–89.

DURING, SIMON, 'Postmodernism or Post-colonialism Today', *Textual Practice*, 1.1 (1987), 32–47.

EAGLETON, TERRY, 'The End of English', *Textual Practice*, 1.1 (1987), 1–9.

FRYKENBERG, ROBERT E., 'The Emergence of Modern "Hinduism" as a Concept and as an Institution: A Reappraisal With Special Reference to South India', in Günther D. Sontheimer and Hermann Kulke (eds.), *Hinduism Reconsidered* (Delhi: Manohar, 1989), 82–107.

GANDHI, M. K. (ed.), 'Not Man's Work?', *Young India*, 7.24 (11 June 1925), 204.

—— 'To the Women of India', *Young India*, 12.15 (10 Apr. 1930), 121.

GEMMILL, JANET P., 'Dualities and Non-Duality in Raja Rao's *The Serpent and the Rope*', *World Literature Written in English*, 12.2 (1973), 247–59.

—— 'The Transcreation of Spoken Kannada in Raja Rao's *Kanthapura*', *Literature East and West*, 18 (1974), 199–202.

—— 'Raja Rao: Three Tales of Independence', *World Literature Written in English*, 15.1 (1976), 135–48.

—— 'Elements of the Folktale in Raja Rao's *Cow of the Barricades*', *World Literature Written in English*, 20.1 (1981), 149–61.

HALAPPA, G. S., 'New Lights on the History of Karnataka', *Journal of Karnataka University (Humanities)*, 8 (1964), 267–77.

HARMAN, CHRIS, 'The Return of the National Question', in Alex Callinicos, John Rees, Chris Harman, and Mike Haynes, *Marxism and the New Imperialism* (London, Chicago, and Melbourne: Bookmarks, 1994).

HARREX, S. C., 'Typology and Modes: Raja Rao's Experiments in Short Story', *World Literature Today*, 62.4 (1988), 591–5.

INDEN, RONALD, 'Orientalist Constructions of India', *Modern Asian Studies*, 20.3 (1986), 401–46.

JALAL AL-'AZM, SADIK, 'Orientalism and Orientalism in Reverse', *Khamsin: Journal of Revolutionary Socialists of the Middle East*, 8 (1981), 5–26.

JAMESON, FREDERIC, 'Third-World Literature in the Era of Multinational Capitalism', *Social Text*, 15 (1986), 65–88.

JANES, REGINA, 'Past Possession in Latin America', *Salmagundi*, 68–9 (1985–6), 291–311.

JANMOHAMED, ABDUL R., 'The Economy of Manichean Allegory: The Function of Racial Difference in Colonialist Literature', in Henry Louis Gates, Jr. (ed.), *'Race,' Writing, and Difference* (Chicago and London: The University of Chicago Press, 1986), 78–106.

—— and LLOYD, DAVID, 'Introduction: Toward a Theory of Minority Discourse', *Cultural Critique*, 6 (1987), 5–12.

KACHRU, YAMUNA, 'Cross-Cultural Texts and Interpretation', *Studies in the Linguistic Sciences*, 13.2 (1983), 57–72.

KAMATH, SURYANATH U., 'Agrarian Agitations and Freedom Movement in Karnataka', *Quarterly Journal of the Mythic Society*, 73.2, 14–21.

KANTAK, V. Y., 'The Language of *Kanthapura*', *The Indian Literary Review*, 3.2 (1985), 15–24.

—— 'Raja Rao's *Kanthapura*', *Chandrabagha*, 13 (1985), 35–49.

KAPLAN, CAREN, and GREWAL, INDERPAL, 'Transnational Feminist Cultural Studies: Beyond the Marxism/Poststructuralism/Feminism Divides', *Positions*, 2.2 (1994), 430–45.

KAPUR, GEETA, 'Contemporary Cultural Practice: Some Polemical Categories', *Social Scientist*, 18.3 (1990), 49–59.

KAVIRAJ, SUDIPTA, 'Imaginary History', *Occasional Papers On History and Society*, 2nd series, no. 7 (New Delhi: Nehru Memorial Museum and Library, 1988), 1–123.

—— 'Signs of Madness: A Reading of the Figure of Kamalakanta in the Work of Bankimchandra Chattopadhyay [Chatterjee]', *Journal of Arts and Ideas*, 17–18 (1989), 9–31.

KAYE, HARVEY J., 'Historical Consciousness and Storytelling: John Berger's Fiction', *Mosaic: A Journal for the Interdisciplinary Study of Literature*, 16.4 (1983), 43–57.

KISHWAR, MADHU, 'Gandhi on Women', *Economic and Political Weekly*, 20.40 (5 Oct. 1985), 1691–702.

KNIPPLING, ALPANA SHARMA, 'R. K. Narayan, Raja Rao and Modern English Discourse in Colonial India', *Modern Fiction Studies*, 39.1 (1993), 169–86.

KOUNDOURA, MARIA, 'Naming Gayatri Spivak' (interview), *Stanford Humanities Review*, 1 (1989), 84–97.

KUMAR, RADHA, 'Contemporary Indian Feminism', *Feminist Review*, 33 (1989), 20–9.

LOOMBA, ANIA, 'Overworlding the "Third World"', *Oxford Literary Review*, 13.1–2 (1991), 164–91.

MACAULAY, THOMAS BABINGTON, 'Indian Education: Minute of the 2nd of February, 1835', in G. M. Young (ed.), *Macaulay: Prose and Poetry* (Cambridge, Mass.: Harvard University Press, 1967), 719–30.

MCCLINTOCK, ANNE, '"No Longer in a Future Heaven": Women and Nationalism in South Africa', *Transition*, 51 (1991), 104–23.

MCROBBIE, ANGELA, 'Strategies of Vigilance: An Interview with Gayatri Chakravorti [sic] Spivak', *Block*, 10 (1985–6), 5–9.

MANI, LATA, 'Contentious Traditions: The Debate on Sati in Colonial India', *Cultural Critique*, 7 (1987), 119–56.

MARX, KARL, 'The British Rule in India' (1853), in *Collected Works of Marx and Engels*, xii (London: Lawrence and Wishart, and Moscow: Progress Publishers, 1979), 125–33.

MEHTA, BALWANTRAY, 'Reflections from the Chair', in M. V. Mathur and Iqbal Narain (eds.), *Seminar on Panchayati Raj, Planning and Democracy, Jaipur 1964* (Bombay: Asia, 1969), 78–93.

MENON, NIVEDITA, 'Orientalism and After', *Economic and Political Weekly*, 27.39 (1992), 2133–6.

MUKHERJEE, MEENAKSHI, 'Raja Rao's Shorter Fiction', *Indian Literature*, 10.3 (1967), 66–76.

NAGARAJAN, S., 'An Indian Novel', *Sewanee Review*, 72 (1964), 512–17.

NAIK, M. K., '*The Cow of the Barricades and Other Stories*: Raja Rao as a Short Story Writer', *Books Abroad: An International Literary Quarterly*, 40.1 (1966), 392–6.

NAJMABADI, AFSANEH, 'Interview with Gayatri Spivak', *Social Text*, 9 (1991), 122–34.

NARASIMHAIAH, C. D., 'Raja Rao: *The Serpent and the Rope*', *The Literary Criterion*, 5.4 (1963), 62–89.

PANDEY, GYANENDRA, 'Modes of History Writing: New Hindu History of Ayodhya', *Economic and Political Weekly*, 29.25 (1994), 1523–8.

PARMESWARAN, UMA, 'Siva and Shakti in Raja Rao's Novels', *World Literature Today*, 62 (1988), 574–7.

PARRY, BENITA, 'Problems in Current Theories of Colonial Discourse', *Oxford Literary Review*, 9.1–2 (1987), 27–58.

PATANKAR, R. B., 'The Three Alternatives', *The Literary Criterion*, 19.1 (1984), 55–6.

PATEL, SUJATA, 'The Construction and Reconstruction of Woman in Gandhi', *Occasional Papers on History and Society*, 1st series, no. 49 (New Delhi: Nehru Memorial Museum and Library, 1984), 1–62.

PATIL, CHANDRASHEKHAR, B., 'The Kannada Element in Raja Rao's Prose: A

Linguistic Study of *Kanthapura*', *Journal of the Karnataka University (Humanities)*, 13 (1969), 143–67.

RAINE, KATHLEEN, 'On the Serpent and the Rope', *World Literature Today*, 62 (1988), 603–5.

RAJAN, B., 'Identity and Nationality', in John Press (ed.), *Commonwealth Literature* (London: Heinemann, 1965), 106–9.

RAO, MADHAVA N., '*Kanthapura*—An Appreciation', *Triveni: Journal of Indian Renaissance*, 44.3 (1975), 55–9.

RAO, RAJA, 'Pilgrimage to Europe', *Jaya Karnataka*, 10.1 (1931), 27–31.

—— 'Jupiter and Mars', *Pacific Spectator*, 8.4 (1954), 369–73.

—— 'Varanasi', *Illustrated Weekly of India* (3 Sept. 1961), 12–15.

—— 'Trivandrum', *Illustrated Weekly of India* (25 Feb. 1962), 12–16.

—— 'André Malraux Among the Gods of India', *United Asia: International Magazine of Afro-Asian Affairs*, 16 (1964), 122–8.

—— 'The Climate of Indian Literature Today', *The Literary Criterion*, 7.1 (1965), 229–31.

—— 'The Gandhian Way: Replies to a Questionnaire on Gandhi', *Illustrated Weekly of India* (14 Feb. 1965), 39.

—— 'The Writer and the Word', *The Literary Criterion*, 7.1 (1965), 76–8.

—— 'The Meaning of India', in P. Lal (ed.), *The First Writers Workshop Literary Reader* (Calcutta: Writer's Workshop, 1972), 35–42.

—— 'The Caste of English', in C. D. Narasimhaiah (ed.), *Awakened Conscience: Studies in Commonwealth Literature* (New Delhi: Sterling, 1978), 420–2.

—— 'Books Which Have Influenced Me', in M. K. Naik (ed.), *Aspects of Indian Writing in English* (Delhi: Macmillan, 1979), 45–9.

—— 'Entering the Literary World', *World Literature Today*, 62 (1988), 537–8.

RORTY, RICHARD, 'Deconstruction and Circumvention', *Critical Inquiry*, 11 (1984–5), 1–23.

SAID, EDWARD W., 'The Problems of Textuality: Two Exemplary Positions', *Critical Inquiry*, 4.4 (1978), 673–714.

—— 'Representing the Colonized: Anthropology's Interlocutors', *Critical Inquiry*, 15.2 (1989), 205–25.

—— 'Rushdie and the Whale', *The Observer* (26 Feb. 1989), 14.

SANGARI, KUMKUM, 'The Changing Text', *Journal of Arts and Ideas*, 8 (1984), 61–73.

—— 'The Politics of the Possible', *Cultural Critique*, 7 (1987), 157–86.

SARKAR, TANIKA, 'Bankimchandra and the Impossibility of a Political Agenda', *Oxford Literary Review*, 16.1–2 (1994), 177–204.

SCHOLES, ROBERT, 'Towards a Poetics of Fiction: An Approach through Genre', *Novel*, 2 (1969), 101–11.

SHARRAD, PAUL, 'Aspects of Mythic Form and Style in Raja Rao's *The Serpent and the Rope*', *Journal of Indian Writing in English*, 12.2 (1984), 82–95.

SHOHAT, ELLA, 'Notes on the "Post-Colonial"', *Social Text*, 31–2 (1992), 99–113.

SLEMON, STEPHEN, 'Post-Colonial Allegory and the Transformation of History', *The Journal of Commonwealth Literature*, 23.1 (1988), 157–68.

SPIVAK, GAYATRI CHAKRAVORTY, 'Three Women's Texts and a Critique of Imperialism', *Critical Inquiry*, 12 (1985), 243–61.

—— 'Imperialism and Sexual Difference', *Oxford Literary Review*, 8.1–2 (1986), 225–40.

—— 'Can the Subaltern Speak?', in Cary Nelson and Lawrence Grossberg (eds.), *Marxism and the Interpretation of Culture* (London: Macmillan, 1988), 271–313.

—— 'Woman in Difference: Mahasweta Devi's "Douloti the Bountiful"', *Cultural Critique*, 14 (1989–90), 105–28.

—— 'Asked to Talk About Myself . . .', *Third Text*, 19 (1992), 9–18.

TANDECIARZ, SILVIA, 'Reading Gayatri Spivak's "French Feminism in an International Frame": A Problem for Theory', *Genders*, 10 (1991), 75–90.

THAPAR, ROMILA, 'Imagined Religious Communities? Ancient History and the Modern Search for a Hindu Identity', Kingsley Martin Memorial Lecture, University of Cambridge, 1 June 1988. Published in *School of Social Sciences Working Paper Series* (New Delhi: Jawaharlal Nehru University, 1988), 1–40.

THUMBOO, EDWIN, 'Encomium for Raja Rao', *World Literature Today: A Literary Quarterly of the University of Oklahoma*, 62.4 (1988), 530–3.

TIFFIN, HELEN, 'Commonwealth Literature and Comparative Methodology', *World Literature Written in English*, 23.1 (1984), 26–30.

—— 'Post-Colonialism, Post-Modernism and the Rehabilitation of Post-Colonial History', *The Journal of Commonwealth Literature*, 23.2 (1986), 169–81.

TODD, LORETO, 'The Role of Vernacular Literatures in Contemporary Commonwealth Writing', *World Literature Written in English*, 23.1 (1984), 243–51.

TROUPE, QUINCEY, 'Decolonizing the Mind', *South: The Third World Magazine* (1983), 19.

VANITA, RUTH, '"Ravana shall be Slain and Sita Freed . . .": The Feminine Principle in *Kanthapura*', in Lola Chatterji (ed.), *Woman/Image/Text: Feminist Readings in Literary Texts* (New Delhi: Trianka, 1986), 188–93.

VASU, S. V., 'Raja Rao: Face to Face', *Illustrated Weekly of India* (5 Jan. 1964), 44–8.

WICKS, ULRICH, 'The Nature of Picaresque Narrative: A Modal Approach', *PMLA*, 89 (1974), 240–9.

YOUNG, ROBERT, 'Neocolonialism and the Secret Agent of Knowledge' (interview with Gayatri Spivak), *Oxford Literary Review*, 13 (1991), 220–51.

# Index